"Christian Collins Winn has written a welcome compelling exposition of 'the Kingdom of God' as it is parsed in the Bible. He has read and digested a remarkable amount of scholarship and put it to good use. Most importantly, he keeps a close eye on the emancipatory dimension of 'the Kingdom' as it pertains to the great emancipatory issues of race, class, and gender among us. Collins Winn has written a thoughtful, judicious manifesto, to which attention must be paid."

—WALTER BRUEGGEMANN
Columbia Theological Seminary

"This is the book I've been waiting for—a clear depiction of the kingdom of God thoroughly grounded in the Old and New Testaments. Collins Winn shows us what Christian faith is all about. He offers a biblical, theological, and ethical vision that speaks directly to those who face injustice and compellingly argues through the psalms, prophets, apocalyptic writers, and Jesus himself that God is on their side. This will be a text I will return to again and again to guide my teaching, preaching, and discipleship."

—JENNIFER M. MCBRIDE
author of *You Shall Not Condemn: A Story of Faith and Advocacy on Death Row*

"With the intimacy of a fireside chat, the precision of a neurological surgeon, the quest of an avid, curious adventurer, the deep compassion of pastoral-prophetic activism, and the artistry of a maestro conducting universal music, Christian Collins Winn provides a tour de force that offers a clarion call for all faith-believers to experience Jesus as the embodiment of the quintessential rule of God, which is ultimate, covenantal, self-giving love.

This work explores the reign of God, a metaphor used and abused to support myriad socio-political-ethical visions of reality. Such interpretive gymnastics often create a miseducated overlay of patriotism and faith. Collins Winn invites us to frame social ethics as responsible liberation. *Jesus, Jubilee, and the Politics of God's Reign* makes a convincing case for Jubilee that exposes powers and principalities steeped in white supremacist, patriarchal, capitalistic misogyny, to interpret theologically the totality of Jesus's life as resurrection justice. This volume is a must-read for those committed to following the way of Jesus and breaking free of traditional, institutionalized theological missteps."

—CHERYL A. KIRK-DUGGAN
scholar, author, and performer

PROPHETIC CHRISTIANITY

Series Editors

Malinda Elizabeth Berry
Peter Goodwin Heltzel

The PROPHETIC CHRISTIANITY series explores the complex relationship between Christian doctrine and contemporary life. Deeply rooted in the Christian tradition yet taking postmodern and postcolonial perspectives seriously, series authors navigate difference and dialogue constructively about divisive and urgent issues of the early twenty-first century. The books in the series are sensitive to historical contexts, marked by philosophical precision, and relevant to contemporary problems. Embracing shalom justice, series authors seek to bear witness to God's gracious activity of building beloved community.

PUBLISHED

Bruce Ellis Benson, Malinda Elizabeth Berry, and Peter Goodwin Heltzel, eds., *Prophetic Evangelicals: Envisioning a Just and Peaceable Kingdom* (2012)

Christian T. Collins Winn, *Jesus, Jubilee, and the Politics of God's Reign* (2023)

Jennifer Harvey, *Dear White Christians: For Those Still Longing for Racial Reconciliation,* 2nd edition (2020)

Peter Goodwin Heltzel, *Resurrection City: A Theology of Improvisation* (2012)

Johnny Bernard Hill, *Prophetic Rage: A Postcolonial Theology of Liberation* (2013)

Grace Ji-Sun Kim, *Embracing the Other: The Transformative Spirit of Love* (2015)

Liz Theoharis, *Always with Us? What Jesus Really Said about the Poor* (2017)

Chanequa Walker-Barnes, *I Bring the Voices of My People: A Womanist Vision for Racial Reconciliation* (2019)

Randy S. Woodley, *Shalom and the Community of Creation: An Indigenous Vision* (2012)

Jesus, Jubilee, and the Politics of God's Reign

Christian T. Collins Winn

William B. Eerdmans Publishing Company
Grand Rapids, Michigan

Wm. B. Eerdmans Publishing Co.
4035 Park East Court SE, Grand Rapids, Michigan 49546
www.eerdmans.com

Published 2023
Printed in the United States of America

29 28 27 26 25 24 23   1 2 3 4 5 6 7

ISBN 978-0-8028-6712-4

Library of Congress Cataloging-in-Publication Data

A catalog record for this book is available from the Library of Congress.

For my two prophets, Jonah and Elijah

"What does the Lord require of you but to do justice, and to love kindness, and to walk humbly with your God?"

Micah 6:8

For all those who struggle and hope, who dream and work for a better world

"Let justice roll down like waters, and righteousness like an ever-flowing stream."

Amos 5:24

CONTENTS

PREFACE

This book owes its original inception to a class I took in New Testament interpretation as a graduate student in the mid-1990s. I was assigned the task of exegeting the concluding clause found in Luke 17:21, which in Greek reads *idou gar hē basileia tou theou entos hymōn estin*. My task was to determine whether the traditional translation of the clause—"the kingdom of God is within you"—was correct. Fully expecting that I would agree with this cherished rendering, I was surprised to discover that for reasons both internal and external to the Greek text, I had to disagree, and I opted instead for the translation "the kingdom of God is in your midst," a translation that more clearly identifies the kingdom with Jesus's person and ministry.

At the time I failed to fully comprehend the theological ramifications of this shift. Nevertheless, as my education continued, I encountered again and again theological voices who pressed the point that the kingdom of God was not simply a vague cipher that could be used to justify just about anything. Rather, it had a concrete shape that could be discerned in the light not only of Jesus's words but also of his actions and the overall shape of his life history. Many of those theological voices also stressed the invariably social and prophetic nature of the kingdom of God as it was lived out in the patchwork portrait of Jesus given to us in the New Testament, and they often gestured toward the social and political implications of Jesus's embodiment of the kingdom. But none of them offered a theological, biblical, or ethical elaboration of the truth to which they pointed. Thus, I found myself needing to write the book that I had hoped I would someday discover in one of the many beloved used bookstores I have visited over the years.

As the reader will discover, my thesis is that Jesus *is* the kingdom of God enfleshed. In his life, death, and resurrection, *Jesus* is the quintessential demonstration of the rule of God in the form of self-giving love, and he is the true covenant partner, embodying active human faithfulness unto death. His life is the concrete embodiment of divine and human fellowship marked by jubilee justice, which is the compassionate justice and mercy of which Micah 6:8 speaks. Through the Spirit, the kingdom that Jesus *is* gets poured out on all flesh, in search of a faithful human response. I develop this thesis over the course of six chapters, three of which are devoted to an exploration of some of the key themes and dynamics found in the Hebrew Scriptures, with the last three chapters committed to an engagement with the New Testament witness. Our discussion begins in the first chapter with an exploration of the psalms. Though there are certainly texts found earlier in the canon that offer important insights regarding God's reign, the psalms offer one of the most comprehensive considerations of kingship in ancient Israel. Through an exploration of the so-called royal psalms and enthronement psalms, we show the deep ambivalence that ancient Israel had regarding human rule and authority and the contrasting vision of God's reign that is marked by compassionate justice and faithful righteousness. The chapter highlights the important theme of Jubilee, which offers the basic contours of what God's will and rule seek to achieve for the good of creation and humankind. In the forms of poetry, song, and prayer, the psalms offer a kind of politics of praise through which oppressed communities find the resources to envision the world that God intends, while also providing an outlet for resistance and an opportunity for God to act on the divine promise that all should be free. We flesh this out through a brief consideration of Black music in North America, specifically the spirituals, and the theo-political role they played in the Black freedom struggle.

Chapter 2 considers the hopes of the prophets. It is in the writings of the exilic and postexilic prophets that God's kingship is set in an eschatological context. The prophetic turn toward eschatology was driven in part by the profound failure of the Israelite monarchy and its ruling class, who did not live into the vision of justice articulated in the law. Given those failures, the prophets emphasize that the only righteous reign will be *God's* reign, and thus it is God who brings the kingdom. As we show, for the prophets, God's future reign presses into the present, bringing both a judgment on current injustice and new life. The experiences of exile and restoration form the essential background for the ways the prophets imagined God's coming reign. Strikingly, the prophets do not see YHWH as an external observer but rather as a direct participant in concrete experiences of exile and restoration. YHWH enters into the judgment that befalls Israel in and through the righteous servant. Here, the prophets introduce a messianic dimension to their reflections on God's reign, for the emphasis on divine agency does not preclude but rather includes a human dimension, as God's partner has a role to play in bringing God's Jubilee justice. And as we show, the prophets imagine the restoration of Israel as a kind of cosmic Jubilee. Lastly, we consider a politics of exile that imagines ways of life that reject exploitation and injustice, and that embrace life-giving forms of community.

Chapter 3 considers the important ways that apocalyptic discourse offers additional layers to the notion of God's coming reign. The writers of apocalyptic literature widen the frame and intensify the dire situation in which not only Israel but also humanity as a whole finds itself. Of great significance for our understanding of Jesus is the enigmatic figure of the Son of Man, who, much like the righteous servant, functions as God's partner in bringing the kingdom but who also begins to take on divine characteristics as a co-regent with God not only on earth but also in heaven. A key ingredient in the production of most apocalyptic literature is a sense of impending crisis. In fact, for some, apocalyptic writing is considered resistance literature, thus it is no surprise that apocalyptic has influenced and informed a variety of resistance and revolutionary movements. To demonstrate this point, and to indicate what an apocalyptic politics might look like, we offer a brief consideration of the Black freedom struggle during the nineteenth century, when apocalyptic notions and the image of Jubilee were key themes shaping the vision and fueling the actions of communities struggling to free themselves from white supremacist rule. The chapter concludes with a brief synthetic recounting of the first three chapters. Taken together, the psalms, prophets, and apocalyptic visionaries offer a vision of God's reign that is fundamentally different from human rule, in that it is animated by God's compassionate justice and faithful righteousness, which is good news for humanity and the earth, and especially to those whose existence is threatened by violence, injustice, and dispossession.

Chapters 4, 5, and 6 take up the background provided by the first three chapters and offer an interpretation of Jesus's life, death, and resurrection. Chapter 4 is especially concerned to offer an outline of Jesus's ministry, including his preaching, his work to release those in bondage, and his extension of table fellowship. We explore these under the broad headings of "release from bondage" and "the great reversal," both of which are deeply rooted in the vision of Jubilee. What emerges is a picture of Jesus, the Son of Man, whose life is dedicated to the proclamation and embodiment of God's reign, a reign that resonates deeply with the Jubilee found in the Hebrew Scriptures and that encounters resistance as it confronts the injustice of the world in an apocalyptic manner.

Chapter 5 is concerned with interpreting Jesus's way to the cross, which is the way of God's reign. As we show, the biblical witness understands the resistance to Jesus's ministry and declaration of God's great Jubilee as deeply human but also ideological and even cosmic. The forces arrayed against Jesus include not only human actors but also larger social forces and the cosmic powers of death and sin. Through a brief discussion of the ideology of white supremacy and racial capitalism, we show that the powers and principalities against which Jesus himself stood continue to provoke, while the Spirit of Jesus continues to call disciples into action. At the same time, the death of Jesus is also an unveiling, revealing the insidious nature of human resistance to the divine call to live into God's loving hope for creation. To this end, we show that all of the Gospels offer a theological interpretation of the events surrounding Jesus's execution in apocalyptic categories. At the same time, this fact should not distract us from the profoundly human character of the event of the cross, an event in which an innocent man is lynched. In this event, God is shown to be the God of the oppressed, for Jesus takes his place among the crucified of history, and by so doing calls into question all forms of dehumanization and shows God's unwavering faithfulness such that God is even willing to enter death to liberate creation. As such, the event of the cross functions as a kind of apex moment, since it reveals the character of God's reign.

Chapter 6 considers the fact that the cross is not the end of the story, neither for Jesus, nor for his followers, nor for the crucified of history. For the Crucified One lives! God raises Jesus from the dead, and in so doing vindicates his way of life. As we argue, the resurrection of Jesus is an affirmation that Jesus's way of life *is in fact God's way of life*—a way of life that death cannot and will never be able to master. With his vindication, justice is done on behalf of the crucified of history, for what happens in and to Jesus is not simply about him alone but about creation as a whole, and especially about those who have been trodden underfoot. But the resurrection is not simply a reality that occurred in the past, or that we await in the future—it is also experienced now through the outpouring of the Spirit. It is the Spirit of freedom who empowers and energizes communities and persons to resist the powers of death and to imagine and work for spaces and places where God's *shalom* can more fully be experienced. We conclude the chapter with a brief consideration of George Floyd Square and the work of the people in south Minneapolis to reassert and reclaim community self-determination, which means justice and hope for those who have lived under regimes designed to dispossess and kill.

Acknowledgments

This book would not have been possible without the encouragement and helpful criticism of many people. First, thanks must go to the countless individuals and communities from whom I have learned and with whom I have often discussed the ideas in this book, especially the animating theme of God's reign. Without those critical conversations, what is offered here would be far poorer in both its content and its aims.

To those many friends, colleagues, and former students who read portions of the argument as it evolved over the years, including Chris Boesel, Donald Dayton, Kait Dugan, Victor Ezigbo, David Felsch, Tyler Gerdin, Stina Jost, Abbey Kisner, Bernon Lee, Sara Misgen, Devorah Schoenfeld, and J. T. Young, I offer my hearty thanks. Thanks also go to Andy Browne for his insights into the struggle for justice and the practices of commoning that have evolved at George Floyd Square in Minneapolis. I am especially grateful to Tyler Davis and Ry Siggelkow, who read the manuscript in its entirety multiple times and offered significant feedback, criticism, and encouragement. Without their insights and prodding, it is quite possible that this project would never have seen the light of day.

To the series editors Peter Goodwin Heltzel, Bruce Benson, and Malinda Elizabeth Berry I owe a large debt of gratitude. They believed in the project from its inception, but most importantly, they sojourned with me as my research and argument evolved over the years. Their patience, cheerfulness, and thoughtful feedback made a significant contribution to seeing the project to completion. I also want to extend my thanks to James Ernest, Andrew Knapp, Laurel Draper, and the whole editorial team at Eerdmans for making the process both smooth and productive.

ACKNOWLEDGMENTS

There have been several communities with which I have traveled over the years of the project's gestation. Few have been as important as Meetinghouse Church, where I currently serve as a minister and member of the community. The peculiar forms of theological exegesis and biblical interpretation offered here were often first attempted in Bible studies and sermons at Meetinghouse, though admittedly without the footnotes and academic jargon. It is not lost on me that I am fortunate not only to have a community to love and to serve but that I get to the do the work of ministry alongside remarkable and graceful people, both lay and clergy, who have a deep commitment to God's love and justice. I am especially grateful to my colleague and friend Sara Wilhelm Garbers for the support, encouragement, and enthusiasm she showed for the project as I shared portions with her. Her willingness to write a foreword for the work is a gift that I shall not soon be able to repay.

Love, care, hope, grace—these and many more are the gifts that my family has given to me. I would never have been able to pursue, let alone complete, this work without the unfailing support of my extended family, the Winns, the Crumrines, and the Kerners. And for those closest to me, my sons Jonah and Elijah, and my wife Julie, I continue to find life with you an unimaginable source of blessing even in the hardest of times. To Julie, my muse and my truest friend, I can only say thank you for your love and confidence in me and in the vision found in these pages. And for my two sons, to whom I dedicate this book, you have reminded me often that life is to be lived and lived to the full. May you continue to find your own voices in a world in desperate need of love and justice and use them for the good of your neighbor.

Finally, I almost abandoned this project several times. But for the living voice I encountered time and time again in Scripture and in life, I would have given up long ago. My truest hope is that I have been able to point to you, the one whose love overcomes all things. May your kingdom come, Lord Jesus!

INTRODUCTION

At the center of Christian faith and life stands the figure of Jesus of Nazareth, and any attempt to understand what Jesus was about requires wrestling with the central theme of his life: the reign of God. This book is concerned with two key questions: *What* is the reign of God about which Jesus speaks? And, what, if anything, does the reign of God have to do with *our social lives*? Unfortunately, there are no simple answers to these questions, as no metaphor from the Bible has suffered so much misunderstanding as the "kingdom of God."[1] Consider the following.

1. Feminist scholarship has pushed for a needed reconsideration of the use of the terminology of "kingdom of God." See Ada María Isasi-Díaz, "Kin-dom of God: A *Mujerista* Proposal," in *In Our Own Voices: Latino/a Renditions of Theology*, ed. Benjamin Valentin (Maryknoll, NY: Orbis, 2010), 171–89, and Ada María Isasi-Díaz, *Mujerista Theology: A Theology for the Twenty-First Century* (Maryknoll, NY: Orbis, 1996), 166n9. Notwithstanding the merit of these criticisms, we will use the language of "reign of God" and, less frequently, "kingdom of God" throughout. We do so for three reasons: first, the language of "reign" or "kingdom" retains the intrinsic political meaning and therefore social and political implications of such language. Second, proposed alternatives such as "kin-dom of God" have their own problematic connotations, including the fact that "family" can be just as fraught and entangled with oppression as other forms of social organization. And third, the history of scholarship, biblical translation, and widespread usage makes such terminology more easily accessible, even though the basic content of the reign of God that will be outlined here shares a great deal with the vision of feminist theology. For feminist theologians who use the language of "kingdom" or "reign of God," see Susanne Guenther Loewen, "'We Are All Meant to Be Mothers of God': Mothering as Embodied Peacemaking," *Vision: A Journal for Church and Theology* 1, no. 1 (Fall 2000): 32–43, and Sharon H. Ringe, *Jesus, Liberation, and the Biblical Jubilee: Images for Ethics and Christology* (Philadelphia: Fortress, 1985).

In March 1957, E. Earle Ellis, a young assistant professor of Bible and religion at Aurora College in Aurora, Illinois, published a short article in *Christianity Today* titled "Segregation and the Kingdom of God." The article bears all the hallmarks of the southern defense of segregationist racial policies, but it does so by appealing to the metaphor of the kingdom of God. Somewhat shockingly, Ellis's argument was that the reign of God was not a single homogenous otherworldly phenomenon but rather was a reality that intersected with this world, affirming and working with the differences found in the world. According to Ellis, these differences were protected more readily in a segregated society than in an integrated one.[2]

This, of course, would have been news to the members of the newly formed Southern Christian Leadership Conference—and especially to Martin Luther King Jr.—who saw themselves as struggling for the "creation of the beloved community,"[3] a provisional or initial appearing of the kingdom of God on earth.[4] In fact, as Eyal Naveh has pointed out, "the concept of the Kingdom of God was undoubtedly central to the most renowned postwar reform group—the civil rights movement."[5] And these two examples are not anomalies.

From Columbus and the Catholic conquistadores to the Puritans, apocalypticism and the attempt to build the kingdom of God were a ubiquitous presence in the early history of the European invasion of the Americas and persist down to the present day as a key metaphor in Christian circles as a way of talking about God's designs for the world.[6] In the history of the

2. See E. Earle Ellis, "Segregation and the Kingdom of God," *Christianity Today* 1, no. 12 (March 1957): 9.

3. Martin Luther King Jr., "Facing the Challenge of a New Age," in *A Testament of Hope: The Essential Writings and Speeches of Martin Luther King, Jr.*, ed. James M. Washington (San Francisco: HarperCollins, 1986), 140.

4. See Eyal Naveh, "Dialectical Redemption: Reinhold Niebuhr, Martin Luther King, Jr., and the Kingdom of God in America," *Journal of Religious Thought* 42, no. 2 (1989-1990): 73-76.

5. Naveh, "Dialectical Redemption," 73.

6. See Charles H. Lippy, "Waiting for the End: The Social Context of American Apocalyptic Religion," in *The Apocalyptic Vision in America: Interdisciplinary Essays in Myth and Culture*, ed. Lois Parkinson Zamora (Bowling Green, OH: Bowling Green University Popular Press, 1982), 37-63; see also John Leddy Phelan, *The Millennial Kingdom of the Franciscans in the New World*, 2nd ed. (Berkeley: University of California Press, 1970); Djelal Kadir, *Columbus and the Ends of the Earth: Europe's Prophetic Rhetoric as Conquering Ideology* (Berkeley: University of California Press, 1992); Avihu Zakai, *Exile and Kingdom: History and Apocalypse in the Puritan Migration to America* (Cambridge: Cambridge University Press, 1992); and Frank Granzano, *The Millennial New World* (Oxford: Oxford University Press, 1999).

United States, appeal to the metaphor of the "kingdom of God" or "reign of God" has been used to justify radically different ethical and social visions, including colonization, slavery, and racism as well as abolition, desegregation, and numerous movements for social equity and justice. It would be hard to find another metaphor from the Bible that has been subject to so many different interpretations.

THE CENTRALITY OF THE "REIGN OF GOD"

Why has the concept of the reign of God played such an outsized role in so many modern social movements?

The Witness of Scripture

One obvious reason that the concept of the reign of God has played such a conspicuous role in the recent history of the Americas is, in part, that it is the core element in the preaching of Jesus. In the Gospel of Mark, widely regarded as the first of the four Gospels to be written, the first words we hear out of the mouth of Jesus of Nazareth are: "The time is fulfilled, and the kingdom of God has come near; repent, and believe in the good news" (1:15).[7] Perhaps counterintuitively, Jesus describes the kingdom proclaimed as a "secret" given to the disciples but conveyed in parables to "those outside" (4:11). The kingdom is that which has come, and yet that which is still to come (9:1). Jesus describes the kingdom as that which comes upon a person (1:15), but also as something that one enters into (10:23-25).

In the Gospel of Matthew, though it is John the Baptist who inaugurates the proclamation of God's reign (3:1), Jesus takes up the theme and makes it central to his own proclamation and teaching (e.g., 4:17). In distinction from Mark, in Matthew Jesus speaks about the "kingdom of heaven" as well as the "kingdom of God," the former being a synonym for the latter. The kingdom belongs to those who are poor in spirit, those who are "persecuted for righteousness' sake" (5:3, 10), and those who care for "the least of these" (25:34-40). Jesus calls into question easy assumptions about who the heirs of the kingdom are (e.g., 7:21; 8:11-12; 19:14, 23-24) and instructs his disciples to pray for the coming of the kingdom (6:10), while also sending them out to proclaim "the good news, 'The kingdom of heaven has

---

7. Biblical quotations follow the NRSV unless otherwise stated.

come near'" (10:7). In Matthew's Gospel, Jesus's ministry of healing and his exorcisms are both explicitly identified with the inbreaking presence of the reign of God (e.g., 9:35; 12:28), and those to whom the "keys of the kingdom" are given are said to have the power to bind and loose both in heaven and on earth (16:19).

In the Gospel of Luke, the announcement of the birth of Jesus is accompanied by the proclamation that his kingdom will have no end (1:33). In concert with Mark and Matthew, the concept of the "kingdom of God" or the rule of God is prominent in Jesus's preaching and teaching (e.g., Luke 4:43; 6:20; 8:1). Jesus is the great teacher of parables, comparing the reign of God to a reality whose beginning is small and of little consequence, and yet grows to become ubiquitous and determinative for life and well-being (e.g., 13:18-21). As in Matthew, events of healing and exorcism are kingdom events (e.g., Luke 9:2, 11; 11:20; 17:20-21). Following Jesus is the costly venture of witness to the reign of God (9:57-62). Even in the Gospel of John, where the terminology of "kingdom" is not as prominent, nevertheless the crucifixion of Jesus is described through the metaphors of kingship and enthronement (e.g., John 3:14; 8:28; 12:32-33).

As this brief overview of the Gospels shows, not only was the kingdom metaphor central to Jesus's message but it was also capable of bearing significantly different meanings. Sifting through the many potential interpretations of the theme of the kingdom or reign of God has been a major occupation of scholars since the 1892 publication of Johannes Weiss's seminal work, *Jesus' Proclamation of the Kingdom of God*.[8] Having agreed that central to the preaching of Jesus was the message of the coming of the kingdom, scholars have nevertheless been divided as to the precise meaning of the phrase.[9] Some questions, however, have been provisionally settled.

For instance, the issue of the kingdom's time signature. Is the reign of God a reality that lies only in the future, or is it present in the here and now, or is it some combination of the two? Weiss and others argued for the fundamentally eschatological and apocalyptic, and therefore future, dimension of Jesus's preaching. The kingdom of God is not the product of history; rather, it will disrupt history at its end. For Weiss and (later) Albert

---

8. Johannes Weiss, *Jesus' Proclamation of the Kingdom of God* (Philadelphia: Fortress, 1971).

9. For surveys of this discussion, see Gösta Lundström, *The Kingdom of God in the Teaching of Jesus: A History of Interpretation from the Last Decades of the Nineteenth Century to the Present Day* (Richmond, VA: John Knox, 1963), and Mark Saucy, *The Kingdom of God in the Teaching of Jesus: In the 20th Century* (Dallas: Word, 1997).

Schweitzer,[10] the kingdom that Jesus preached had not yet arrived; rather, it was to be understood in an almost exclusively futuristic sense.[11]

This position was later countered by C. H. Dodd, who argued for a present or realized eschatology,[12] which emphasized the presence of the kingdom in the ministry of Jesus. For Dodd, in the person of Jesus, the kingdom "is not merely immanent; it is here."[13] Dodd's position was eventually modified by George Eldon Ladd, who developed what has come to be called an "inaugurated eschatology" characterized by the tension of an "already, not yet" dialectic in which the kingdom has truly arrived in the ministry of Jesus but has not yet been revealed in all its fullness.[14] As Ladd puts it, "The Kingdom of God involves two great moments: fulfillment within history, and consummation at the end of history."[15] Ladd's configuration has become the dominant way that theologians and others speak about the presence and future of God's reign.

Another important question scholars have been debating is, does the "kingdom of God" as used by Jesus, and anticipated in Jewish thought, refer primarily to a realm or space where God rules, or does it refer more

10. See Albert Schweitzer, *The Quest of the Historical Jesus* (New York: Macmillan, 1968); Albert Schweitzer, *The Mystery of the Kingdom of God* (Buffalo, NY: Prometheus, 1985); Albert Schweitzer, *The Kingdom of God and Primitive Christianity* (New York: Seabury, 1968).

11. See Lundström, *The Kingdom of God*, 69–95.

12. See Lundström, *The Kingdom of God*, 113–24.

13. C. H. Dodd, *The Parables of the Kingdom* (New York: Charles Scribner's Sons, 1961), 33.

14. George Eldon Ladd, *The Presence of the Future: The Eschatology of Biblical Realism*, rev. ed. (Grand Rapids: Eerdmans, 1974). Ladd's work is preceded by Werner G. Kümmel and his seminal work, *Promise and Fulfillment: The Eschatological Message of Jesus* (Naperville, IL: Allenson, 1957).

15. Ladd, *Presence of the Future*, 218. Ladd utilized two relatively distinct forms of Jewish eschatology—the prophetic and the apocalyptic—to delineate this present-future tension. Though the central insight that there is a tension in the preaching of Jesus between the present and the future has generally stood the test of time, Ladd's division between a prophetic-present and an apocalyptic-future has proven to be more problematic, as the whole of Jesus's life, death, and resurrection bears unmistakable apocalyptic characteristics. As an example, see Brant Pitre, *Jesus, the Tribulation, and the End of the Exile: Restoration Eschatology and the Origin of the Atonement* (Grand Rapids: Baker Academic, 2005). "Kingdom" language in the New Testament is incorrigibly eschatological and apocalyptic and must be interpreted against that backdrop. This is not an uncontested claim, however. See, for example, the various essays in Robert J. Miller, ed., *The Apocalyptic Jesus: A Debate* (Santa Rosa, CA: Polebridge, 2001), and John S. Kloppenborg, with John W. Marshall, eds., *Apocalypticism, Anti-Semitism, and the Historical Jesus: Subtexts in Criticism* (London: T&T Clark International, 2005).

to the active ruling of God? Though too sharp a contrast between rule and realm should probably be avoided, nevertheless, the general consensus of biblical scholarship—one that also informs the approach of this book—is that the kingdom about which Jesus spoke refers to the active reign of God rather than a specific realm.[16]

Finally, scholars have also come to the conclusion that in order to get clarity on the meaning of the "kingdom of God," one has to understand that the phrase is multilayered and includes "a complex set of associations."[17] This insight has expanded the conceptual and semantic field for understanding the realities about which kingdom discourse speaks well beyond the specific utterances of the term "kingdom of God" found in the biblical text.[18] There is now a general consensus that understanding what Jesus's kingdom language referred to requires attending to the imagery and events that include kingship, power, authority, etc., as well as the eschatological and apocalyptic contours found in other parts of the biblical witness, and in other texts that would have influenced Jesus and the early Christian movement.[19]

The Reign of God and Our Social Arrangements

Even with these clarifications, there is still confusion regarding what precisely the reign of God might be. This is a pressing matter not just for biblical interpretation but also because the term has often either influenced or appeared in the discourse of different social movements as a justification for human social action as we have already noted. And there is good reason why communities and individuals have appealed to the kingdom metaphor, because it so clearly speaks about power, especially social power. For when

16. See Jeremy R. Treat, *The Crucified King: Atonement and Kingdom in Biblical and Systematic Theology* (Grand Rapids: Zondervan, 2004), 41.

17. Karl Allen Kuhn, *The Kingdom according to Luke and Acts* (Grand Rapids: Baker Academic, 2015), 24.

18. Several approaches to this have been developed over the years. See, for example, Norman Perrin, *Jesus and the Language of the Kingdom* (Philadelphia: Fortress, 1976); H. Leroy Metts, "The Kingdom of God: Background and Development of a Complex Discourse Concept," *Criswell Theological Review* 2, no. 1 (Fall 2004): 51–82; and Anne Moore, *Moving beyond Symbol and Myth: Understanding the Kingship of God of the Hebrew Bible through Metaphor* (New York: Lang, 2009).

19. See Stephen Voorwinde, "The Kingdom of God in the Proclamation of Jesus," in *The Content and Setting of the Gospel Traditions*, ed. Mark Harding and Alanna Nobbs (Grand Rapids: Eerdmans, 2010), 329–53.

Jesus came preaching the "kingdom of God," he was, at the very least, proclaiming that there was another power at work in the world, a power that was superior to that of Caesar—and fundamentally different.

Such a claim offers something like "a 'narrative substructure' for making sense of and articulating God's intentions for creation, Israel's identity as God's people, the current state of reality, and what the future would hold."[20] According to one scholar, the overarching story of the kingdom of God contained three key elements: "1. Yahweh is King of Israel and Ruler of the universe. 2. The current order of creation and state of God's people are not in alignment with God's will. 3. God will act to reorder creation into alignment with God's intentions."[21] Stories or histories of this type create meaning and purpose while offering direction for action in the midst of chaos. Functioning like a foundation myth, whose central task is to animate a community with a particular vision of the world that will inform how they should act in that world,[22] the story of God's reign is also invariably political and ethical.[23] The narrative of the rule of God offers to communities and persons of faith an alternative way of viewing reality, and thereby contributes to the conditions for an alternative way of being social.

As we have noted, however, this metaphor has been used for very different purposes, many of which most Christians, and frankly most people of good will, would describe as antithetical to the life and ministry of Jesus. How then do we discern where the kingdom or reign of God is truly at work? In other words, how do we decide which of the two antithetical kingdom visions described at the beginning of this introduction is actually faithful to the vision of Jesus? This book attempts to answer this question by offering a biblical and theological description of God's reign that is rooted in the life, death, and resurrection of Jesus, for the purpose of helping communities of faith to discern in outline what God's reign looks like and how they might join in with God's good work of repairing the world.

20. Kuhn, *The Kingdom*, 25.
21. Kuhn, *The Kingdom*, 25.
22. See Kevin J. Vanhoozer, *Remythologizing Theology: Divine Action, Passion, and Authorship* (Cambridge: Cambridge University Press, 2010), 5-8.
23. For some recent discussions of the role of myth in the construction of nationalism and the state, see Anthony D. Smith, *Chosen Peoples: Sacred Stories of National Identity* (Oxford: Oxford University Press, 2003), and Bruce Lincoln, *Gods and Demons, Priests and Scholars: Critical Explorations in the History of Religions* (Chicago: University of Chicago Press, 2012).

Jesus Is the Reign of God Enfleshed

The thesis of this book is that Jesus *is* the kingdom of God. In his life, death, and resurrection, *Jesus* is the quintessential demonstration of the rule of God in the form of self-giving love, and he is the true covenant partner, embodying active human faithfulness unto death. His life is the concrete embodiment of divine and human fellowship marked by Jubilee justice, which is the compassionate justice and mercy of which Micah 6:8 speaks. In him, God has entered the cosmos in a definitive fashion, overthrowing the politics of death that stands behind the ways of much of our world. His resurrection, among other things, is a vindication of his way of life, a way of life that death cannot master.

The rule of God that Jesus *is* calls forth the response of faithfulness. The form of that faithfulness is parabolic. Jesus is singular, unique, and unrepeatable. His death and resurrection declare the true end of the politics of death and sin, by illuminating the indestructibility of the politics of God. But the centrality of divine action in Jesus does not erase human agency. It creates space for it in the form of parabolic expressions of faithfulness. Through the Spirit of the Messiah, the rule of God has now been poured out in a new and provisional fashion, to be experienced and lived out in the here and now. Thus, the politics of Jesus calls for a politics of discipleship that is Spirit-empowered, and parabolic (i.e., not exhaustive nor directly identifiable with God's rule embodied in Jesus).

Kingdom—Jubilee—Apocalypse

As the unfolding argument shows, the metaphor of the kingdom is bound up especially with two other broad conceptual fields found in Scripture: Jubilee and apocalyptic. If the kingdom of God refers to the active reign of God that is both present and future, then Jubilee, a notion first developed in the book of Leviticus and then taken up by the prophets, visionaries, and eventually Jesus himself, points to the concrete shape of God's reign. The Jubilee laws in Leviticus 25 envision a form of social redistribution and reconciliation. As we discuss in chapter 1, they called for the cancellation of debts, freeing of prisoners, and a restoration of the land. The Day of Jubilee, which was supposed to occur once every fifty years, was nothing less than a revolution that imagined a society marked more by equity and justice than rampant accumulation and the concentration of power. The prophets and visionaries took over this vision and widened its scope, such that when they spoke of the salvation and restoration of the earth, it was seen as a kind of cosmic Jubilee. As we point out, Jesus took over this tradition and framed his own ministry as an expression of God's great Jubilee.

The word "apocalyptic" is derived from the Greek term *apokalypsis*, which means to "unveil," "disclose," or "reveal."[24] As we discuss in chapter 3, the term has several important component parts, but above all it makes clear the confrontational nature of God's reign with the ruling powers of the world. In other words, when God's reign presses into the present, it challenges the structures and ways of the world. Though many of the apocalyptic texts that highlight this element often utilize violent imagery, the underlying point is that God's reign is going to overthrow present unjust and dehumanizing arrangements so that creation can be set free to flourish.

Both Jubilee and apocalyptic figure prominently in the imagery, words, and actions of Jesus, and are especially helpful for elaborating how Jesus understood and sought to embody the kingdom of God of which he spoke. When taken together, kingdom, Jubilee, and apocalypse form a threefold cord. Kingdom refers to God's active embodied reign that is made uniquely manifest in Jesus, is poured out in the Spirit, and is both present and future. Jubilee then offers a way of talking about the contours of the life that God's reign seeks to establish, while apocalyptic offers a way of imaging what happens when this radically different mode of life confronts or is confronted by the powers and principalities that currently rule human imaginations and arrangements.

However, of even more significance for our argument and approach is Jesus himself, as he is portrayed in the biblical narratives. Though the concepts kingdom or reign of God, Jubilee, and apocalyptic all have important antecedent histories that give shape and meaning to our understanding, it is Jesus who is most determinative. Through his ministry and teaching, and in his life, death, and resurrection, these concepts take on a distinctly christological coloring. Thus, the Jubilee life that God's reign points to is seen most clearly in the life of the humble Jesus, who kept faith with God and humankind, was welcoming to the stranger and the sinner, and concerned with the liberation of the body, spirit, and social dimensions of human life, and whose commitment to these realities led him to become one who was faithful unto death. His life history constitutes a kind of apocalypse, a challenge to the status quo, which is a clear demonstration of God's desire for life and the overthrow of death.

---

24. See Wilhelm Mundle, "Revelation," in *The New International Dictionary of the New Testament*, ed. Colin Brown (Grand Rapids: Zondervan, 1986), 3:310-16.

The Liberating Spirit

This book offers a theological and theo-political meditation on the biblical narrative. My introduction to Christian theology came through a reading of James Cone's *God of the Oppressed*[25] in a college class on religion and American culture. For a young white male who had grown up in the southern United States, reading Cone's work was something like an earthquake. It removed my own blinders to the racial formation and arrangements of injustice in which I had been living and showed me the profoundly anti-Christian nature of much of what passed for Christianity in the United States.[26]

Aside from the trenchant critique of racial injustice, three other elements from that work have stayed with me and informed my approach in the present book. The first was the deadly seriousness with which Cone took Scripture. His work was marked by a consistent attending to the Bible in all its problematic beauty and power. It impressed upon me the profound ways in which the Christian church—and individual Christians, including myself—doesn't always read Scripture very carefully or closely. The current volume bears the impact of Cone and others in that it offers an argument that is deeply rooted in the witness of Scripture.

The second aspect of Cone that has remained with me was his pronounced Christocentrism. For Cone, following in the wake of both the Black church tradition and the dialectical theology of Karl Barth, Dietrich Bonhoeffer, and others, it is Jesus who most clearly reveals who God is. Jesus is God enfleshed, who in his own life, death, and resurrection reveals God's deepest intentions, truest character, and unyielding solidarity with a humanity and creation in thrall to death.

In Jesus we are given a vision of the *way* that God is God. That is, in Jesus God is revealed as the partisan of the poor, the one who stands alongside the oppressed, and the liberator of the captives. As Cone himself notes, "it is impossible to speak of the God of Israelite history, who is the God revealed in Jesus Christ, without recognizing that God is the God *of* and *for* those who labor and are overladen."[27] This commitment to the crucified of history is made plain in Jesus's willing and faithful journey, which ends

---

25. James H. Cone, *God of the Oppressed*, rev. ed. (Maryknoll, NY: Orbis, 1997).

26. See, for instance, Cone's reframing of the issue of heresy in *God of the Oppressed*, 33-35.

27. James H. Cone, *A Black Theology of Liberation*, fortieth anniversary ed. (Maryknoll, NY: Orbis, 2016), 1.

with his dehumanizing rejection via the cross—an experience Cone has powerfully connected to the African American experience of lynching in the nineteenth and twentieth century.[28] For Cone, what the Gospels show is that Jesus positions himself, his message, and his ministry—and therefore God positions Godself—to be in solidarity with those on the margins or underside of history, and as such he reveals himself to be Black, or one who lives especially among those who in the modern world have found themselves disinherited and dehumanized.[29]

Thus, Cone's Christocentrism bears an essentially liberative stamp. This leads then to the last element in Cone's vision and work that has stayed with me over the years: his unrelenting commitment to the concrete way in which God is God, a way that is fundamentally *liberative*. Cone's theology avoids abstractions and moves always toward the concrete and the particular. To be more specific, it moves toward and is inspired by the concrete struggle for Black freedom, a freedom that is in fact expansive and potentially inclusive of all peoples and creatures, but that begins with the oppressed.

As the reader will find, I too have been shaped by Cone and others, having become convinced that God's deepest intentions for creation and for all creatures is that they have access to a flourishing life in fellowship and freedom. In a world marked by death-dealing ideologies like racial capitalism, such a divine intention expresses itself as an apocalypse of liberation, a fact to which the biblical witness and the lives and struggles of oppressed communities attest. The present book is inspired by these witnesses, but it is also an attempt to rethink the form of the Christian faith that was initially passed on to me not so much by leaving behind the biblical witness but rather by reengaging it with different eyes. The form of Christian faith and culture that I inherited was indelibly shaped by the assumptions of the racialized political economy prevalent in the United States.[30] My own

---

28. See James H. Cone, *The Cross and the Lynching Tree* (Maryknoll, NY: Orbis, 2011).

29. See Cone, *God of the Oppressed*, 122-26; see also Cone, *Black Theology of Liberation*, 8-9.

30. "Racial capitalism" is a term that was first developed in response to the apartheid state of South Africa after 1948, though it is now used to name the key dynamics and practices bound up with the social and political economy that evolved from the late medieval era into modern racial regimes. Among other things, it names the fact that racism and racialization are the products of a capitalist political economy predicated on the extraction of cheap or free labor and the enclosure of common lands and resources. See, among others, Eric Williams, *Capitalism and Slavery* (Chapel Hill: University of North Carolina Press, 1944); Cedric J. Robinson, *Black Marxism: The Making of the Black Radical*

longing is and has been to find a way out of this enclosure and into God's capacious Jubilee reign. Thus, this is an exercise in attempting to see the text of Scripture and our world from the perspective of the "crucified of history" so as to struggle for a more just and life-giving world. My hope is to find others who are either on the journey or who long to begin.

The Call to Discipleship

The reign of God is more than a story or an idea. It is an ongoing reality that makes a claim on our lives. The way of Jesus is a way of life in the face of death. Echoing Moses at Mount Sinai, the ancient Christian text the Didache speaks about the way of death and the way of life, calling for the early Christians to enter into the way of life.[31] This call still echoes into our own time, even if the challenges we face are different.

Our world, much like the ancient world, continues to be organized by death-dealing powers and ideologies. But God is also at work in our world, working to repair that which is broken, to lift up the lowly, to heal the broken and the brokenhearted, to bring justice and mercy where there is only injustice and despair. The call of discipleship is the call to turn toward the God of life, whose reign is embodied in Jesus. It is the call to receive the Spirit of freedom in the here and now and to enter into the struggle for life for all of humankind and creation, and especially for those who have little or no access to the flourishing life that God intends. Let us choose the way of Jesus, the way of life, the way of God's reign, the way of love!

Tradition (Chapel Hill: University of North Carolina Press, 2000); and Peter Linebaugh and Marcus Rediker, *The Many-Headed Hydra: Sailors, Slaves, Commoners, and the Hidden History of the Revolutionary Atlantic* (Boston: Beacon, 2000).

31. See Aaron Milavec, *The Didache: Text, Translation, Analysis, and Commentary* (Collegeville, MN: Liturgical Press, 2016).

Chapter One

"YHWH HAS BECOME KING"

Jesus is the kingdom of God enfleshed. The purpose of the following chapters is to ground this statement in the biblical witness and to offer a theological and theo-political interpretation of its most salient points. Before we focus on Jesus and the New Testament portrayal of him, however, we will map out some of the most important background concepts and dynamics found in the Old Testament and Jewish apocalyptic traditions. Our story begins with the declaration that "YHWH has become king," a notion that is central to the message of Psalms.[1]

For many scholars, Israel's liturgical book, Psalms, offers an important starting point for understanding biblical conceptions of divine and human kingship because "The theme of the reign or sovereignty of God is here both prominent and pervasive."[2] An important declaration of Psalms is that "YHWH has become king!" What does this mean? Does the proclamation of the rule of God refer to a past, present, or future reality in Psalms? What is the quality of God's kingship? How does God's reign intersect with and critique human forms of rule? We will consider these questions through a brief discussion of the "royal" (e.g., Pss. 2; 18; 20; 21; 45; 72; 89; 101; 110; 132; 144)

The title of this chapter is derived from insights developed by Sigmund Mowinckel in his seminal *The Psalms in Israel's Worship* (Grand Rapids: Eerdmans, 2004).

1. Out of deference to the Jewish tradition, and following the advice of Robert Jenson, we will be using YHWH for the divine personal name, which identifies the God of Israel and Father of Jesus Christ. See Robert W. Jenson, *Systematic Theology*, vol. 1, *The Triune God* (Oxford: Oxford University Press, 1997), 44.

2. Paul Joyce, "The Kingdom of God and the Psalms," in *The Kingdom of God and Human Society*, ed. R. S. Barbour (Edinburgh: T&T Clark, 1993), 42.

and "enthronement" (e.g., Pss. 24; 47; 93; 95–100) psalms. We note the deep ambivalence and even hostility toward human kingship. We also sketch out the difference between God's reign and the reign of human powers and principalities, which is the establishment of righteousness and justice. As we note, the righteousness and justice that YHWH brings is reminiscent of the proclamation of the Year of Jubilee, so that one can describe the kingdom of God as the appearance of the righteousness and justice of God's Jubilee reign.

THE ENTHRONEMENT OF YHWH

The precise phrasing *basileia tou Theou* ("the kingdom of God" or "the reign of God") does not appear in the Septuagint or Greek Old Testament.[3] Nevertheless, the theme of kingship or the rule of God can be found throughout the Old Testament. The Hebrew root *mlk*, which corresponds roughly to the Greek *basileia*, has a number of associative meanings, including "'kingship,' 'royal power,' 'royal dignity,' 'dominion' and 'kingdom.'"[4] Added to this is a variety of word groups that evoke the royal apparatus, or what we might call the imagery of ruling. These include words associated with God's throne or enthronement, the act of judging or judgment, and glory or exaltation.[5] These are employed by various authors to evoke the specter of God's present or future rule.

The theme of YHWH's kingship and the attendant ideas associated with it developed unsystematically, finding different expressions in the preexilic, exilic, and postexilic eras of Israel's existence. Though YHWH's kingship is portrayed across a number of early texts,[6] it is with the psalms that any discussion of Israelite notions of kingship should begin.[7] Robert D.

---

3. See G. R. Beasley-Murray, *Jesus and the Kingdom of God* (Grand Rapids: Eerdmans, 1986), 17.

4. Stephen Voorwinde, "The Kingdom of God in the Proclamation of Jesus," in *The Content and Setting of the Gospel Traditions*, ed. Mark Harding and Alanna Nobbs (Grand Rapids: Eerdmans, 2010), 329.

5. See Robert D. Rowe, *God's Kingdom and God's Son: The Background to Mark's Christology from Concepts of Kingship in the Psalms* (Leiden: Brill, 2002), 15–16.

6. Notwithstanding possible editorial accretions, these texts would include Exod. 15:18, Num. 23:21, Deut. 33:5, and Isa. 6:5, among others. Meredith G. Kline has argued that the whole of the Old Testament, beginning especially in Genesis, is concerned with the confrontation between the kingship of YHWH and the pseudokingship of other powers and forces. See his *Kingdom Prologue: Genesis Foundations for a Covenantal Worldview* (Eugene, OR: Wipf & Stock, 2006).

7. In considering the key places in the OT where the concept of the "kingdom of God"

Rowe goes so far as to argue that "it is in the Psalms that Israelite conceptions of kingship attain their highest expression."[8] Whether Rowe's assessment is correct or not, the pervasive royal imagery found throughout the psalms[9] and the inclusion of two significant and interrelated conceptions of kingship—the human and the divine—mean that the psalms must be taken seriously. Add to that the fact that the psalms also display some of the deep ambivalence toward human kingship that comes to such prominent expression in the subsequent writings of the prophets and apocalyptic traditions, and the Psalter becomes even more important for understanding the biblical vision of the reign of God.

The Royal Psalms

Divine and human kingship are prominent themes in the literature of Psalms. Since the twentieth century, scholars have called attention to two groups of psalms that deal with these themes: the "royal psalms" and the "enthronement psalms." Hermann Gunkel was the first to draw attention to the former (e.g., 2; 18; 20; 21; 45; 72; 89; 101; 110; 132; 144).[10] These hymns were marked by the special attention they paid to the figure of the king, who was generally not to be confused with YHWH but who was nevertheless placed in close relationship. Dating these psalms precisely is difficult, but they probably bear a preexilic stamp, having been constructed in association with coronation or enthronement festivals for the kings of Israel and Judah. In this endeavor, the psalmists reflect the influence of ancient Near Eastern ideas regarding the person of the king:

> The king is Yahweh's anointed, and as such he is endowed with the spirit of Yahweh (1 Sam. 10.6, 9ff.; 11.6f.; 16.13) and with supra-normal faculties and powers (Ps. 89.22; Mic. 5.3; Num. 24.17). He is chosen by Yahweh

---

comes to light explicitly, Martin J. Selman argues that the language and imagery of Psalms provide the source material for other texts, including the histories and the prophets. See his "The Kingdom of God in the Old Testament," *Tyndale Bulletin* 40, no. 2 (November 1989): 161-83.

8. Rowe, *God's Kingdom*, 13.

9. Because of its pervasive presence, James L. Mays argues that "the Lord reigns" should be understood as the root metaphor for the whole Psalter. See his *The Lord Reigns: A Theological Handbook to the Psalms* (Louisville: Westminster John Knox, 1994), 12-22.

10. See Hermann Gunkel, *Introduction to Psalms: The Genres of the Religious Lyric of Israel* (Macon, GA: Mercer University Press, 1998).

(1 Sam. 10.24; 16.1ff.; 2 Sam. 7.8; Pss. 45.8; 89.21), adopted and fostered by him (Pss. 2.2; 18.35; 89.27f.). He is the son of Yahweh. . . . He is endowed with "eternity" (1 Kgs. 1.31; Pss. 21.5; 72.5) i.e., superhuman life-force, even divinity (Ps. 45.7). . . . He is the people's source of strength, its "breath of life" (Lam. 4.20), "equal to ten thousand of us" (2 Sam. 18.3), "Israel's lamp" (2 Sam. 21.7), the bearer of divine forces, without whom Israel cannot live (Hos. 3.4), the protector in whose "shadow" it lives (Lam. 4.20). He is endowed with an extraordinary quality of success (Pss. 20.5f.; 72.6, 17; 2 Sam. 23.3f.), with victory and glory (Pss. 110.2, 5ff.; 72.9; 45.4–6), with righteousness (Pss. 72.1, 4f., 12–14; 45.7f.; 101), wisdom (2 Sam. 14.7; 1 Kgs. 3.5ff.), and piety (Pss. 20.4; 72.1; 18.21ff.). As the son of the highest god, Yahweh, and his viceroy on earth he is entitled to world sovereignty (Pss. 2.8; 72.8–11; 89.26ff.). This is the style in which he speaks, like one of the great rulers on the Euphrates or the Nile.[11]

The parallels with Egyptian and Mesopotamian notions of kingship are striking not only in their mythic or theological structure but especially in the possible political implications that they entailed.

Endowing the king with the authority of YHWH was a sword that could, and probably did, cut both ways. On the one hand, if the king ruled with justice and mercy, then his reign could be interpreted as an expression of God's grace. On the other hand, if the king chose to identify more with the spectacle of rule, military glory, and the opulence of wealth, his identification with YHWH as depicted in these psalms could provide a shield against criticism—the king is, after all, the Lord's Anointed. Walter Brueggemann, following Sigmund Mowinckel, has theorized that the liturgical setting for such psalms was probably enthronement festivals wherein the king was either enthroned for the first time or his enthronement was reinscribed in the memory of the people. Either way, "the liturgy of enthronement, as it was sung and enacted in the Jerusalem Temple, is closely tied to the politics of the city of Jerusalem, the Temple establishment, and finally to the Davidic dynasty."[12] As such, it represented a temptation to the kings of Israel—the temptation to empire, to a self-sustaining existence based on the exploitation of others.[13] We must therefore note one of the most

11. Mowinckel, *Psalms in Israel's Worship*, 53.

12. Walter Brueggemann, *Israel's Praise: Doxology against Idolatry and Ideology* (Philadelphia: Fortress, 1988), 60.

13. See J. J. M. Roberts, "The Enthronement of Yhwh and David: The Abiding Theolog-

important elements that mark the royal psalms off from their ancient Near Eastern parallels: the real theme of these psalms is the "sovereignty of Yahweh."[14]

Already in the royal psalms themselves, significant ambivalence shrouds the status of the king. Though named a "son of God," the king is not such by nature, but only through adoption. As Hans-Joachim Kraus puts it: "The king in Jerusalem becomes the 'son of God' by being called to that status and installed in a ceremony that confers power and authority."[15] Thus the declaration of the king as "son of God" is neither a metaphysical nor a mythological declaration, as might have been the case for an Egyptian monarch.[16] Likewise, almost all the other divine characteristics to be exercised by the king are ultimately endowments rooted not in the king's nature but the gifting of YHWH, the implication being that the king is not free to exercise sovereignty in any way that he sees fit, but only in conformity to the ways of YHWH.[17]

The built-in critical assessment of the Israelite monarch displayed in these psalms makes sense, given that the phenomenon of human kingship seems to have arisen later in the life of Israel, and appears from the very beginning to have been a contentious issue. In fact, 1 Samuel portrays the call for a king as an act of solemn unfaithfulness to YHWH, and the prophet describes the eventual course that the history of the kings of Israel and Judah will take:

> And the LORD said to Samuel, "Listen to the voice of the people in all that they say to you; for they have not rejected you, but they have rejected me from being king over them. Just as they have done to me, from the day I brought them up out of Egypt to this day, forsaking me and serving other gods, so also are they doing to you now. Now then, listen to their voice; only—you shall solemnly warn them, and show them the ways of the king who shall reign over them."

---

ical Significance of the Kingship Language of the Psalms," *Catholic Biblical Quarterly* 64 (2002): 682.

14. Rowe, *God's Kingdom*, 37.

15. Hans-Joachim Kraus, *Theology of the Psalms* (Minneapolis: Fortress, 1992), 113.

16. "Thus it is that in the Old Testament, 'the king was not "son of God" by nature, nor did he by his ascending the throne necessarily enter into the sphere of the divine, but by a decision of Israel's God he was *declared* to be son at his entry into the office of king' (Noth, 1957c, p.222)." Kraus, *Theology of the Psalms*, 113.

17. See Roberts, "Enthronement of Yhwh," 683.

So Samuel reported all the words of the LORD to the people who were asking him for a king. He said, "These will be the ways of the king who will reign over you: he will take your sons and appoint them to his chariots and to be his horsemen, and to run before his chariots; and he will appoint for himself commanders of thousands and commanders of fifties, and some to plow his ground and to reap his harvest, and to make his implements of war and the equipment of his chariots. He will take your daughters to be perfumers and cooks and bakers. He will take the best of your fields and vineyards and olive orchards and give them to his courtiers. He will take one-tenth of your grain and of your vineyards and give it to his officers and his courtiers. He will take your male and female slaves, and the best of your cattle and donkeys, and put them to his work. He will take one-tenth of your flocks, and you shall be his slaves. And in that day you will cry out because of your king, whom you have chosen for yourselves; but the LORD will not answer you in that day." (1 Sam. 8:7-18)

Through the mouth of the prophet, YHWH predicts the voracious appetite of empire, which will leave none of the people untouched. Though an undoubtedly more positive view of kingship arose under the Davidic-Solomonic reign, the contentious history of the later prophets with the kings of Israel and Judah shows that even a more positive Israelite conception of kingship was to be highly qualified.[18]

In light of our theme, the reign of God, the key point here is that from very early on the psalms and other strands of the biblical witness certainly link human rule and divine rule—as we find throughout the ancient Near East. They offer a theological interpretation of the monarchical political ideology that would come to be associated with Jerusalem. At the same time, however, there is an attempt to clearly subordinate the monarchy located in Jerusalem to YHWH's kingship, a fact that may have been rooted in a general suspicion of monarchical aspirations. As illustrated in the story of the anointing of Saul, the purported first king of Israel, the desire for a human king was interpreted as a misplaced longing that was tantamount to betrayal.

18. Brueggemann makes this point by drawing attention to the trappings of an imperial ideology in the reign of Solomon, which was counter to the social vision articulated in much of the Torah. See his *The Prophetic Imagination*, 2nd ed. (Minneapolis: Fortress, 2001), 21-37.

The Enthronement Psalms

According to Martin Buber, a consistent ambivalence toward human kingship in Israel predated the existence of the Israelite state, and was rooted in another claim: that YHWH alone is king.[19] Whether Buber's argument for a prestate-Israel dating of divine kingship can be confirmed or not,[20] the "other" kingship of which he speaks finds expression in the so-called enthronement psalms. Though these psalms share a great deal of overlap with the royal psalms, they are differentiated in that they are explicitly concerned with the kingship and enthronement of YHWH alone. Included in this category are Psalms 47, 93, and 95-100, though other psalms can also be included, especially Psalm 24.

A significant characteristic of these psalms is the dynamic language used to speak about God's kingship. God not only *is* king, but more importantly, has *become*, and to some extent, is *becoming* king in the present. Sigmund Mowinckel, the first major scholar to draw attention to these psalms, describes the dynamic: "The characteristic phrase in the enthronement psalms proper—one which often appears in the introduction—is 'Yahweh has become King,' *Yahweh mālakh* (93.1; 97.1; 47.8; 96.10). . . . The poet's vision is of something new and important which has just taken place: Yahweh has now become king; hence the new song of joy and praise to be sung."[21] Mowinckel argued that these psalms originally found their setting in the context of an autumnal New Year's festival, during which YHWH was symbolically depicted as, after having conquered the gods, entering the temple and being "enthroned."[22] Such a setting helped to explain the peculiar verbal construction in the psalms of a present action: "Yahweh has become king."[23]

Regardless of whether one accepts the cultic reconstruction offered by Mowinckel, the verbal phrasing that casts the rule of God in a dynamic-

---

19. See Martin Buber, *Kingship of God*, 3rd ed. (Amherst, NY: Humanity Books, 1967).

20. See Sigmund Mowinckel, *He That Cometh: The Messiah Concept in the Old Testament and Later Judaism* (Grand Rapids: Eerdmans, 2005), 461-62.

21. Mowinckel, *Psalms in Israel's Worship*, 107.

22. See Mowinckel, *Psalms in Israel's Worship*, 109-89.

23. For an explanation of the grammatical and theological peculiarities at issue in this translation, see Mowinckel, *Psalms in Israel's Worship*, 222-24. For a discussion of the various responses to Mowinckel's thesis, see J. J. M. Roberts, "Mowinckel's Enthronement Festival: A Review," in *The Book of Psalms: Composition and Reception*, ed. Peter W. Flint and Patrick D. Miller Jr. (Leiden: Brill, 2005), 97-115.

CHAPTER ONE

historical fashion rather than as a static ontological reality is of great theological importance for understanding YHWH's kingship as portrayed in the
Old Testament. Walter Brueggemann echoes this point when he calls attention to the imperative *basar* (i.e., "declare") in Psalm 96:2: "Declare his glory
among the nations, his marvelous works among all the peoples." The term
basar carries the connotations of "gospel," which implies the announcement
of the news of a recent event that has happened elsewhere (usually an event
of some import, such as a victory in battle), to a specific audience.[24]

The point is that the declaration that the psalmist enjoins is not meant
to describe a static transcendent reality (though this is of course not ruled
out—for God certainly *is* king eternally), but to point to a dynamic historical happening through which God's kingship has been demonstrated and
enacted. A kingship that is effective and real in the here and now, but which
is also eschatological. "For the psalmists all moments blend to affirm and
confirm God's rule. God's throne is 'ancient' (Ps. 93:2), reminding us that in
one sense *God has always been king*, which is to say, God's kingship is rooted
in acts of power and creation that long precede our attempts to express
in song and prayer the meaning of God's rule. And yet, in another quite
radical sense, *God becomes king in the present*," and even further, "God is
coming to rule; God's rule has not yet been established."[25] In other words,
the rule of YHWH envisioned in these psalms is not primarily a static ontological claim regarding divine power but is tied to a history of events—past,
present, and to some extent future—in which YHWH enacts and thereby
reveals the quality of the divine rule.[26]

The identification of God with a history of events is in keeping with a
pervasive pattern in the biblical witness as a whole. Pointing out the Old
Testament pattern, Robert Jenson notes that Israel understood that God
was "'Whoever rescued us from Egypt.'"[27] The name of God—YHWH—and

24. See Brueggemann, *Israel's Praise*, 30-35. Brueggemann is especially concerned here
to discuss the way in which the psalms function in creating a doxological vision, in contrast
to the vision of human empire. Though not necessarily ignoring this point, we are employing his insights to understand the nature of YHWH's kingship.

25. J. David Pleins, *The Psalms: Songs of Tragedy, Hope, and Justice* (Maryknoll, NY: Orbis,
1993), 137.

26. "While there is no doubt that the root idea of kingship is supreme authority, power
or leadership, the most important feature of the kingship of Yahweh in the Psalms is his
historical relationship with Israel as his covenant people." Rowe, *God's Kingdom*, 22. See
also Mowinckel, *Psalms in Israel's Worship*, 115.

27. Jenson, *Systematic Theology*, 1:44.

the narrative events of rescue and liberation, then, are all tied together so that one knows *who* YHWH is by attending to *what* YHWH has done and will do. This perspective is also normative for understanding God's kingship.

YHWH's kingship is rooted in a specific history of events. Buber presses this point by contrasting the biblical understanding of God's kingship, expressed in the psalms and elsewhere, with conceptions of the Canaanite *baals*. "That which I regard as a most ancient religious idea, more correctly as the central one among the ancient religious ideas of Israel, is something which emerges from a wealth of early texts . . . ; it can be expressed in the words: *JHWH leads us*."[28] The "leading" described by Buber, and envisioned in the Old Testament witness, is no mere abstraction (i.e., a static concept of providence, etc.), but is rooted in the very specific history of God with the people of Israel. Again Buber: "Not in theological metaphorics, but in all concreteness is JHWH revered and trusted as *the God who leads the community*. . . . Even in His relation to nature He does not appear as without history like the *baals*, but as the Lord of history, the 'King.'"[29] YHWH is the "One-who-leads-us," the "One-who-goes-before," the "One-who-sojourns-with-us."[30] Thus, one could say that "YHWH is what YHWH does."

From this dynamic perspective regarding YHWH's reign, the events to which the psalms typically point are primarily the subduing of the chaos of creation (e.g., 93; 95:3–5; 96:5), the exodus from Egypt, and the establishment of the covenant (e.g., 47:2–4; 93:4; 95:6–11; 97:2–6; 98:1–3; 99; 100:3). Importantly, in the mouth of the psalmists, the events of creation, exodus, and covenant—all of which come from the distant past—are described as contemporaneous happenings. The kingship of God is God's act of subduing the chaos that threatens creation, liberating the people from bondage, and establishing a covenant relationship that constitutes the people Israel. These past events, however, are understood as *current* or *present* realities. In and through them YHWH is portrayed "with thunder and lightning (Pss. 97.2ff.; 29.3, 7ff.), with storm (29.5; 48.8), earthquake (29.6,8; 46.7; 97.4), clothed in his wonderful armor, to which belongs also the girdle of strength (93.1)"[31]—all the accoutrements of an Old Testament theophany or event of revelation.

---

28. Buber, *Kingship of God*, 23.

29. Buber, *Kingship of God*, 23, 106.

30. "So strong, so central i[n] JHWH's manifestation is the character of the God walking-on-before, the leading God, the *melekh* [king]." Buber, *Kingship of God*, 99.

31. Mowinckel, *Psalms in Israel's Worship*, 143.

Through the psalmists' language, the redeclaration of these revelatory events or epiphanies discloses the identity of a living and active God. Of the dynamic-historical events to which the psalms allude, creation is more clearly portrayed in categories taken from Ugaritic and Babylonian creation myths, wherein a divine warrior figure violently subdues the forces of chaos.[32] The central difference is that in the psalms, YHWH's mere appearance topples the gods and brings the created order into harmony. The other gods "are struck with horror at the very appearance of Yahweh, and tremblingly throw themselves down, paying homage to him."[33] All the other so-called gods are revealed to be mere idols (e.g., 96:5), powerless in the face of the living Lord. However, as we will see, the issue is not simply about power or sovereignty but is about the radical contrast between God's rule and the rule of human beings.

THE RIGHTEOUSNESS AND JUSTICE OF GOD'S JUBILEE REIGN

What makes YHWH's rule victorious? Has YHWH, through sheer power alone, simply overpowered the enemies of the divine and thereby vanquished them? Is this the theological equivalent, and therefore the root of all such claims, that "might makes right"? And how exactly is this different from the ways in which human rule manifests itself?

The Righteousness and Justice of YHWH

The answer of the psalmists is that what overpowers the death-dealing kings and empires of the earth is the epiphany of God's life-giving justice (*mishpat*) and righteousness (*tzedakah*). As Psalm 96:13 describes it,

> He is coming,
>   for he is coming to judge the earth.
> He will judge the world with righteousness,
>   and the peoples with his truth.

Psalm 89, depicting YHWH as a conquering king, describes God's rule by an appeal to justice and righteousness, declaring,

---

32. The exception here is the so-called song of Miriam, found in Exod. 15.
33. Mowinckel, *Psalms in Israel's Worship*, 149.

> you scattered your enemies with your mighty arm. . . .
> Righteousness and justice are the foundation of your throne;
> steadfast love and faithfulness go before you. (89:10, 14)

That which overpowers the unruly powers of nature, the gods, or the human kingdoms that oppose YHWH is not power as such, but the effective and life-giving power of God's justice and righteousness.

Fleming Rutledge's observation that the moralistic connotations that the term "righteousness" carries in the English language have little to do with the biblical notion of righteousness is helpful here. "The meaning of the word 'righteousness' in Hebrew . . . is a world away from our idea of legalism or moralism. When we read in the Old Testament that God is just and righteous, this doesn't refer to a threatening abstract quality that God has over against us. It is much more like a verb than a noun, because it refers *to the power of God to make right what has been wrong*."[34] In other words, "justice" and "righteousness" in reference to God do not refer to an abstract quality of the divine being but to God's act of "setting things right," or "rectifying."

YHWH's righteousness is not an abstract concept. "Jahweh's righteousness was not a norm, but acts, and it was these acts which bestow salvation."[35] YHWH's righteousness is a relational concept, a way of life that creates and sustains the loving bond between God and the creature.[36] As such, the divine righteousness is a manifestation of the deepest intentions of God's love, and so is an expression of radical divine self-consistency.[37] It is another way of naming the divine *faithfulness*. The parallelism in Psalm 89:14 quoted above—between "righteousness and justice" on the one hand and "love and faithfulness" on the other—underscores the character of this righteousness: it consists in salvific acts of liberation and compassion. In other words, YHWH's righteousness and justice are life-giving, while the adversaries of YHWH are death-dealing. God's justice has to do

---

34. Fleming Rutledge, *The Crucifixion: Understanding the Death of Jesus Christ* (Grand Rapids: Eerdmans, 2015), 134.

35. Gerhard von Rad, *Old Testament Theology*, vol. 1, *The Theology of Israel's Historical Traditions* (New York: Harper & Row, 1962), 373.

36. See Rad, *Old Testament Theology*, 1:327. See also James L. Mays, *Amos: A Commentary* (Philadelphia: Westminster, 1969), 92–93.

37. For a discussion of the divine attribute of righteousness as an expression of self-consistency, whose fundamental character is not at odds with God's mercy, see Karl Barth, *Church Dogmatics* II/1 (Edinburgh: T&T Clark, 1957), 376–77.

with the act of establishing the conditions for life, and not just bare life, but the flourishing life of a creation in fellowship with God, the source of life itself.

For the psalmists, God's righteousness and justice are that which sustain creation, making life possible. YHWH is the king

> from of old,
>> working salvation in the earth.
> You divided the sea by your might;
>> you broke the heads of the dragons in the waters. (Ps. 74:12–13)

As Mowinckel notes: "That Yahweh (again) creates, means that out of threatening chaos (*tōhû wābhōhû*), he makes an ordered cosmos, an earth where men can live (Isa. 45.18). He (again) establishes the 'right order,' without which heaven and earth cannot exist. It is this establishment of the right order which the Hebrews express by the verb *šāphaṭ* and the noun *mišpāṭ*, usually translated by 'judge' and 'judgment.' The words express His 'saving activity,' his *ṣedheq* or *ṣedhāqâ*, usually translated 'justice.'"[38] God's intention to establish "right order" does not refer to an abstract or impartial notion of equilibrium, along the lines of something like the "laws of nature." Rather, righteousness here, and throughout the biblical witness, refers to God's will to be in covenantal relation with creation. In the context of this ancient worldview, the implications would be clear: "when the gods and their respective nations ignore justice and righteousness and allow the wicked to oppress the poor, it is not just human society that suffers; indeed the very structures of reality are threatened."[39] In the context of creation, then, God's justice and righteousness aim at the creation of the conditions for life, and not simply bare life, but a life of fellowship.

As such, God's justice and righteousness, and the judgments that proceed from them, are fundamentally compassionate and are aimed especially at aiding those who are barred from a flourishing life. According to Abraham Heschel, justice and righteousness are both expressions of YHWH's "burning compassion for the oppressed . . . His being merciful, compassionate."[40] Justice and righteousness "does not refer to the proper execution of justice, but rather expresses, in a general sense, social justice and equity, which is

38. Mowinckel, *Psalms in Israel's Worship*, 146.
39. Roberts, "Enthronement of Yhwh," 681.
40. Abraham J. Heschel, *The Prophets* (New York: HarperOne, 2001), 256-57.

bound up with kindness and mercy."[41] Justice in the scriptural witness is always already social, because it has to do with the securing of the conditions that make all life possible. When individuals, classes of people, whole communities, or even creation itself is not given access to the conditions of a flourishing life because of arrangements of injustice, then God's justice takes on an indelibly confrontational and liberative character.

Along this line, Glen Stassen has argued that God's justice is singularly concerned with liberation and rescue, and therefore is intrinsically compassionate: "Justice in the Bible is *delivering* justice, justice that *delivers* the poor, the needy, the outcasts, the dominated, the victims of violence, and *restores* them to community."[42] Karl Barth intensifies this point, noting that "God's righteousness, the faithfulness in which He is true to Himself, is disclosed as help and salvation, as a saving divine intervention for man directed *only* to the poor, the wretched and the helpless as such, while with the rich and the full and the secure as such, according to His very nature He can have nothing to do."[43]

The justice and righteousness of the rule of God that confront and vanquish the other "gods" then are not expressions of naked power, but refer to God's undying will that creation should live in covenant with God. As such, they also clearly show a special concern for the most vulnerable.[44] Justice and righteousness are not depicted as abstract principles but envision a state of existence in which all creatures—especially the oppressed and the dispossessed—can thrive in relation to one another and to their Creator. "Justice is not important for its own sake; the validity of justice and the motivation for its exercise lie in the blessings it brings to men."[45] The setting right of wrongs that the judgment of justice brings, therefore, is meant ultimately for life and not for death, for liberation and not for condemnation.

The appearance of God's righteousness, an event that confronts both human unrighteousness and the so-called gods, is an expression of God's

41. Moshe Weinfeld, "'Justice and Righteousness'—משפט וצדקה—the Expression and Its Meaning," in *Justice and Righteousness: Biblical Themes and Their Influence*, ed. Henning Graf Reventlow and Yair Hoffman (Sheffield: JSOT Press, 1992), 238.

42. Glen Stassen, "The Ten Commandments: Deliverance for the Vulnerable," *Perspectives in Religious Studies* 35, no. 4 (Winter 2008): 362 (emphasis mine).

43. Barth, *Church Dogmatics* II/1, 387 (emphasis mine).

44. As we will see in our next chapter, God's compassionate justice doesn't just have to do with God's extension of life to others, but also with God's coming alongside those who suffer to suffer with them.

45. Heschel, *The Prophets*, 276.

will for the creature to be in relationship with the Creator, even in the face of the creature's unfaithfulness.[46] "The righteous God is not the wrathful and punishing Judge but the gracious Lord, who offers his creatures salvation."[47] The appearing of the just and righteous reign of God that the psalmists proclaim and anticipate means liberation and salvation.

Jubilee Justice and Righteousness

YHWH's justice and righteousness as expressions of compassion are also evident in God's covenant with Israel.[48] The establishment of the covenant itself, in its Mosaic form, represented an act of liberation and compassion. YHWH liberated Israel from bondage in Egypt, setting them free for a joyful vocation of justice and righteousness as a holy priesthood (e.g., Exod. 19:5-6).[49] Their calling in the midst of the nations was nothing less than to do justice. "The justice commanded by YHWH, moreover, is not the retributive justice of 'deeds-consequences' wherein rewards and punishments are meted out to persons and the community according to conduct. Rather, Israel understands itself as a community of persons bound in membership to one another, so that each person-as-member is to be treated well enough to be sustained as a full member of the community."[50] This is especially evident in Leviticus 25, the pinnacle chapter of the so-called Holiness Code, wherein YHWH declares every fifty years to be a Jubilee Year in which all debts are to be forgiven, land is to be returned, and anyone sold into slavery is to be released.

The chapter is framed by the broad themes of Sabbath rest, the right of return, forgiveness of debts, and the liberation of slaves. The Jubilee

---

46. "The answer lies in the basic conception of the Old Testament: that God is Israel's covenant partner and remains such even when punitive. His righteousness is expressed precisely in the fact that he keeps covenant with his people, continually enforces it, and correspondingly requires that the partner shall not behave in any other way. If Israel breaches the covenant, punishment ensues that still reveals God's faithfulness.... It reveals that the creature is never rid of its Creator." Ernst Käsemann, "The Righteousness of God in an Unrighteous World," in *On Being a Disciple of the Crucified Nazarene: Unpublished Lectures and Sermons*, by Ernst Käsemann (Grand Rapids: Eerdmans, 2010), 183.

47. Ernst Käsemann, "The Righteousness of God in Paul," in Käsemann, *On Being a Disciple of the Crucified Nazarene*, 16.

48. See Mowinckel, *Psalms in Israel's Worship*, 154

49. See Enrique Nardoni, *Rise Up, O Judge: A Study of Justice in the Biblical World* (Peabody, MA: Hendrickson, 2004), 42-67.

50. Walter Brueggemann, *An Unsettling God: The Heart of the Hebrew Bible* (Minneapolis: Fortress, 2009), 27.

Year follows in the logic of the Sabbath and the Sabbath Year, in which the images of rest and release from labor were applied to all members of the community and to the land itself.[51] As Patrick Miller observes, "Human toil is built into the system and the story of creation has made that clear (Gen. 2:15; 3:14–4:2). Work is required for human survival. The issue is not getting work done but making sure that it does not go on all the time and that one may let it go—and let it go regularly."[52] Thus, the Sabbath commandment was a gift, meant to provide refreshment, rest, and liberation from the constant toil of life.

Following in this train of thought, Leviticus 25:1–7 recapitulates earlier injunctions regarding the Sabbath Year, including Exodus 23:10–11: "For six years you shall sow your land and gather in its yield; but the seventh year you shall let it rest and lie fallow, so that the poor of your people may eat."[53] Sabbath practice envisioned an alternative form of economics, echoing the communities' trek through the wilderness, where it was sustained through the sharing of manna. No one had too much, and no one had too little. The Sabbath ordinances made evident that YHWH is the one who orders the life of the community by ordering its time and providing for its life.

The Jubilee legislation, which spans verses 8–55, extends the provisional wilderness experience into the more settled existence of the community, imagining a people marked by sharing and compassion.[54] Beginning on the Day of Atonement, a fact to which we will return shortly, Jubilee indicates liberation and return for the people: a return to equitable social relations and therefore to one another; a return to YHWH and YHWH's righteousness; a return to the original vision of creation. Jubilee is to be a homecoming for all the people, as the text commands the Jubilee to be proclaimed "throughout the land to all its inhabitants" (Lev. 25:10).[55] The unfaithfulness of the community embodied in unjust relations especially between the rich and poor will be set right through the enacting of Jubilee legislation.

---

51. See Ross Kinsler and Gloria Kinsler, *The Biblical Jubilee and the Struggle for Life: An Invitation to Personal, Ecclesial, and Social Transformation* (Maryknoll, NY: Orbis, 1999), 9–17.

52. Patrick D. Miller, *The Ten Commandments* (Louisville: Westminster John Knox, 2009), 121.

53. For a discussion of the backgrounds of the Levitical texts, see Sharon H. Ringe, *Jesus, Liberation, and the Biblical Jubilee: Images for Ethics and Christology* (Philadelphia: Fortress, 1985), 16–25.

54. See Ringe, *Jesus, Liberation*, 33–39.

55. I am borrowing this image of "homecoming" from Ephraim Radner. See his *Leviticus* (Grand Rapids: Brazos, 2008), 265–78.

As the true owner of the land and the redeemer of the people, the Jubilee Year is a divine act of liberation and compassion by YHWH. In the Levitical legislation, persons who could not redeem themselves could be redeemed by another, usually a close family member (cf. 25:25). However, if no one was able to come to the rescue of a person or a whole family, then during the Jubilee Year they were to be set free anyway (cf. 25:28). The justification for this lay with YHWH. It was YHWH who owned the land (25:23). "Just as the laws of Exodus 21 and 23 assume God as the actual covenantal ruler of Israel, so in Leviticus 25 the sovereign God is the royal owner of the land who alone can determine its distribution."[56] Furthermore, the whole of the people of Israel were to be servants of YHWH, and therefore could not truly be slaves of one another (cf. 25:55). As Ephraim Radner puts it, "Servitude and slavery are to be regularly expunged from the land and from lived relations (25:39-41, 47-55), for the people as a whole as servants to God (25:55), whom God alone orders and redeems."[57] In the Jubilee, then, YHWH ransoms the people from their own injustice and unfaithfulness.

The compassionate justice seen here follows a pattern established in the exodus narratives: "The year of the Lord's favor [i.e., the Jubilee Year] thus focuses on liberation as God's primary intention for God's people."[58] Equitable social relations and liberation from oppression are to be the norm in Israel.[59] As noted above, the Sabbath evokes God as the one who orders time and as the source of life and sustenance. This fact produces a leveling in the community: rich and poor alike are dependent on God.[60]

This leveling becomes even more startling when placed next to the proclamation of "release" in the Jubilee legislation. This was not simply meant to be a nice idea, but was to occur every seven years, until finally in the fiftieth year Jubilee is proclaimed. "Every seven years, and double on the forty-ninth and fiftieth, the rich learn 'worry,' such as the poor always have (Deut. 28:67); but they also learn complete and utter dependence upon God, which is the practical purpose of the laws."[61] Both rich and poor are affected by the legislation throughout its duration, and to some extent beyond it. The rich are brought low while the poor are raised up,

56. Ringe, *Jesus, Liberation*, 26.

57. Radner, *Leviticus*, 271.

58. Kinsler and Kinsler, *The Biblical Jubilee*, 17.

59. See Walter Brueggemann, *An Introduction to the Old Testament: The Canon and Christian Imagination* (Louisville: Westminster John Knox, 2003), 72-73.

60. See Radner, *Leviticus*, 270-72.

61. Radner, *Leviticus*, 271.

effecting a reversal and redistribution of capital.[62] This is not an absolute reversal of fortune, such that the wealthy are now on the bottom. Rather, the text imagines a more equitable relationship, wherein all in the society can flourish.

A significant caveat must be noted here. Leviticus 25:44-46 clearly establishes a differentiation between the manumission of Israelite slaves and the treatment of foreign slaves, who do not have to be released. There is no doubt a contradiction here to what appears to be the deeper intention of the Jubilee legislation as a whole: freedom. Though it does not resolve the contradiction here, nevertheless, this text should be read next to other Levitical texts such as 19:18, 33-34, and 24:22, which intone upon the Israelites the obligation to love the alien and stranger just as they would love a fellow Israelite.[63]

The challenge that the Jubilee Year presented to the community is evident both in the historical record and in the fact that the year was to be inaugurated on the Day of Atonement. In regard to the historical record, there is no evidence that Israel ever sought to put into practice the Jubilee legislation.[64] The only other text to deal in some sense historically with enacting the Jubilee legislation is Jeremiah 34:8-22, and the underlying point there is to show the failure of the wealthy and powerful to fully embrace the vision of the Jubilee Year.

Of more theological consequence is the fact that the Jubilee Year begins on the Day of Atonement. The prominent placement of this purifying festival at the onset of the year of the Lord's favor indicates that entering into Jubilee necessitates cleansing and conversion. In the Levitical imagery, the Day of Atonement symbolically marked just such a transition or conversion for the whole community. The Day of Atonement, described in detail in Leviticus 16, was the "day of purgation"[65] or cleansing, an annual event in which all of Israel came together before YHWH to confess their sins and participate in cultic rites that cleansed the sanctuary and effected communal purgation, forgiveness, and restoration. The acting subject who makes the rites efficacious is YHWH, who is represented by the priest,[66]

---

62. See André Trocmé, *Jesus and the Nonviolent Revolution* (Maryknoll, NY: Orbis, 2003), 36-41.

63. See Miller, *The Ten Commandments*, 146-47.

64. See Christopher J. H. Wright, "Year of Jubilee," in *The Anchor Bible Dictionary*, ed. David Noel Freedman and Gary Alan Herion (New York: Doubleday, 1992), 3:1027-28.

65. This is the heading used to describe the ritual by Jacob Milgrom in his magisterial *Leviticus 1-16* (New York: Doubleday, 1991), 1009-84.

66. See Milgrom, *Leviticus 1-16*, 1083-84. "Rather than propitiation of God's wrath or

while the primary phenomenon or reality with which the rituals aim to deal is sin or impurity, which are associated with death.[67] With YHWH as acting subject, and sin as the principal target of YHWH's cultic action, the rites performed on the Day of Atonement were not propitiatory attempts to appease an angry God but, rather, liberative expiatory actions meant to cleanse the community of its sin, and so to set it free from its bondage to death. Sin—or the power of death—was understood to be removed and done away with by the gracious act of YHWH, while the community was reclaimed and transferred to the realm of life.[68]

The social meaning of the rituals and cleansing was evident from early on,[69] being associated with the story of the betrayal of Joseph by his brothers, as recounted in Genesis 37.[70] From the perspective of the community, the Day of Atonement enacted the restoration of intercommunal relationships of peace, especially through the symbolic removal of sin via the scapegoat, which thereby restored the community's relationship to YHWH.[71] In effect, there was no difference between the restoration of communal harmony and the restoration of relationship with YHWH. They occurred simultaneously. Once purgation was accomplished, the restored people were prepared once again for their work as the holy priesthood of God. In the context of the Jubilee, once transformed through purgation, the community would then be able to make their atonement truly concrete as the members of the community "returned to one another" through the remission of debts, the liberation of the enslaved, and the redistribution of the land.[72]

---

payment of penalty to God, atoning sacrifice was the God-provided means by which God-self acted to remove sin, guilt, and impurity and so cleanse pollution from the holy place, things, and people that are consecrated to God's service." Darrin W. Snyder Belousek, *Atonement, Justice, and Peace: The Message of the Cross and the Mission of the Church* (Grand Rapids: Eerdmans, 2012), 189.

67. See Milgrom, *Leviticus 1–16*, 1002–3.

68. See Milgrom, *Leviticus 1–16*, 1002–3.

69. See Jacob Milgrom, "Israel's Sanctuary: The Priestly 'Picture of Dorian Gray,'" *Revue biblique* 83, no. 3 (July 1976): 390–99.

70. This association is evidenced in a rather striking way in the Second Temple text Jubilees. See Anke Dorman, "'Commit Injustice and Shed Innocent Blood': Motives behind the Institution of the Day of Atonement in the Book of Jubilees," in *The Day of Atonement: Its Interpretation in Early Jewish and Christian Traditions*, ed. Thomas Hieke and Tobias Nicklas (Leiden: Brill, 2012), 49–61.

71. See Calum Carmichael, *Illuminating Leviticus: A Study of Its Laws and Institutions in the Light of Biblical Narratives* (Baltimore: Johns Hopkins University Press, 2006), 37–52.

72. See Carmichael, *Illuminating Leviticus*, 133–34.

The presence of the Day of Atonement at the beginning of the Jubilee Year helpfully highlights a key pattern associated with the appearing of God's rule: *judgment* and *new life.*[73] YHWH's reign is marked by the judgment of injustice *and* the establishment of God's compassionate justice, just as the cleansing of the Day of Atonement occurs in tandem with the freedom declared in the Jubilee Year. Furthermore, in the economy of God's rule, judgment and new life do not stand in a kind of yin and yang relationship. Rather, *judgment is meant to serve new life.* The judgment of atonement—wherein sins are confessed and restitution is made—produces a conversion that is meant to be in service to a new form of life. The implication here is clear: God's righteous reign comes not finally for destruction but to make new life in fellowship possible.

The practices of Jubilee are one of the most startling expressions of YHWH's compassionate justice, as they move decidedly toward the poor, the dispossessed, the oppressed, and the marginal. They make concrete the idea that YHWH's righteousness is not a neutral concept but rather is decidedly partisan, siding with the powerless, poor, dispossessed, and oppressed, for the purpose of removing the shackles that keep them from accessing a flourishing life. "God's sovereignty is presented as a fact bearing on people's daily life and structuring their relationships with one another and with the rest of the created order."[74] The Levitical Jubilee Year was understood to be the proper imitation of YHWH's own justice, which was a justice that bent toward compassion and life.[75]

The Politics of Praise

Coming back to our original focus, it is fair to say that the righteousness of God declared in Psalms belongs on a kind of continuum with the Jubilee vision of Leviticus 25, since the revelation of YHWH's kingship that Psalms

---

73. Leviticus 25 is ambiguous regarding precisely when the Jubilee declaration was to occur vis-à-vis the rituals associated with the Day of Atonement. This ambiguity opens up the possibility that the announcement of Jubilee was to be understood as coincident with atonement rather than consequent.

74. Ringe, *Jesus, Liberation*, 28.

75. Brueggemann, *An Unsettling God*, 26–30. Nardoni makes the argument that coordination of divine rule and human justice that the Jubilee assumes is even more clearly established in Lev. 19. See his *Rise Up, O Judge*, 86.

declares is concerned especially with the righting of social, national, and cosmic wrongs. The reign of God is marked by justice, mercy, and peace, in contrast to the injustice, violence, and chaos found either in the realm of nature, among the nations, or among the people Israel (e.g., Pss. 9:7–12, 18; 10; 22:25–28; 68:5, 6; 74:19; 82:4; 145:14; 146:5–9).[76]

Karl Barth once noted that to invoke God was to engage in an act that was "a supremely social matter, publicly social, not to say political, even cosmic."[77] Walter Brueggemann offers a way of conceptualizing Barth's claim, proposing that the doxology or praise we find in Psalms is inherently "world-making."[78] In the context of worship, Israel recounts its history with YHWH—including its experiences of suffering, disobedience, and liberation—not simply as a series of past events but as events that have present purchase. As this happens, the way in which the community perceives the world is altered.

Speaking in regard to Psalms, he notes that "Israel's world-making is counter world-making, counter to the empire and its oppressions, counter to the imperial gods and the exploitative ordering of the regime. It is counter to conventional idolatry and routine ideology. Israel's liturgy at its best is not triumphalist, not self-serving of Zion, but it must 'tell among the nations' that there is a new governance in heaven and in earth. In heaven the new governance has defeated the powers of death and oppression. On earth, the regimes of injustice and unrighteousness are placed in a final jeopardy by the new governance of Yahweh."[79] Such praise is not mere fantasy. Rather, it is authorized by past actions, though it also looks forward, eschatologically anticipating future acts of God's deliverance and concomitant instantiations of righteousness.

Psalms's acclamation of YHWH's kingship, the righteousness and justice of God's coming Jubilee reign, creates a context in which the community can envision new and creative ways to live and act in the light of YHWH's past faithfulness and coming reality. As such, Psalms offers not only substantive content in regard to the actual contours and shape of YHWH's coming

76. "An Israel that perverted justice and oppressed the poor was just as much a threat to the stability of the created order as any other sinful nation; and thus Israel was just as much a potential object of divine judgment as any other nation." Roberts, "Enthronement of Yhwh," 681.

77. Karl Barth, *The Christian Life: Church Dogmatics* IV/4; *Lecture Fragments* (Grand Rapids: Eerdmans, 1981), 95.

78. See Brueggemann, *Israel's Praise*, passim.

79. Brueggemann, *Israel's Praise*, 158.

reign, but it enacts a kind of politics, what we might call the politics of praise. Through their world-making power, the psalms create the "possibility for energy, courage, hope, and imagination that orders political power differently."[80] Though this will entail acts of justice, what we are especially concerned with here is the way the psalms as lived Scripture are able to reshape the vision of the community. "The settled social arrangements of the status quo are thoroughly probed as the community lifts up its words of lament, trust, thanksgiving, praise, and its psalms of kings, both earthly and divine."[81]

If God comes to establish righteousness, justice, and mercy that are oriented toward the poor and lowly, then it stands to reason that the corresponding human politics that these psalms seek to inculcate will conform to that vision in some way. These psalms and their recitation envision a "zone of social possibility outside the ideology of the powerful."[82] In such a space and time, the community can take up, in provisional and creative ways, the Jubilee declaration to set free the captives, to heal the brokenhearted, and to raise up the poor and oppressed.

This very same dynamic can be discerned in the spirituals, the blues, jazz, and hip-hop. In all these forms of music, created by Africans and African Americans living in the dehumanizing cauldron of white supremacy, one can hear "the voice, sometimes strident, sometimes muted and weary, of a people for whom the cup of suffering overflowed in haunting overtones of majesty, beauty and power!"[83] As a form of explicitly religious music, the relationship between the psalms and the spirituals can be more readily discerned. As described by Cheryl Kirk-Duggan, "Both the Psalms and the Spirituals are poetic pilgrimage songs of faith, of homecomings, of life-giving vitality. They express the religious creativity of exiled peoples, the stories of their suffering and of their longing for freedom and justice."[84] The concrete material reality that produced the spirituals was chattel slavery in the United States. The spirituals express the longings for freedom and justice of Black women and men caught up in the material and ideo-

---

80. Walter Brueggemann, "Psalms 9–10: A Counter to Conventional Social Reality," in *The Bible and the Politics of Exegesis*, ed. David Jobling et al. (Cleveland: Pilgrim, 1991), 13.

81. Pleins, *The Psalms*, 173.

82. Brueggemann, "Psalms 9–10," 13.

83. Howard Thurman, "The Negro Spiritual Speaks of Life and Death," in *Deep River and the Negro Spiritual Speaks of Life and Death*, by Howard Thurman (Richmond, IN: Friends United Press, 1975), 12.

84. Cheryl A. Kirk-Duggan, *Exorcizing Evil: A Womanist Perspective on the Spirituals* (Maryknoll, NY: Orbis, 1997), 63.

logical machinery of racial capitalism. Through the language of devotion, hope, lamentation, and joy, the spirituals give voice to the Black refusal to accept enslavement as either just or divinely sanctioned.

As James Cone notes, "The divine *liberation* of the oppressed from slavery is the central theological concept in the Black spirituals.... The basic idea of the spirituals is that slavery contradicts God; it is a denial of God's will. To be enslaved is to be declared *nobody*, and that form of existence contradicts God's creation of people to be God's children."[85] The spirituals wrestled with the radical contradiction that life in North America presented to the enslaved. In their great profundity, they imagined a different future and world. With an expectant, apocalyptic imagination, "These songs emphasized the inability of the present to contain the reality of the divine future."[86] As with the psalms, the singing of the spirituals was itself a kind of help, as the world contained in the music offered an alternative interpretation of reality than the one proffered by the slavocracy of the plantation bloc.[87]

Important to remember is that these truths were not only negotiated via the lyrics, rhythms, melodies and harmonies, shouts, or tonal key, but also through the embodied communal context in which the songs were usually expressed. "The flexible, improvisational structure of the spirituals gave them the capacity to fit an individual slave's specific experience into the consciousness of the group. One person's sorrow or joy became everyone's through song."[88] The call-and-response structure found in many of the spirituals was an expression of the "communal support" that each person needed to survive the hell of slavery and injustice.[89]

Many of the spirituals were also adapted to later historical struggles. Kirk-Duggan's historical genealogy of the adaptations of "Oh, Freedom" is apposite here: "The original unredacted text grew out of more than one hundred slave revolts. African Americans met in secret, urged escape, and laid out northern escape routes. 'Oh, Freedom' was a marching song of Black regiments during battle, a cry of victory after Emancipation, a chant

---

85. James H. Cone, *The Spirituals and the Blues: An Interpretation* (Maryknoll, NY: Orbis, 1992), 32–33.

86. Cone, *Spirituals and the Blues*, 90.

87. For a historical discussion and a political, economic, and ideological analysis of the ongoing entity described here as the "plantation bloc," see Clyde Woods, *Development Arrested: The Blues and Plantation Power in the Mississippi Delta* (London: Verso, 2017).

88. Albert J. Raboteau, *Slave Religion: The "Invisible Institution" in the Antebellum South* (Oxford: Oxford University Press, 2004), 246.

89. Raboteau, *Slave Religion*, 246.

during a race riot in downtown Atlanta, Georgia, in 1906, and a rallying song during the radical 1930s union activity. During the 1960s, the song was a moving, powerful, hand-clapping, striking jubilee."[90]

The structure of the song invited innovation and participation.[91] The original version gave a basic structure that later singers could adjust to new situations:

> Oh, freedom, oh, freedom,
> Oh, freedom, oh, freedom over me;
> And before I'll be a slave,
> I'll be buried in my grave;
> And go home to my Lord and be free.
>
> No more moanin', no more moanin',
> No more moanin' over me . . .
> No mo' weepin' . . .
> There'll be singin' . . .
> There'll be shoutin' . . .
> There'll be prayin' . . . [92]

The lyrics, rhythm, and tonal center conveyed the truth that "God is creator, protector, parent, liberator; God is far and near; God is the northern abolitionist, and God is in one's soul."[93] The infernal powers that enslave both body and mind would not finally have the last word. During the civil rights movement of the 1960s, singing such songs provided strength and sustenance in the face of injustice, and through full communal participation expressed solidarity and the sharing of power.[94] The very act of singing such songs was an attempt to offer an alternative vision of social life, one in which the death-dealing powers were put on notice, resisted, and rejected, while the possibility of life in freedom was affirmed as God's truest intention for creation and the creature. And though we cannot develop the point in more depth here, the blues, jazz, and hip-hop should also be

90. Kirk-Duggan, *Exorcizing Evil*, 210.

91. See Kirk-Duggan, *Exorcizing Evil*, 218.

92. *Songs of Zion* 12, United Methodist Church Supplemental Worship Resources (Nashville: Abingdon, 1981, 1982), 102, as quoted in Kirk-Duggan, *Exorcizing Evil*, 210.

93. Kirk-Duggan, *Exorcizing Evil*, 222.

94. See Kirk-Duggan, *Exorcizing Evil*, 213-17, 218-19, 223-24.

understood as artistic revolts against the "unlivable"[95] by those who have and have had their "backs against the wall."[96]

As we shall see, the connection between YHWH's coming Jubilee reign and corresponding human actions here and now continues, and in some cases intensifies, in the prophets, the apocalyptic traditions, and the witness of the New Testament.

CONCLUSION

In this first chapter we began to take up the challenge of rooting our argument that Jesus is the reign of God in the larger biblical witness. We began with a discussion of Psalms. Psalms is widely regarded as containing the "highest expression"[97] of early Israelite conceptions of divine and human kingship.

Our discussion engaged both the royal psalms and the enthronement psalms. Here we saw coordination between the Davidic monarchy and God's own rule, a fact that could cut both ways. But we also noted that even in those psalms most positively disposed toward the monarchy, there was already a deep ambivalence regarding human rule. Rather, the real claim, standing behind and critiquing the king in Jerusalem, was the fact that "YHWH has become king!" In the psalms, this acclamation pointed not so much to an ontological claim about God's sovereignty as to a living history, which in the psalms is focused primarily on creation, exodus, and covenant. Especially in the enthronement psalms, these episodes from the history of Israel are not described primarily as past occurrences but rather as present dynamic events that in the here and now disclose what it means that YHWH rules.

We also noted that central to the ambivalence toward the monarchy in Jerusalem, and outright hostility toward other rulers, human or otherwise, was the fact that God rules in a way that is fundamentally different. God's reign is distinct from that of all other "gods" and from human rule in general, in that it is marked by compassionate justice and righteousness. The divine righteousness that comes against human unrighteousness refers to God's faithfulness to the divine decision that creation should live

95. Franklin Rosemont, preface to *Blues and the Poetic Spirit*, by Paul Garon (New York: Da Capo, 1975), 8, as quoted in Woods, *Development Arrested*, 39.

96. Howard Thurman, *Jesus and the Disinherited* (Boston: Beacon, 1996), 11.

97. Rowe, *God's Kingdom*, 13.

and should live a flourishing life in fellowship with God. In this regard, we discussed the significant image of the Jubilee Year, which serves as a kind of subterranean resource for the psalms. The Jubilee justice outlined in Leviticus 25 and alluded to in the psalms imagines a community set right through judgment and new life. This combination of righteousness and the images of Jubilee will become more and more pronounced as we move into the prophetic and apocalyptic literature.

Finally, we briefly noted that though there is a definite ambivalence and even hostility toward human rule, the psalms do nevertheless enact a kind of politics of praise that opens up a space in which to imagine political or social action that does not conform to the dominant mode of politics or political realities. Rather, it recalls or anticipates events of liberation, healing, restoration, and the establishment of God's compassionate justice. As an illustration of this dynamic, we briefly discussed the ways in which Black music in North America, specifically the spirituals, offered an alternative vision of the world, provided an outlet for resistance, and called on the God who liberates to act. Though we have left these insights relatively undeveloped here, as we move into the prophetic, apocalyptic, and New Testament literature, the world that the psalms (and spirituals) envision and what human action might look like in light of that vision will become more fully fleshed out. Suffice it to say, human communities and individuals are called to enact improvisational parables that seek in a limited, though faithful, fashion to conform to God's compassionate justice.

It was the prophets who pointed out the total failure of human faithfulness to God's compassionate justice in Israel. They paint a portrait of almost total social collapse in this regard. In the face of this collapse, the prophets did not fall into total despair but looked toward the future, toward an eschatological appearance of God's righteous rule that would include a human face in the person of the Messiah, variously styled. They also envisioned a kind of anticipatory politics as they awaited the arrival of God's reign. To their hopes we now turn.

Chapter Two

THE HOPES OF THE PROPHETS

The present chapter extends our discussion of the rule of God by exploring the eschatological vision of the prophets. Decisive and liberative acts that addressed injustices done especially toward the most vulnerable in society were supposed to mark the rule of the earthly monarch in Jerusalem. This vision, however, was not to be realized by the kings of Israel, or by many of her people, a fact that the prophets vigorously pointed out. Regardless of where one historically places the failures of the monarchy (i.e., whether the prophetic texts reflect a preexilic, exilic, or postexilic viewpoint)—and notwithstanding the scriptural picture offered to us of David's reign (e.g., 2 Sam. 8:15)—a considerable gap developed between the idealization of kingly rule as described in the "royal psalms" and the reality on the ground as experienced by the people. Into this gap stepped what has been called, for want of a better term, prophetic eschatology.

The prophets were more than social critics. Living in the shadow of the collapse of the monarchy and the judgment of exile, the exilic and postexilic prophets, in particular, also held out hope for a future redemptive act of YHWH. Having judged the injustice of Israel, God would judge the injustice of the nations and restore God's beloved. As such, it is in the literature of the writing prophets that we begin to find the conception of the reign of God set even more prominently in an eschatological context. Furthermore, it is also with the prophets that we begin to see the hope-filled outline of God's final intentions for Israel, the nations, and creation as such: life with God through a decisive Jubilee. Taking up the twofold dynamic of judgment and new life, the prophets placed the historical experience of Israel's exile and return within a larger eschatological framework.

Historically speaking, though Moses was considered a prophet, what we are concerned with under the heading "prophetic eschatology" or "the hopes of the prophets" is the fruit of those figures who witnessed the rise and fall of the monarchies of Israel and Judah. In regard to the concept of the "reign of God," they are in deep continuity with the tradition that emphasized YHWH's kingship, though they were also concerned with issues of covenantal fidelity through the doing of justice, and the Davidic kingship, albeit in a different register. That is, it is really with the prophets that the human figure of the king begins to be read futuristically and eventually in messianic fashion. In what follows we will sketch the basic contours of the hopes of the prophets, highlighting their most salient points in reference to the reign of God.

Finally, it is also with the prophets that one begins to discern the depth and extent of YHWH's compassion, and not only toward the most vulnerable. This becomes especially clear in the so-called Servant Songs found in Isaiah. In these texts, the divine agent or messiah not only pursues or establishes justice, he also willingly undergoes the radical judgment that is meant to purify the people. The image of a suffering messiah is concurrent with questions about God's own willingness to suffer alongside the people of God, and by extension the whole of humanity, for the purpose of the liberation of the cosmos.

THE ESCHATOLOGICAL TURN OF THE PROPHETS

A central mark of continuity between the psalms' declaration of YHWH's kingship and the writings of the prophets was "its actuality."[1] YHWH sojourned with the people, leading them in their exodus from Egypt, through the wilderness, and into the land. For the prophets, as for the psalmists before them, God's sojourn with the people had not come to an end. To the contrary, "the prophets paid serious attention to the theory that Jahweh accompanied Israel along her road through history, and they were particularly concerned with the obligations which this involved, in a way which was markedly different from their contemporaries who were, apparently, no longer very greatly aware of these things."[2] The central difference between the psalms and the prophets was the sense that God was doing or

---

1. Gerhard von Rad, *Old Testament Theology*, vol. 2, *The Theology of Israel's Prophetic Traditions* (New York: Harper & Row, 1965), 115.
2. Rad, *Old Testament Theology*, 2:112.

was about to do something new, which was nevertheless in continuity with God's previous actions in that the soon-coming events would be decisive, both for this life and beyond.[3] This shift of register to the future can also be described as the eschatological turn of the prophets.[4]

In the psalms, God's kingly rule was linked primarily to events in the past (i.e., creation and exodus), which were nevertheless understood to be contemporaneous and effective in the cultic setting of Israel's festivals. In the prophets, God's advent is now configured as an approaching event, set in the future but effective in the here and now. To be clear, Israel was not working with a theory of time but with a sense of history, or rather, of events in history that were of such significance that they marked and filled up time. These are the events of God's actions with the people Israel that give to the community its identity, sense of place, and history.[5] In this sense, even the older events of creation and exodus should be understood under the concept of advent.

The Latin term *adventus*, from which we derive our word "advent," is a rendering of the Greek word *parousia*, a term that carries at least three significant meanings: presence, coming, and arrival.[6] The first meaning is generally used in reference to a divine presence and carries the sense of the palpable or effective presence of an individual or event. It is in this sense that the past events of which the psalms speak have an advent quality, because they speak of divine events in the past from which God, so to speak, arises and comes forth into the present. As the distance between past and present is traversed, the past actions and their effects become presently effective or at hand.

Of course, of even more importance for our understanding of prophetic eschatology is the meaning of *parousia* and advent as pointing to an event located not in the far distant future to which we must travel, but to an event that is *coming* or *coming forth* from the future into the present.[7] Finally, and intimately connected with both the first and second meaning, is the sense in which a future event comes toward the present and, as it does so, is effective in the present. This is the sense of an *arrival*, or "at-handed-ness."[8]

---

3. Eschatology is the area of discourse that deals with final things, or *eschata*. See Hans Schwarz, *Eschatology* (Grand Rapids: Eerdmans, 2000), 25-26.

4. See Rad, *Old Testament Theology*, 2:115.

5. See Rad, *Old Testament Theology*, 2:99-106.

6. See G. Braumann, "Parousia," in *The New International Dictionary of New Testament Theology*, ed. Colin Brown (Grand Rapids: Zondervan, 1986), 2:898-901.

7. See Jürgen Moltmann, *The Coming of God: Christian Eschatology* (Minneapolis: Fortress, 1996), 25-26.

8. I am borrowing this term from Christopher Morse, *The Difference Heaven Makes: Rehearing the Gospel as News* (London: T&T Clark, 2010), 21-25.

Just as the psalms spoke of the at-handed-ness of YHWH's act of subduing the chaos threatening creation and of overthrowing Pharaoh and establishing covenant in the exodus event, so also do the prophets speak of the at-handed-ness of the coming new event of God's judgment and salvation. Thus, alongside the Torah and the psalmist's claim that, in Buber's words, YHWH is the One who leads us,[9] the prophets proclaim that YHWH is the One who *comes forth from the future*.[10]

Finally, for the prophets, the coming forth of YHWH marks the end. Eschatology deals with "last things" or "the end."[11] "End," in this context, bears two meanings. First, it refers straightforwardly to the ending of a specific reality or situation. The inauguration of YHWH's rule means an end to the absolute sovereignty of the ways of death, embodied for the prophets in the waywardness of Israel and the lawlessness of the nations.

The second meaning is connected to the Greek word *telos*, which means "end" in the sense of "goal." From this perspective, the coming realization of YHWH's rule can be understood as the goal toward which all things move. This movement, however, is not the result of the evolution of history or of some other immanent process. Rather, it is the result of YHWH's faithfulness. In the prophets, it is YHWH who declares, "I will be their God, and they shall be my people" (Jer. 31:33). Thus, the reign of God comes not by human hands or by any other cosmic powers, but by an act of divine power that disrupts history. When integrated, both meanings of the word "end" highlight the fact that it is *God's* reign that comes; no one but God can bring the kingdom; and when YHWH arrives, the reign of death will end, because no power, whether natural or supernatural, will be able to withstand the living Lord.

THE POLITICS OF JUDGMENT IN THE FACE OF INJUSTICE

When taken as a whole, the vision of the prophets includes both negative and positive elements. What initially drove the turn toward a future advent, however, was present injustice and infidelity—a repudiation of God's righteousness as embodied especially in the Jubilee. The action that Israel

---

9. See Martin Buber, *Kingship of God*, 3rd ed. (Amherst, NY: Humanity Books, 1967), 23.

10. Thus, rather than eschatological discourse focusing primarily on the last things (*eschata*) or the last time (*eschaton*), Christian eschatology should be focused more properly on the coming of the Last One (*Eschatos*). See Moltmann, *The Coming of God*, 23–24. See also Adrio König, *The Eclipse of Christ in Eschatology: Toward a Christ-Centered Approach* (Grand Rapids: Eerdmans, 1989), 1–47.

11. See Schwarz, *Eschatology*, 24–25.

could anticipate as the coming action of God was *judgment*, or the setting right of wrongs.

Walter Brueggemann locates the injustice and infidelity of which the later prophets speak in the corrosive effects of the later reign of Solomon. Affluence, oppression, and a static view of God all colluded to produce a situation of stupefaction.[12] The people became numb to the dynamic presence of YHWH, who had called them to sojourn in the land as a people marked by justice and righteousness. What marked the royal ideology of the kings was an attempt to provide security and stability through the means of empire. A mortal threat to the vision of Sinai,[13] the royal ideology, as it developed after Solomon, moved away from the doing of justice and righteousness and toward a radically stratified society in which the most vulnerable were treated as mere objects to be controlled, leveraged, and exploited.

Though writing much later than Solomon, Amos details the initial fruit of this vision:

> Thus says the LORD:
> For three transgressions of Israel,
>   and for four, I will not revoke the punishment;
> because they sell the righteous for silver,
>   and the needy for a pair of sandals—
> they trample the head of the poor into the dust of the earth,
>   and push the afflicted out of the way;
> father and son go in to the same girl,
>   so that my holy name is profaned;
> they lay themselves down beside every altar
>   on garments taken in pledge;
> and in the house of their God they drink
>   wine bought with fines they imposed. (2:6-8)

And Amos's accusation was not merely leveled at a few "bad apples." Rather, the problem was systemic. In one of the most famous chapters in the book of Amos, he speaks about a legal system rife with corruption:

---

12. See Walter Brueggemann, *The Prophetic Imagination*, 2nd ed. (Minneapolis: Fortress, 2001), 21-37.

13. Brueggemann describes this vision as one of a "counter-community" that envisioned a world beyond triumphalism and oppression, which he argues is rooted in the Mosaic vision of the freedom of God. See *The Prophetic Imagination*, 1-9.

Seek the LORD and live,
>   or he will break out against the house of Joseph like fire,
>   and it will devour Bethel, with no one to quench it.
Ah, you that turn justice to wormwood,
>   and bring righteousness to the ground! . . .
They hate the one who reproves in the gate,
>   and they abhor the one who speaks the truth.
Therefore because you trample on the poor
>   and take from them levies of grain,
you have built houses of hewn stone,
>   but you shall not live in them;
you have planted pleasant vineyards,
>   but you shall not drink their wine.
For I know how many are your transgressions,
>   and how great are your sins—
you who afflict the righteous, who take a bribe,
>   and push aside the needy at the gate.
Therefore the prudent will keep silent in such a time;
>   for it is an evil time.
Seek good and not evil,
>   that you may live;
and so the LORD, the God of hosts, will be with you,
>   just as you have said.
Hate evil and love good,
>   and establish justice at the gate;
it may be that the LORD, the God of hosts,
>   will be gracious to the remnant of Joseph. (5:6-7, 10-15)

"Gate" throughout this oracle refers to the location of the courts.[14] According to Amos, bribery, exploitation, oppression, and dispossession were the characteristic marks of the social order *as a whole*. "The justice administered in the courts had been changed by the alchemy of greed to bitter calamity."[15] The practices of injustice were firmly entrenched as sys-

14. "*The gate* was the regular place in which the local courts of Israel's towns and cities was held (Ruth 4.1, 10f.; Amos 5.12, 15). It was a fortified building set in the walls, which protected the entrance to the city and provided a place where the legal assembly convened to regulate the life and property of the citizens according to the accepted ethos." James L. Mays, *Amos: A Commentary* (Philadelphia: Westminster, 1969), 93.

15. Mays, *Amos*, 91.

temic realities, residing in the courts and, by implication, in the policies of the king.

To be sure, the nations were also guilty of ruthlessness and violence, and Amos, not one to withhold the word of judgment, also brings them in for scathing critique (e.g., 1:1–2:3). The criticisms of both Israel and the nations were motivated out of the deep conviction that "The Exodus/Sinai traditions spoke of a God whose special concern is for the helpless of the earth. . . . Wherever human beings are mistreated, Yahweh is offended."[16] The theme of the critique of the nations stretches back well into the pre-exilic period and usually carries with it the promise that YHWH, the Great King, would deliver the people in their hour of need. But in Amos, the day of deliverance will not be a happy day. Rather, the "day of the LORD" will be "darkness, not light" (5:18).

When the king of Israel that Amos anticipates comes, he will bring a day of terror for those who do not practice justice and compassion. It is impossible to ignore the political-theological dimension of this critique. In the ancient Near East, human rule was legitimized through identification with divine rule—and as our discussion of the royal psalms showed, Israel was no exception to this. Paul Hanson offers a useful outline to this political-theological strategy: "First, the political leader was presented as the designated deputy of the deity, a concept often construed in terms of divine sonship and implying a prerogative handed down from father to son (hence, dynastic succession). Second, the imperial cult manifested the special status of the nation by virtue of the presence of the patron deity's image in the central sanctuary. Two important political consequences arose from these strategies: The political leadership was permanent and beyond human reproof, and the nation enjoyed special entitlements within the family of nations relating to trade and conquest."[17] In an effort to expose the corruption, limitations, and pretensions of human rule in Israel, Amos, in an ironic twist, appeals to one of the long-standing politico-theological idioms of Israel (i.e., "the day of the LORD," which had originally referred to the day of YHWH's rescue),[18] not as a sign of hope but as the hour of undoing. Israel believes they are chosen, and that this chosenness makes them im-

---

16. David E. Gowan, *Theology of the Prophetic Books: The Death and Resurrection of Israel* (Louisville: Westminster John Knox, 1998), 32, 33.

17. Paul D. Hanson, "Prophetic and Apocalyptic Politics," in *The Last Things: Biblical and Theological Perspectives on Eschatology*, ed. Carl E. Braaten and Robert W. Jenson (Grand Rapids: Eerdmans, 2002), 53.

18. For a brief discussion of the origin and meaning of the image "the Day of the Lord," see Mays, *Amos*, 103-5.

mune to criticism. But Amos's announcement shows precisely the opposite: the election of Israel is the ground of their judgment (e.g., Deut. 3:2). As Gowan notes, "This was election for privilege, yes; they had been saved from slavery and they had been given a land that once belonged to others. But privilege involves responsibility as well. . . . Amos asserts that they have enthusiastically claimed the privilege, but have forgotten the responsibility."[19] The message of the prophet is meant to remind them of this responsibility and to call the people to repentance, to turn to a different way of life, to a different politics—to "establish justice in the gate" (Amos 5:15).[20]

The oracle of the prophet points to the coming rule of God, a righteous and compassionate rule that stands in stark contrast to human rule. Though the people ultimately do not respond to the call, the prophets themselves represent an alternative form of politics, in that they embody a critical orientation toward imperial claims, whether those of Israel or Assyria or Babylon.[21]

God alone is sovereign. In driving home this message, the prophets were often moved to engage in a kind of prophetic guerilla theater; to serve as human parables. Hosea was commanded by God to take an adulteress as his wife and to have children with her, which was to be a sign of Israel's own unfaithfulness to YHWH.[22] Isaiah stripped down and purportedly walked around Jerusalem for three years naked and barefoot as a sign that Israel's hope of rescue from the Assyrians by the Egyptians was ill-placed.[23] The book of Jeremiah offers multiple places where the prophet is called to embody some element of God's message,[24] including the striking image of judgment in which Jeremiah must carry a yoke to symbolize Israel's eventual submission to Babylon (i.e., Jer. 27–28), and his subsequent purchase of his uncle's field as an image of the coming redemption of Israel that YHWH will effect (i.e., Jer. 32). The book of Ezekiel is also filled with such enactments.[25] The point here is that the message and oracles of the prophets elicited modes of action that challenged, even if only obliquely, the hegemony of injustice.

---

19. Gowan, *Theology of the Prophetic Books*, 30.

20. See Abraham J. Heschel, *The Prophets* (New York: HarperOne, 2001), 42–46; Rad, *Old Testament Theology*, 2:181. Though it may be true formally that Amos holds out hope for repentance, Gowan argues that it is a feigned hope. See *Theology of the Prophetic Books*, 35.

21. See Hanson, "Prophetic and Apocalyptic Politics," 51–57.

22. Hos. 1:2–9; 3:1–5.

23. See Isa. 20.

24. E.g., Jer. 16:1–13; 19:1–14; 32.

25. E.g., Ezek. 4:1–17; 5:1–17; 12:1–19.

Exile as Death

Though there is a hope for repentance in the prophets, an overwhelming sense of inevitability looms: the people will not listen; they have turned away; they have hardened themselves and in turn been hardened by God; the catastrophe of judgment moves swiftly toward Israel.[26] The failure to act with compassionate justice, to live according to the ethics of Jubilee, leads to the judgment of exile (cf. Lev. 26:14-39).

As understood in the prophetic writings, exile was nothing short of death. The dream that was once Israel has gone into eclipse. The sentence of exile is the inevitable end of the pretensions to empire. Rather than embodying a different mode of existence, as their vocation of election had called for—a mode of existence marked by justice, righteousness, and mercy; an existence marked by fundamental reliance on YHWH as a people marked more by peace than by violence—Israel had wanted to be like the nations, and thus she experiences the true *telos* of such a desire: death.

"Exile meant deportation, destruction, and death."[27] In one of the most harrowing descriptions of the judgment to befall Israel, Jeremiah appeals to the image of de-creation:

> I looked on the earth, and lo, it was waste and void;
>> and to the heavens, and they had no light.
> I looked on the mountains, and lo, they were quaking,
>> and all the hills moved to and fro.
> I looked, and lo, there was no one at all,
>> and all the birds of the air had fled.
> I looked, and lo, the fruitful land was a desert,
>> and all its cities were laid in ruins
>> before the LORD, before his fierce anger. (4:23-26)

The first line of the oracle points to the devolution of creation, its return to a "waste and void" (literally "uninhabitable"), the state of chaos out of which it had come (Gen. 1:2).[28] From this perspective, exile means life is impossible. The creation imagery appealed to here "functions to voice a complete,

---

26. That Israel had come to this state is the sad truth conveyed in Jer. 36, where King Jehoiakim burns the prophet's scroll and refuses to listen to God's rebuke.

27. Tamara C. Eskenazi, "Exile and the Dreams of Return," *Currents in Mission and Theology* 17, no. 3 (June 1990): 195.

28. See also Isa. 24:1-20.

unreserved, elemental negation of all that makes life livable, a negation that could hardly be uttered without such large language. . . . It is an *end*— what happened in 587 is an end of the royal line, the end of a certain kind of temple practice, the end of a certain social cohesion and coherence."[29] Speaking in light of the existential experience of anguish and shame from the contemporary Palestinian perspective, Edward Said's remarks drive home the point: "There has always been an association between the idea of exile and the terrors of being a leper, a social and moral untouchable."[30] For Israel, whether at the hands of Assyria or Babylon, exile was death, not something to be welcomed, nor something to be easily borne.

THE SUFFERING SERVANT OF YHWH

In the midst of Israel's judgment and death, one might be forgiven for viewing God as an imperious taskmaster. Even if Israel has exploited, killed, been unfaithful to the covenant, etc., does her very existence really need to be extinguished? Is that what exile means? It is here that a twist can be discerned in the prophets regarding exile as judgment and God's agency in the event. Israel's exile is both an act of YHWH and the true *telos* of the desire of Israel to "be like other nations" (1 Sam. 8:20). It is the judgment (i.e., the setting right) of the injustice of Israel.

At the same time, and perhaps even more importantly, the judgment that befalls sinful Israel also falls on YHWH. "Israel's God is 'the Lord,' and yet he is simultaneously experienced as 'Israel's servant': he carries the torch ahead of Israel in the wilderness; he provides for Israel's needs like a slave; he bears Israel with her sins; he offers himself up for Israel."[31] "In all their distress he too was distressed" (Isa. 63:9 NIV), or as Heschel translates the passage, "In all their affliction He was afflicted."[32] This was

---

29. Walter Brueggemann, *Like Fire in the Bones: Listening for the Prophetic Word in Jeremiah* (Minneapolis: Fortress, 2006), 44, 87.

30. Edward Said, *Representations of the Intellectual* (London: Vintage, 1994), 35. See also Ada María Isasi-Díaz's personal reflections on exile in *Mujerista Theology: A Theology for the Twenty-First Century* (Maryknoll, NY: Orbis, 1996), 35-56.

31. Jürgen Moltmann, *The Spirit of Life: A Universal Affirmation* (Minneapolis: Fortress, 2001), 48. "So Israel's shame is God's shame too, Israel's exile is God's exile, Israel's sufferings are God's sufferings; for everyone who attacks Israel attacks God's honor and the name which God allows to be sanctified in his people" (49).

32. Heschel, *The Prophets*, 193.

the "pathos of God,"[33] which would lead the talmudic tradition to argue that God sojourned with Israel as she went into exile. A rabbinic saying captures the sentiment well: "So precious is Israel that, wherever they have been carried away into exile, the Presence of God is with them."[34] The death that Israel experienced was also experienced by God.

The suffering of God in the exile raises profoundly difficult questions, especially in our modern context, after the dispossession of indigenous lands through colonialism, after chattel slavery, after Auschwitz, after Cambodia, after Srebrenica . . . and the list could go on.[35] From the perspective of the exile, the mystery of human suffering is not itself dissolved through appeals to divine cosuffering. Suffering *as such* is not redemptive. On the contrary—it is meaningless. For Israel, the experience of exile is the experience of meaninglessness; it is the experience of the dissolution of creation itself (e.g., Jer. 4:22–26). Nothing can be more meaningless than this. However, another voice comes alongside this one, wherein the suffering of exile is opened up to the divine to move toward an end that is different from meaninglessness and death. This is what Elizabeth Johnson describes as a compassionate cosuffering: "In the midst of the isolation of suffering the presence of divine compassion as companion to the pain transforms suffering, not mitigating its evil but bringing an inexplicable consolation and comfort."[36] In the context of the exile, the most significant example of this is found in the Servant Songs of Deutero-Isaiah (42:1–4; 49:1–6; 50:4–9; 52:13–53:12).

Though in regard to suffering we are especially interested in the depiction of the suffering servant in 52:13–53:12, this passage ought not to be di-

33. See Heschel, *The Prophets*, 285–98.
34. Jacob Neusner, *Theological Dictionary of Rabbinic Judaism*, part 3, *Models of Analysis, Explanation, and Anticipation* (Lanham, MD: University Press of America, 2006), 162.
35. See, for example, Elie Wiesel, "God's Suffering: A Commentary," in *Wrestling with God: Jewish Theological Responses during and after the Holocaust* (Oxford: Oxford University Press, 2007), 682–84. "We know that God suffers, because He tells us so. We know of His role as an exile, because He offers us vivid descriptions. . . . I confess, however, that sometimes it is not enough for me. Nothing is enough for me when I consider the convulsions our century has endured. God's role is important in that context. How did God manage to bear His suffering added to our own? Are we to imagine the one as justification for the other? Nothing justifies Auschwitz. Were the Lord Himself to offer me a justification, I think I would reject it. Treblinka erases all justifications and all answers. . . . He could have—should have—interrupted His own suffering by calling a halt to the martyrdom of innocents" (638).
36. Elizabeth Johnson, *She Who Is: The Mystery of God in Feminist Theological Discourse* (New York: Crossroad, 1997), 267.

vorced from its context or from the other Servant Songs. This is especially important as the first Servant Song (i.e., Isa. 42:1-4) casts the servant in royal imagery:

> Here is my servant, whom I uphold,
>> my chosen, in whom my soul delights;
> I have put my spirit upon him;
>> he will bring forth justice to the nations.
> He will not cry or lift up his voice,
>> or make it heard in the street;
> a bruised reed he will not break,
>> and a dimly burning wick he will not quench;
>> he will faithfully bring forth justice.
> He will not grow faint or be crushed
>> until he has established justice in the earth;
>> and the coastlands wait for his teaching. (Isa. 42:1-4)

The servant is authorized by the Great King and commissioned to establish the rule of God, YHWH's compassionate justice.[37] The second Servant Song (i.e., Isa. 49:1-6) widens the aperture to show that the establishment of God's reign means the end of exile (49:1-5), and what is more, the salvation of the nations (49:6). In this song, the appearance of the servant himself is the appearance of God, and though the servant is not directly described in royal imagery, the event is nonetheless theo-political, as the kings and princes of the earth will be astonished at what YHWH performs through the servant.

The final Servant Song (i.e., Isa. 52:13–53:12) reveals the instruments of God's confrontation with the powers—the representative suffering of the righteous servant of YHWH and the servant's subsequent return.[38] Though there are parallels among the prophets,[39] only here is such representative suffering described as effective (i.e., it produces the repentance and con-

---

37. For a useful discussion of this text and a contemporary application, see S. Daniel Breslauer, "Power, Compassion and the Servant of the Lord in Second Isaiah," *Encounter* 48, no. 2 (Spring 1987): 163-78.

38. Here I am following Darrin W. Snyder Belousek's argument regarding the difference between "representative" and "substitutionary," wherein the former refers to a corporate model as opposed to a transactionary model as implied by the latter. See his *Atonement, Justice, and Peace: The Message of the Cross and the Mission of the Church* (Grand Rapids: Eerdmans, 2012), 265-91.

39. E.g., Jer. 16:1-4; Ezek. 12:17-20.

version of the people).[40] Because of its importance, the passage is worth quoting in its entirety.

> See, my servant shall prosper;
>> he shall be exalted and lifted up,
>> and shall be very high.
> Just as there were many who were astonished at him
>> —so marred was his appearance, beyond human semblance,
>> and his form beyond that of mortals—
> so he shall startle many nations;
>> kings shall shut their mouths because of him;
> for that which had not been told them they shall see,
>> and that which they had not heard they shall contemplate.

> Who has believed what we have heard?
>> And to whom has the arm of the LORD been revealed?
> For he grew up before him like a young plant,
>> and like a root out of dry ground;
> he had no form or majesty that we should look at him,
>> nothing in his appearance that we should desire him.
> He was despised and rejected by others;
>> a man of suffering and acquainted with infirmity;
> and as one from whom others hide their faces
>> he was despised, and we held him of no account.

> Surely he has borne our infirmities
>> and carried our diseases;
> yet we accounted him stricken,
>> struck down by God, and afflicted.
> But he was wounded for our transgressions,
>> crushed for our iniquities;
> upon him was the punishment that made us whole,
>> and by his bruises we are healed.
> All we like sheep have gone astray;
>> we have all turned to our own way,
> and the LORD has laid on him
>> the iniquity of us all.

40. See Gowan, *Theology of the Prophetic Books*, 161.

He was oppressed, and he was afflicted,
    yet he did not open his mouth;
like a lamb that is led to the slaughter,
        and like a sheep that before its shearers is silent,
        so he did not open his mouth.
By a perversion of justice he was taken away.
    Who could have imagined his future?
For he was cut off from the land of the living,
        stricken for the transgression of my people.
They made his grave with the wicked
    and his tomb with the rich,
although he had done no violence,
    and there was no deceit in his mouth.

Yet it was the will of the LORD to crush him with pain.
When you make his life an offering for sin,
    he shall see his offspring, and shall prolong his days;
through him the will of the LORD shall prosper.
    Out of his anguish he shall see light;
he shall find satisfaction through his knowledge.
    The righteous one, my servant, shall make many righteous,
    and he shall bear their iniquities.
Therefore I will allot him a portion with the great,
    and he shall divide the spoil with the strong;
because he poured out himself to death,
    and was numbered with the transgressors;
yet he bore the sin of many,
    and made intercession for the transgressors.

We must note immediately that YHWH's relationship to the suffering of the servant is not as straightforward as is usually assumed, given that verse 10 can also be translated: "Yet Yahweh took pleasure in him [who was crushed]."[41] In this rendering, God does not pour out wrath upon the servant but allows the purifying judgment to befall the servant.[42] The ser-

---

41. Claus Westermann, *Isaiah 40-66: A Commentary* (Philadelphia: Westminster, 1969), 254. See also Belousek, *Atonement, Justice, and Peace*, 227-28.

42. "Now, one might be tempted to infer here that God directly imposes a punishment of death upon the Servant in place of the people (per penal substitution). [However] . . . the

vant's undeserved, though active, suffering is the object of YHWH's delight and is vindicated as a truly righteous (i.e., compassionate) suffering, by resurrection (53:10b–12).[43]

Here a crucial distinction needs to be made between suffering as the medium of God's self-giving and God's self-giving as such. God is life and is the source of life.[44] In the act of creation God gives life to that which is not God, giving it a share in God's own life—God's very self. As such, for God to give God's self is to give life. In the case of the servant, rather than suffering ending finally *only* in death, it gives way to God's irrepressible life, rendered in this Servant Song somewhat obliquely as a resurrection.

Even here, in the midst of the servant's trial, suffering ought not to be reified or freighted with redemptive qualities *in and of itself*; rather, only as a medium for God's self-giving, only *because* the servant is YHWH's servant, can one speak in such a way. That such a way of speaking is in fact justified in the present context is confirmed in the particular form of the servant and the eventual verdict on that form. The servant's faithfulness unto death (i.e., its form) is an expression of YHWH's compassion, in that it is done representatively (53:4–6) and in that it brings *shalom* (53:5b), the mark of a repentant community. Furthermore, the faithfulness unto death of the servant is declared to be righteous (53:11). Such a declaration refers to the fact that the servant's faithfulness is in keeping with God's own righteousness or faithfulness to the divine determination that creation should have life and that such a life should be flourishing and marked by fellowship with God and the community of creation.

---

popular account, that the Servant is 'struck down by God,' is wrong, for 'we' have unjustly killed him (vv. 4b–5a, 8). Nonetheless, the text and its context do emphasize God's active role in the drama: God desires that the Servant interpose himself between the people and the consequences of their rebellion in order to deal with their guilt (vv. 10b, 12c); God lets the people's rebellion strike down the Servant (v. 6c); and thus the Servant suffers and dies according to God's will (v. 10a). It does not follow from this that God purposed to put his Servant to death, but rather that God desires that this righteous one intercede on behalf of the unrighteous many, even to the point of suffering himself the deathly consequences of others' sins." Belousek, *Atonement, Justice, and Peace*, 240.

43. See Sigmund Mowinckel, *He That Cometh: The Messiah Concept in the Old Testament and Later Judaism* (Grand Rapids: Eerdmans, 2005), 204–5.

44. "The definition that we must use as a starting-point is that God's being is *life*. Only the Living is God. Only the voice of the Living is God's voice. Only the work of the Living is God's work; only the worship and fellowship of the Living is God's worship and fellowship. So, too, only the knowledge of the Living is knowledge of God." Karl Barth, *Church Dogmatics* II/1 (Edinburgh: T&T Clark, 1957), 263.

Finally, the servant's faithfulness unto death is vindicated by a kind of resurrection (53:10–12). Echoes of the scapegoat ritual of the Day of Atonement, which inaugurated the Jubilee Year, can be discerned here; though now, the servant of YHWH stands in as a kind of scapegoat figure. Notwithstanding that in Isaiah the servant is clearly distinct from YHWH,[45] the servant is YHWH's instrument (49:1–3, 6), and therefore seeing the servant as the medium through which YHWH participates in the exilic suffering of the people—bearing their suffering, and bearing it away, in order to give life and a new future to Israel—is no stretch.

Though we will be led to add further meaning to this passage in the light of the Gospels, in its literary context, which is the context of exile, suffering here must be interpreted as the destruction experienced by Israel at the hands of Babylon; a suffering at the hands of empire and therefore also a theo-political suffering. Though somewhat muted, the passage implies a confrontation between different modes of rule. The kings of the earth, who throughout the prophets are described as filled with malice, violence, and injustice,[46] are astonished at the act of self-giving performed by YHWH through the servant (52:15). When taken together, the internal logic of the Servant Songs establishes a link that offers one possible meaning for the servant's suffering: the act of establishing justice and mercy (as seen in the earlier songs)—presumably through a lived existence of faithfulness— has led to the servant's destruction.[47] The world cannot abide justice. The

45. The identity of the servant has also been debated. Is this corporate Israel, a prophetic figure (perhaps someone from the prophet's circle), a small group of prophets, or is it messianic? These need not be mutually exclusive options in regard to how the authors understood the passage. Texts such as these are capable of multiple meanings, a fact that cannot be stressed too much given the eventual importance of the text for early Christians as they sought to understand the significance of Jesus's death. I am convinced, however, by David Gowan and others that the key to understanding the text does not reside in the identity of the servant but in realizing that the servant is the instrument of YHWH's will, and therefore is the medium through which YHWH draws near to the people's suffering. See Gowan, *Theology of the Prophetic Books*, 159. For discussions of the debates and theories surrounding the identity of the servant, see Christopher R. North, *The Suffering Servant in Deutero-Isaiah: An Historical and Critical Study*, 2nd ed. (Oxford: Oxford University Press, 1956); Tryggve Mettinger, *A Farewell to the Servant Songs: A Critical Examination of an Exegetical Axiom* (Lund: Gleerup, 1983); Bernd Janowski and Peter Stuhlmacher, eds., *The Suffering Servant: Isaiah 53 in Jewish and Christian Sources* (Grand Rapids: Eerdmans, 2004); and Jaap Dekker, "The Servant and the Servants in the Book of Isaiah," *Sárospataki Füzetek* 3, no. 4 (2012): 33–46.

46. E.g., Isa. 13; 14:3–23; Ezek. 25; Amos 1:1–2:3; Nah. 3.

47. See Jon Sobrino, *Jesus the Liberator: A Historical-Theological View* (Maryknoll, NY: Orbis, 1993), 229.

servant is oppressed and afflicted (53:7), a victim of injustice (53:8) whose bad fortune can only lead those who view the world from the perspective of power and empire to view him as cursed (53:4, 8). And yet, through all of this the very thing that the so-called kings of the earth would have desired is given to the servant:

> Therefore I will allot him a portion with the great,
>   and he shall divide the spoil with the strong. (53:12a)

Indeed, the description of the servant as "exalted and lifted up" (52:13), which occurs at the very beginning of the oracle, is an allusion to the act of enthronement and an identification of the servant with YHWH's own kingship and rule (e.g., 42:1-4), though it is indeed a "hidden and paradoxical" glory (49:3).[48] As we noted in the psalms, there is also here a radical contrast and confrontation between *different ways* of being king. The servant triumphs, "not by defeating the nations in battle but by establishing justice among them (Isa. 42:1-4), becoming a light to them (Isa. 49:6), and discomfiting them through his suffering on their behalf (Isa. 52:13-53:12)."[49] As opposed to the rapacious ways of empire and human rule, YHWH's rule, as exemplified by the servant, is marked not only by justice, righteousness, and mercy but also by a radical and active self-giving.[50]

When refracted through the lens of the Servant Songs, the compassionate justice of YHWH takes on an added dimension. Compassion literally means "co-passion" or "cosuffering." As Jürgen Moltmann puts it, "Anyone who 'has compassion' participates in the suffering of the other, takes another person's suffering on himself, suffers for others by entering into community with them and bearing their burdens."[51] As an act of YHWH,

---

48. Westermann, *Isaiah 40-66*, 209. See also Shirley Lucass, *The Concept of the Messiah in the Scriptures of Judaism and Christianity* (London: T&T Clark International, 2011), 106-9; Richard Schulz, "The King in the Book of Isaiah," in *The Lord's Anointed: Interpretation of Old Testament Messianic Texts*, ed. Philip E. Satterthwaite, Richard S. Hess, and Gordon J. Wenham (Carlisle, UK: Paternoster, 1995), 141-65; and Risto Santala, "The Suffering Messiah and Isaiah 53 in the Light of Rabbinic Literature," *Springfielder* 39, no. 4 (March 1976): 177-82.

49. Joel Marcus, *The Way of the Lord: Christological Exegesis of the Old Testament in the Gospel of Mark* (London: T&T Clark International, 1992), 190.

50. See Robert D. Rowe, *God's Kingdom and God's Son: The Background to Mark's Christology from Concepts of Kingship in the Psalms* (Leiden: Brill, 2002), 70-82.

51. Jürgen Moltmann, *The Way of Jesus Christ: Christology in Messianic Dimensions* (Minneapolis: Fortress, 1993), 179.

the suffering of the servant is an act of cosuffering that is declared righteous, but which also establishes God's righteous rule. It is an expression of solidarity, in which God is made vulnerable, in which God is not in the position of power but of weakness, the situation in which victims of oppression always find themselves. As such, it is an affirmation of those who find themselves living in the shadow of death. But—and this is the unique element of the servant's suffering—it is an affirmation that is meant to effect liberation or the setting right of that which is wrong. The compassion displayed by the servant not only affirms Israel in its passage through the death of exile, but it also bears the suffering of the people away, setting them in a new and broad place. From this perspective, then, the establishment of God's righteousness is not simply an event of power, but of power expressed in weakness.

CAN THESE BONES LIVE?

As seen above, because YHWH is in the midst of the suffering of the people, exile is not the end. In fact, it is out of the experience of exile that a new Israel will come forth as a source of blessing to the nations.[52]

The Resurrection of Israel

Alongside the reality of exile must be placed the promise of restoration. These two themes are so pervasive that one scholar subtitled their overview of the theology in the writings of the prophets "the death and resurrection of Israel."[53] The most striking image of the dialectic of exile/restoration is undoubtedly found in Ezekiel 37:1-14:

> The hand of the LORD came upon me, and he brought me out by the spirit of the LORD and set me down in the middle of a valley; it was full of bones. He led me all around them; there were very many lying in the valley, and they were very dry. He said to me, "Mortal, can these bones live?" I answered, "O Lord GOD, you know." Then he said to me, "Prophesy to these bones, and say to them: O dry bones, hear the word of the LORD. Thus says the Lord GOD to these bones: I will cause breath to enter you, and you shall live. I will lay sinews on you, and will cause flesh to come upon you,

---

52. See Brueggemann, *Like Fire*, 99–115.
53. Gowan, *Theology of the Prophetic Books*.

and cover you with skin, and put breath in you, and you shall live; and you shall know that I am the LORD."

So I prophesied as I had been commanded; and as I prophesied, suddenly there was a noise, a rattling, and the bones came together, bone to bone. I looked, and there were sinews on them, and flesh had come upon them, and skin had covered them; but there was no breath in them. Then he said to me, "Prophesy to the breath, prophesy, mortal, and say to the breath: Thus says the Lord GOD: Come from the four winds, O breath, and breathe upon these slain, that they may live." I prophesied as he commanded me, and the breath came into them, and they lived, and stood on their feet, a vast multitude.

Then he said to me, "Mortal, these bones are the whole house of Israel. They say, 'Our bones are dried up, and our hope is lost; we are cut off completely.' Therefore prophesy, and say to them, Thus says the Lord GOD: I am going to open your graves, and bring you up from your graves, O my people; and I will bring you back to the land of Israel. And you shall know that I am the LORD, when I open your graves, and bring you up from your graves, O my people. I will put my spirit within you, and you shall live, and I will place you on your own soil; then you shall know that I, the LORD, have spoken and will act," says the LORD.

The image of a valley of dry bones that are strewn and therefore no longer connected drives home the reality of exile—it is death. The judgment of exile is real, radical, and thoroughgoing. The former Israel has passed away.[54] The only proper human response to such a situation is a funeral, and the exilic community is depicted as singing just such a dirge (Ezek. 37:11). The vision of dry bones is meant to serve as more than a vivid description of death, however. Rather, it points to the new thing that YHWH is about to do. Countering the entirely understandable human response of a funeral, YHWH asks the question, "Mortal, can these bones live?" To which the prophet provides another entirely understandable human response: "O Lord GOD, you know." Through the voice of the prophet, YHWH speaks "the dead back to life," recapitulating the two stages of creation as found in Genesis 2: "first the body (Ezek. 37:7-8), then the 'breath of life' (37:9-10)."[55]

54. For a detailed discussion of the hardships of exile, see Daniel L. Smith, *The Religion of the Landless: The Social Context of the Babylonian Exile* (Bloomington, IN: Meyer-Stone Books, 1989).

55. Robert W. Jenson, *Ezekiel* (Grand Rapids: Brazos, 2009), 282.

The metaphor of resurrection underlines the fact that Israel's restoration will be akin to nothing less than a re-creation, a new being and form of existence. "They are, in other words, not simply restored but *re-created*, transformed from a wicked and idolatrous people into one capable (probably for the first time, in Ezekiel's thinking) of giving the Lord the obedience that is his by right."[56] In the midst of the discontinuity of exile, continuity is maintained by a divine act of re-creation, but not in such a way that there is no connection to that which had come before. Rather, covenantal obedience is implied, providing a connecting point between YHWH and the Israel of Sinai. At the same time, the relation is not left unchanged, as the promise of restoration given to Israel portends a new reality, not simply the reappearing of the old.

The content of the promises makes clear the newness of Israel's coming existence. Restoration includes forgiveness;[57] return to the land,[58] which is described as supernaturally blessed, fruitful, and filled with justice;[59] the rebuilding of Jerusalem,[60] and the temple or abode of YHWH on earth;[61] the just rule of YHWH and YHWH's servant;[62] the fundamental transformation of the human heart;[63] and the transformation of social relations,[64] and even the cosmos itself.[65] When taken as a whole, the portrait of restoration is tantamount to a cosmic Jubilee.

The return to the land, rebuilding of Jerusalem and the temple, inauguration of just rule, and transformation of social relations clearly root these hopes in history. But their close proximity to hopes that move beyond normal expectations, that which makes them resurrection-like, gives an eschatological stamp to the restoration. Though these may be historically demonstrable hopes, they move beyond the mere calculus of history. The giving of a new heart in Isaiah, Jeremiah, and Ezekiel;[66] the final, eschatological appearing of YHWH, the Great King, in the temple in Ezekiel's

---

56. Jon D. Levenson, *Resurrection and the Restoration of Israel: The Ultimate Victory of the God of Life* (New Haven: Yale University Press, 2008), 160.

57. E.g., Isa. 33:24; Jer. 31:34; 33:8; Ezek. 16:63; Hos. 14:4-7; Mic. 7:18-20.

58. E.g., Isa. 49:8-23; Ezek. 39:21-29.

59. E.g., Isa. 30:23-26; 35; 51:1-3; 55:13; Jer. 30:10-11, 18-22; 31:1-14.

60. E.g., Isa. 44:26, 28.

61. E.g., Isa. 44:28; Ezek. 40–48; Hag. 1:1–2:9; Zech. 1:16.

62. E.g., Isa. 9:1-7; 11:1-9; 32:1-8; 33:17-24; Jer. 23:5-8; 33:14-26.

63. E.g., Isa. 44:3-5; Jer. 31:31-34; Ezek. 36:26-27.

64. E.g., Isa. 32:16-20.

65. E.g., Isa. 11:6-9; 25:6-10; 54:1–56:8; 65:17-25.

66. I.e., Isa. 44:3-5; Jer. 31:31-34; Ezek. 36:26-27.

vision;[67] and the transformation of the cosmos as depicted in Isaiah, which culminates in the overthrow of death,[68] the last and greatest of the enemies of God—these are all eschatological, even apocalyptic, events.

They are also events that the prophets associate with the royal rule of YHWH, much as the psalmists had done before with regard to creation and the exodus event.[69] As Mowinckel argues:

> The fundamental idea in the future hope is always *the kingly rule of Yahweh*, His victorious advent as king, and His reckoning with His enemies. Yahweh's victory is followed by the manifestation of His kingship. . . . As king, Yahweh will gather His people and lead them home; as king, He will then be enthroned in their midst; to pay homage to the king, Yahweh, the Lord of hosts, all nations will stream to Jerusalem on the day of His festival. The kingly rule of Yahweh is the central idea round which are grouped all other ideas and conceptions, and by which they are explained.[70]

The kingship of YHWH, the reign of God, is the underlying motif that holds together the various themes found in the promises of restoration.[71] The God of life, the Great King, intends to give a genuinely *new* life to Israel as an expression of divine rule.

The Messianic Hope

To be sure, though the prophets have soured regarding the earthly kings of Israel, they have not given up altogether. The Davidic king is now portrayed in messianic terms, or "*the future, eschatological realization of the ideal of kingship*."[72] In the psalms and the prophets, the "anointed of YHWH" (i.e., the Messiah) is identified primarily as a royal figure, the "son of David," a fully human figure whose promised presence indicates YHWH's faithfulness to the covenant.[73] At the same time, Messiah also names the human face of the coming redemption—the "Servant of YHWH" has been empow-

---

67. I.e., Ezek. 40–48.

68. I.e., Isa. 25:6–10; 65:17–25.

69. See Peter R. Ackroyd, *Exile and Restoration: A Study of Hebrew Thought of the Sixth Century B.C.* (Philadelphia: Westminster, 1968), 128–29.

70. Mowinckel, *He That Cometh*, 143, 144–45.

71. Mowinckel, *He That Cometh*, 146–47.

72. Mowinckel, *He That Cometh*, 156.

73. See Daniel I. Block, "My Servant David: Ancient Israel's Vision of the Messiah,"

ered to rescue the people. As such, the category "Messiah" functions typo-
logically, sometimes applied to a future figure from Israel (e.g., Isa. 11:1),
while at other times, figures outside of Israel are described messianically—
most notably the Persian king Cyrus (e.g., Isa. 45).[74] Serving as part of the
connective tissue to the former promises made to Israel in the person of
David, the coming Messiah will participate in God's work of redemption
and repair by supernaturally governing justly,[75] in humility and peace,[76]
and even in suffering on behalf of the community.[77]

One of the most striking passages coordinates the inauguration of the
rule of the Messiah with the realization of the Jubilee justice envisioned in
Leviticus 25 and later in the psalms:

> The spirit of the Lord GOD is upon me,
>   because the LORD has anointed me;
> he has sent me to bring good news to the oppressed,
>   to bind up the brokenhearted,
> to proclaim liberty to the captives,
>   and release to the prisoners;
> to proclaim the year of the LORD's favor,
>   and the day of vengeance of our God;
> to comfort all who mourn;
> to provide for those who mourn in Zion—
>   to give them a garland instead of ashes,
> the oil of gladness instead of mourning,
>   the mantle of praise instead of a faint spirit. (Isa. 61:1–3a)

The themes of the Jubilee described in Leviticus 25 are carefully woven in
with words of comfort that portend a liberation for those in exile, creating

---

in *Israel's Messiah in the Bible and the Dead Sea Scrolls*, ed. Richard S. Hess and M. Daniel
Carroll R. (Grand Rapids: Baker Academic, 2003), 17–56.

74. For a discussion of the theo-political dimension of the identification of Cyrus in
messianic terms, see Joseph Blenkinsopp, "The Theological Politics of Deutero-Isaiah,"
in *Divination, Politics, and Ancient Near Eastern Empires*, ed. Alan Lenzi and Jonathan Stökl
(Atlanta: Society for Biblical Literature, 2014), 129–43.

75. E.g., Isa. 9:1–7; 11:1–9; 32:1–8.

76. E.g., Zech. 9:9–10.

77. E.g., Isa. 52:13–53:12; Zech. 12:9–11; 13:5–7. For a discussion of the interconnections
between the suffering servant of Isaiah and the messianic king, see Schulz, "The King,"
141–65, and Anthony R. Peterson, *Behold Your King: The Hope for the House of David in the
Book of Zechariah* (New York: T&T Clark, 2009).

an identification between YHWH's kingly work of restoration and the realization of YHWH's compassionate justice. In continuity with the psalms,
the Messiah is subordinated to YHWH and is the instrument through which
YHWH rules.[78] The real object of hope is YHWH, the one whose personal
advent marks the coming reign of God.[79] For it is YHWH who loves justice
and hates "robbery and wrongdoing" (Isa. 61:8).

Throughout the prophets, YHWH is the principal actor in the astonishing events that will unfold. At the same time, in the figure of the Messiah
humanity is given a share in YHWH's rule. But human participation in
YHWH's coming new reality does not end with the Messiah. Rather, the
task of Jubilee justice is democratized to become the vocation of Israel as
a whole. The people *as a whole*, and not merely the Messiah, are exhorted
to participate in the divine rule expressed in Jubilee:

> Is not this the fast that I choose:
>> to loose the bonds of injustice,
>> to undo the thongs of the yoke,
> to let the oppressed go free,
>> and to break every yoke?
> Is it not to share your bread with the hungry,
>> and bring the homeless poor into your house;
> when you see the naked, to cover them,
>> and not to hide yourself from your own kin?
> Then the light shall break forth like the dawn,
>> and your healing shall spring up quickly;
> your vindicator shall go before you,
>> the glory of the LORD shall be your rear guard.
> Then you shall call, and the LORD will answer;
>> you shall cry for help, and he will say, Here I am. (Isa. 58:6–9)

78. "It is clear that God is the source of both the authority of the speaker and the hope
underlying this passage. It is also clear that what is envisioned is not merely a historical
event such as the return of the Jews to Palestine, but the advent of God's eschatological
reign. Nevertheless, the visionaries who produced the passage make it clear that the consequences of what is hoped for are experienced in the institutions of everyday life and the
attributes of the social order." Sharon H. Ringe, *Jesus, Liberation, and the Biblical Jubilee:
Images for Ethics and Christology* (Philadelphia: Fortress, 1985), 31.

79. See Mowinckel, *He That Cometh*, 169-73.

The true worship that should mark the people is found in their active performance of the Jubilee justice of YHWH's reign.[80] This is the *new form*, made possible by the *new heart*,[81] which YHWH will give to the *new Israel* as it comes forth from the death (i.e., atoning judgment) of exile.

A Gospel to the Nations

The unfolding drama of the coming restoration moves beyond Israel to become a gospel for the nations.

> How beautiful upon the mountains
> > are the feet of the messenger who announces peace,
> who brings good news,
> > who announces salvation,
> > who says to Zion, "Your God reigns."
> Listen! Your sentinels lift up their voices,
> > together they sing for joy;
> for in plain sight they see
> > the return of the LORD to Zion.
> Break forth together into singing,
> > you ruins of Jerusalem;
> for the LORD has comforted his people,
> > he has redeemed Jerusalem.
> The LORD has bared his holy arm
> > before the eyes of all the nations;
> and all the ends of the earth shall see
> > the salvation of our God. (Isa. 52:7-10)

It is an announcement of YHWH's sovereignty and an invitation to the nations. As recounted in Ezekiel, "It is not for your sake, O house of Israel, that I am about to act, but for the sake of my holy name, which you have profaned among the nations to which you came. I will sanctify my great

---

80. "To fast in the name of a 'liberator' God and at the same time to practice the enslavement of persons is supremely incoherent, and Yahweh does not accept it." José Severino Croatto, "From the Leviticus Jubilee Year to the Prophetic Liberation Time: Exegetical Reflections on Isaiah 61 and 58 in Relation to the Jubilee," in *God's Economy: Biblical Studies from Latin America*, ed. Ross Kinsler and Gloria Kinsler (Maryknoll, NY: Orbis, 2005), 103.

81. Cf. Isa. 44:3-5; Jer. 31:31-34; Ezek. 36:26-27.

name, which has been profaned among the nations, and which you have profaned among them; and the nations shall know that I am the LORD, says the Lord GOD, when through you I display my holiness before their eyes" (Ezek. 36:22–23).

YHWH's holiness, or otherness, is seen in the astonishing work of grace in the restoration of Israel, which is now extended to the nations:

> Turn to me and be saved,
>> all the ends of the earth!
>> For I am God, and there is no other. (Isa. 45:22)

This is a theo-political claim to which there is no doubt that the nations will succumb:

> By myself I have sworn,
>> from my mouth has gone forth in righteousness
>> a word that shall not return:
> "To me every knee shall bow,
>> every tongue shall swear." (Isa. 45:23)

As with Israel, so also for the nations, submission to the kingship of YHWH involves the human response of compassionate justice. The nations are called to "maintain justice, and do what is right" (Isa. 56:1), for YHWH is "coming to gather all nations and tongues" (Isa. 66:18).

Finally, the gospel of God's reign envisions a feast of reconciliation (lit. "YHWH's coronation feast") for the nations and the end of the last great oppressor:

> On this mountain the LORD of hosts will make for all peoples
>> a feast of rich food, a feast of well-aged wines,
>> of rich food filled with marrow, of well-aged wines
>>> strained clear.
> And he will destroy on this mountain
>> the shroud that is cast over all peoples,
>> the sheet that is spread over all nations;
>> he will swallow up death forever.
> Then the Lord GOD will wipe away the tears from all faces,
>> and the disgrace of his people he will take away from all
>>> the earth,

>   for the LORD has spoken.
>   It will be said on that day,
>   Lo, this is our God; we have waited for him, so that he
>   might save us.
>   This is the LORD for whom we have waited;
>   let us be glad and rejoice in his salvation. (Isa. 25:6–9)

The promises of restoration move out from Israel to encompass the nations. The realization of YHWH's liberation from the death of exile now includes the liberation of all creation from bondage to death:

>   For I am about to create a new heavens
>   and a new earth;
>   the former things shall not be remembered
>   or come to mind. (Isa. 65:17)

The hopes of the prophets have become universal.

A POLITICS OF EXILE

The promise of restoration creates meaning in exile; it gives hope to those who live in the shadow of death. In the light of YHWH's promise as displayed in the hopes of the prophets, exile takes on a creative function, marking a transition point away from one form of life to another. That which was meant to die in exile were the ways of unfaithfulness and injustice, while that which is meant to come alive in restoration is a people marked by YHWH's compassionate justice.

In a well-known passage from the book of Jeremiah, one of the most important contours of restoration emerges in the midst of exile: "Build houses and live in them; plant gardens and eat what they produce. Take wives and have sons and daughters; take wives for your sons, and give your daughters in marriage, that they may bear sons and daughters; multiply there, and do not decrease. But seek the welfare of the city where I have sent you into exile, and pray to the LORD on its behalf, for in its welfare you will find your welfare" (Jer. 29:5–7). Steed Vernyl Davidson has pointed out that Jeremiah's letter can be read as a capitulation to the ways of empire embodied in Babylon, or it can be read "from below," from the perspective of the deportees. In the latter case, "the letter provides the mechanisms needed by the deportees to maintain their unique identity and subjectivity in the context of diaspora."[82] Economic (i.e., building houses and planting vineyards), domestic (i.e., marriage and family life), and religious (i.e., prayer and cultic life) practices are all marshaled to resist the imperial designs of Babylon, the colonization, effacement, and disappearance of its subject peoples.[83]

All three of these practices allude to conditions in the future post-restoration period of the people, especially the economic aspects (e.g., Isa. 65:21-23; Ezek. 28:26).[84] But, as Brueggemann has pointed out, the appearance of the word *shalom* (translated in the NRSV as "welfare"), both here and in the text of promise that follows it (Jer. 29:10-14), offers a clue regarding the theo-political dynamic at play.[85]

Shalom is one of the conditions of restoration, the holistic peace that comes as a result of YHWH's reign (Isa. 52:7), and consequently of Israel's liberation from Babylon. However, here, in Jeremiah's letter, the exiled Israelites are encouraged to seek the welfare, or *shalom*, of *Babylon*. Though one could read Jeremiah's instruction as only a self-serving command, the means by which the people's continued existence will be assured, it can also be read as a counterintuitive form of politics.[86] The encouragement to seek the *shalom* of Babylon is a command to seek *the end of imperial modes of life from inside the empire*. As such, *it means finding ways to liberate Babylon from itself.*[87] It means the dismantling of the structures of oppression and the disruption of the practices of violence that sustain empire, such that Babylon as "empire" comes to an end. Another way of putting it is that seeking the welfare, or *shalom*, of Babylon doesn't necessarily mean Babylon's utter ruin and end; rather, it means its transformation. This can hardly be interpreted as merely a self-serving command meant to secure the survival of the people.

---

82. Steed Vernyl Davidson, *Empire and Exile: Postcolonial Readings of the Book of Jeremiah* (Edinburgh: T&T Clark, 2011), 152-53.

83. Davidson shows that the marshaling of these resources is not necessarily unproblematic, especially as regards the status of women. See *Empire and Exile*, 165-67.

84. See Davidson, *Empire and Exile*, 159.

85. See Walter Brueggemann, *A Commentary on Jeremiah: Exile and Homecoming* (Grand Rapids: Eerdmans, 1998), 256-60.

86. See Smith, *Religion of the Landless*, 132-37.

87. On Jeremiah's ultimately anti-Babylonian posture, see David J. Reimer, "Political Prophets? Political Exegesis and Prophetic Theology," in *Intertextuality in Ugarit and Israel*, ed. Johannes C. de Moor (Leiden: Brill, 1998), 138-39.

The promises spoken by the prophets are given to a people in dire need of hope. They promise comfort, but they also provide reason for the people to reinhabit their original vocation as the holy priesthood of YHWH, though now in a situation that is markedly different. In such a reading, exilic politics offers a posture toward the practices of empire. It effectively coordinates a posture of sojourning with the practices of Jubilee justice. God's compassionate justice is neither relegated to the future nor confined only to Israel, but is something that can be experienced and enacted in the here and now, a practice meant to liberate all.

The experience of exile is to be akin to a conversion, for it means the end of one form of being and the emergence of another, even in the midst of exile. What comes under judgment is an imperial mode of life, one based on exclusionary, violent, and exploitative practices. These were embodied in Israel's desire to "be like other nations." In turn, Israel was overwhelmed by the very nations she desired to emulate. What YHWH envisions emerging even in the midst of exile is a new *exilic* (re: repentant) form of existence. As we noted in our description above, this was a form of existence marked by liberation from violence and exploitation and the enactment of YHWH's Jubilee justice.[88]

This doesn't, however, mean an existence disconnected from the land; it means, rather, an existence marked by a new relation to the land. In view of Jeremiah 29, exilic existence can be enacted in situations of landlessness (cf. 29:5–9) or landedness (cf. 29:10–14). In regard to the latter, what is imagined, to use an image from Alain Epp Weaver, is an exilic form of landedness or politics based on the labors of *shalom* and compassionate justice.[89] In the context of return, exilic landedness is but another way of naming the humble enactment of Jubilee justice.

In the Jubilee legislation of Leviticus 25, dispossession of inheritable land through economic misfortune is forbidden, not because Israel owns the land but because YHWH does. The Israelites are "but aliens and ten-

---

88. See Smith, *Religion of the Landless*, 201–16.

89. See Alain Epp Weaver, *Mapping Exile and Return: Palestinian Dispossession and a Political Theology for a Shared Future* (Minneapolis: Fortress, 2014), 59–90. Weaver builds critically on the work of John Howard Yoder, who argued for "exile" as a way of naming what should be the missional vocation of Jews and Christians. Yoder's paradigm suggested that a posture of exile—which is another way of saying that one is not in charge—produced a critical posture toward power and the state (and economic) structures that tended to dominate and deploy such power. See his "Exodus and Exile: The Two Faces of Liberation," *Cross Currents* 23, no. 3 (Fall 1973): 297–309.

ants" (Lev. 25:23), whom YHWH has given to share in the land. Such a conception of the land has embedded within it the practice of compassionate justice that should lead to a posture of humility. Though exile is judgment, YHWH uses it to refocus the vision of Israel's vocation and to imagine a nonviolent politics of compassion. To refuse ownership of the land is not to abandon the land but to renounce the exclusionary and violent practices of rule that control of the land often implies, in favor of a politics shaped by the rule of Israel's one true king, the living God whose reign bends toward compassion and *shalom*.[90]

CONCLUSION

The prophets speak primarily of YHWH's rule as future or eschatological. The impending rule of God is understood to come forth from the future into the present, marking an end of the current state of affairs and the inauguration of a new reality. As such, God's rule is marked by both judgment and new life. Both exile (judgment) and restoration (new life) are expressions of God's rule in the prophets. The old state of affairs is one marked by the ways of death, seen especially in the unfaithfulness of Israel and the lawlessness of the nations. While the new state of affairs is characterized by God's Jubilee justice and *shalom*.

The prophets also emphasize divine agency in the coming of God's reign. The coming kingdom of God is initiated by God and is rooted in YHWH's faithfulness. YHWH comes to the rescue of the people, and through them, to the nations. At the same time, it is not as though YHWH has not been present with Israel as they have been sent into exile. Rather, God is with Israel in their suffering and is depicted by Isaiah as suffering alongside the people—even bearing the judgment of exile—in the figure of the servant whose representative action brings about the repentance and conversion of the people. God's compassionate justice means God's cosuffering for the purpose of bearing the sufferings and sins of the people away, bringing forth new life and a new existence.

Human agency, though significantly relativized and subordinated to divine agency, still plays an important role in relation to the reign of God. First, in the prophetic literature we encounter a litany of human figures

90. See Daniel L. Smith-Christopher, *A Biblical Theology of Exile* (Minneapolis: Fortress, 2002), 189-203.

that are depicted as the human face of God's rule. The Davidic messiah and the suffering servant are both traditions that appear in various ways in the prophetic literature. Both are eschatological figures, associated with the appearing of YHWH, and both are subordinated to YHWH, depicted as faithful servants and instruments through which God rules Israel and the nations.

Second, the prophetic tradition calls for human response in the here and now. Fueled by the notion that YHWH's cosmic rule comes from the future into the present, these writings imagine ways of life that reject exploitation and injustice and that embrace life-giving forms of community (i.e., they echo God's Jubilee justice). While the community awaits the coming of God, it is called to humbly live and act in the light of that coming; to live in such a way that the life-giving ways of Jubilee are more determinative than scarcity and violence.

Chapter Three

THE DAY OF YHWH'S APOCALYPSE

In the prophets, YHWH's kingship is revealed as both imminent and immanent. Coming from the future into the present, it is a reality that shapes the here and now both epistemologically and politically as those who receive the word of the prophet *see the world differently* and are called *to live in the world differently*. It is ultimately YHWH who is awaited, and who comes toward Israel and the nations. The eschatological hopes of the prophets have not merely to do with the arrival of "last things" (*eschata*) or a "last time" (*eschaton*), but with the arrival of the Last One (*eschatos*). A helpful tensive metaphor that draws together all three of these aspects—that is, the last things, last time, and Last One—is found in the important concept of the Day of the Lord, "for wherever it occurs in prophecy, the statements culminate in an allusion to Jahweh's coming in person."[1]

The metaphor of "That Day" has a variety of associations in the biblical witness. It is a day of judgment on Israel,[2] but it is also a day of judgment on the nations,[3] the unjust,[4] and creation.[5] It is a day of salvation (even resurrection) for Israel,[6] and for the just,[7] but it is also a day of blessing

---

1. Gerhard von Rad, *Old Testament Theology*, vol. 2, *The Theology of Israel's Prophetic Traditions* (New York: Harper & Row, 1965), 119.
2. E.g., Amos 5:18-24; Joel 2:1-3ff.
3. E.g., Isa. 24:21-22; Joel 3:9-16; Zech. 12:2-9.
4. E.g., Dan. 12:1-3; Mal. 3:5; 4:1.
5. E.g. Isa. 24:1, 3-13.
6. E.g., Isa. 26:1–27:13; Mic. 4:6; Zech. 6:15.
7. E.g., Dan. 12:1-3; Mal. 4:2.

for the nations,[8] and the restoration or re-creation of the cosmos.[9] It is the day of the inauguration of YHWH's Jubilee justice,[10] and the day of the destruction of death.[11] "The day of the Lord" is another way of naming the eschatological appearing of God and God's reign, with its dual pattern of judgment and new life, and is clearly present in the writings of the prophets. But in later portions of Scripture and beyond, it comes to take on what might be called apocalyptic contours.

The apocalyptic tradition, which emerged during the Second Temple period (515 BCE–70 CE), makes the cosmic claims of YHWH's kingship all the more central, as it envisions a confrontation between the God of life and the powers of death. The restoration of Israel is a sign that points to the transformation of the cosmos as a whole. Definitional debates on "apocalyptic" have been especially vigorous over the past fifty years.[12] Though in the popular imagination "apocalyptic" has unfortunately come to be associated with scenarios about the "end times,"[13] in the biblical witness and in later Jewish texts from the Second Temple period, "apocalyptic" can have a wide range of meanings.[14] In addition, the relationship between the hopes of the prophets and "apocalyptic eschatology" is by no means clear,[15] with significant affinities that point toward multiple sources out of

8. E.g., Isa. 19:18–25; Joel 2:28–32.

9. E.g., Isa. 65:17; Joel 3:18.

10. E.g., Isa. 28:5–6.

11. E.g., Isa. 25:6–10.

12. The most relevant literature includes D. S. Russell, *The Method and Message of Jewish Apocalyptic* (Philadelphia: Westminster, 1964); Paul D. Hanson, *The Dawn of Apocalyptic: The Historical and Sociological Roots of Jewish Apocalyptic Eschatology*, rev. ed. (Philadelphia: Fortress, 1979); Christopher Rowland, *The Open Heaven: A Study of Apocalyptic in Judaism and Early Christianity* (New York: Crossroad, 1982); John J. Collins, *The Apocalyptic Imagination*, 3rd ed. (Grand Rapids: Eerdmans, 2016); Bernard McGinn, John J. Collins, and Stephen J. Stein, eds., *The Continuum History of Apocalypticism* (New York: Continuum, 2003); John J. Collins, ed., *The Oxford Handbook of Apocalyptic Literature* (Oxford: Oxford University Press, 2014); and Colin McAllister, ed., *The Cambridge Companion to Apocalyptic Literature* (Cambridge: Cambridge University Press, 2020).

13. I am thinking here about the popular Left Behind novels. For a short critique of this pernicious form of apocalyptic, see Barbara R. Rossing, "Prophecy, End-Times, and American Apocalypse: Reclaiming Hope for Our World," in *Compassionate Eschatology: The Future as Friend*, ed. Ted Grimsrud and Michael Hardin (Eugene, OR: Cascade, 2011), 257–59.

14. See the various essays in Collins, *The Oxford Handbook of Apocalyptic Literature*.

15. See Leslie C. Allen, "Some Prophetic Antecedents of Apocalyptic Eschatology and Their Hermeneutical Value," *Ex Auditu* 6 (1990): 15–28; Benjamin Uffenheimer, "From Prophetic to Apocalyptic Eschatology," in *Eschatology in the Bible and in Jewish and Chris-*

which apocalyptic arose, including Babylonian and Chaldean texts,[16] as well as the Jewish wisdom tradition.[17]

In the most basic sense, "apocalyptic" derives from the Greek word *apokalypsis*, meaning to "unveil," "disclose," or "reveal."[18] As a type of writing, an apocalypse is "a genre of revelatory literature with a narrative framework, in which a revelation is mediated by an otherworldly being to a human recipient, disclosing a transcendent reality which is both temporal, insofar as it envisages eschatological salvation, and spatial insofar as it involves another, supernatural world."[19] Even this definition has been contested, and scholars have gone on to further delineate subtypes within the overarching genre.[20] Though there were clearly antecedents in earlier prophetic and wisdom literature, the texts usually grouped under the heading "apocalyptic literature" emerged primarily during the Second Temple period, and especially as a response to national distress.[21]

It is, however, neither our task to delineate the many aspects of apocalyptic literature or eschatology, nor to review the many different ways in which that literature and eschatology have been interpreted, let alone to determine which interpretation is the most correct. Rather, in what follows we highlight the contribution that "apocalyptic" modes of thought make to the notion of the coming reign of God as we have outlined in the psalms and prophets. That is, what are the most salient dimensions of apocalyptic thought that shape the New Testament witness to the "kingdom of God" and, by extension, the subsidiary theme of Jubilee? At the conclusion of this chapter, we offer a final synthetic description of the loosely related, though conceptually coherent, dynamics and themes associated with the notion of the reign of God as found in the psalms, the prophets, and the apocalyptic traditions.

---

tian Tradition, ed. Henning Graf Reventlow (Sheffield: Sheffield Academic Press, 1997), 200-217; and Lester L. Grabbe and Robert D. Haak, eds., *Knowing the End from the Beginning: The Prophetic, the Apocalyptic, and Their Relationships* (London: T&T Clark, 2003).

16. See Collins, *The Apocalyptic Imagination*, 32-41.

17. See Matthew Goff, "Wisdom and Apocalypticism," in Collins, *The Oxford Handbook of Apocalyptic Literature*, 52-68, and Grant Macaskill, *Revealed Wisdom and Inaugurated Eschatology in Ancient Judaism and Early Christianity* (Leiden: Brill, 2007).

18. See Wilhelm Mundle, "Revelation," in *The New International Dictionary of the New Testament*, ed. Colin Brown (Grand Rapids: Zondervan, 1986), 3:310-16.

19. John J. Collins, ed., *Apocalypse: The Morphology of a Genre*, Semeia 14 (Missoula, MT: Society of Biblical Literature, 1979), 9.

20. See Collins, *The Apocalyptic Imagination*, 5-14.

21. See Collins, *The Apocalyptic Imagination*, 23-40.

THE COSMIC FRAME

One of the central themes that we noted in our discussion of the prophetic literature was the impending confrontation between YHWH and the nations, between the rule of God and the rule of human beings. In the prophets, this confrontation is portrayed as more readily rooted in a situation marked by the specific historical and political realities that faced the community. In such a framework, the prophets announce that YHWH comes to overthrow Assyrian arrogance, Egyptian opulence, Babylonian cruelty, etc. Without losing their connection to the political, apocalyptic texts bring out even more clearly the *cosmic* or *transcendent* dimension of God's coming kingdom. "For the prophets the most significant action takes place on earth. Even if a decision is taken in the divine council, it is acted out on earth, in 'plain history.' For the apocalypticists however, the most significant action takes place between heavenly mythological beings, in the conflict of God and Belial, Christ and Anti-Christ, angels and demons, sons of light and sons of darkness."[22] Apocalyptic writings envision an impending confrontation and liberation that will leave no one and nothing in all creation untouched. YHWH's confrontation with the earthly powers is now transposed into a new key. It is raised to a higher level where heavenly or demonic "powers and principalities"—often styled in mythological language—stand behind history, influencing specific historical actors as the real foe of God and God's people. In light of this shift, God's action is framed as determinative not only for immediate political or social protagonists, but even more importantly, the outcome of the confrontation will be determinative for all of history and for every community.

The historical reasons for this shift between the prophetic and apocalyptic literature are probably rooted in the less-than-hoped-for outcome of Jewish emancipation under the Persians—which can historically be described as little more than an exchange of Babylonian hegemony for Persian hegemony—coupled with the rise of the Seleucid superpower in the fourth century BCE.[23] Put straightforwardly, the new imperial regimes in the ancient Near East appeared to be foes of almost unlimited power, in the

22. John J. Collins, "Apocalyptic Eschatology as the Transcendence of Death," *Catholic Biblical Quarterly* 36, no. 1 (1974): 30.

23. See Daniel L. Smith-Christopher, "Reassessing the Historical and Sociological Impact of the Babylonian Exile (597/587–539 BCE)," in *Exile: Old Testament, Jewish, and Christian Conceptions*, ed. James M. Scott (Leiden: Brill, 1997), 22–23.

face of which a subjugated and relatively powerless group like the Jewish community might be tempted to despair.[24] It was in this context of resistance to the superpowers that the book of Daniel was compiled. Though there are a variety of apocalyptic antecedents in the canonical writings of the prophets, the book of Daniel, and specifically chapters 7–12, "is the only full-scale apocalypse within the Hebrew Bible."[25] Daniel's visions in chapters 7–12 are a good expression of the transcendental or cosmic perspective of apocalyptic.

Cosmic Confrontation and Liberation

In chapter 7, Daniel sees in a vision four different earthly human kingdoms emerge out of the mythological sea of chaos.[26]

> In the first year of King Belshazzar of Babylon, Daniel had a dream and visions of his head as he lay in bed. Then he wrote down the dream: I, Daniel, saw in my vision by night the four winds of heaven stirring up the great sea, and four great beasts came up out of the sea, different from one an-

24. As DiTommaso puts it, "Theodicy is the mother of apocalypticism." "Deliverance and Justice: Soteriology in the Book of Daniel," in *This World and the World to Come: Soteriology in Early Judaism*, ed. Daniel M. Gurtner (London: T&T Clark, 2011), 81. Anathea E. Portier-Young has painstakingly detailed the hegemonic claims and means of deploying power utilized under Antiochus IV Epiphanes (215–164 BCE) in her important work *Apocalypse against Empire: Theologies of Resistance in Early Judaism* (Grand Rapids: Eerdmans, 2011), 49–216. Comparing Antiochus IV's reign to that of previous rulers, Poiter-Young notes: "Prior to the persecution of Jews under Antiochus IV Epiphanes, this *dominio* expressed itself through conquest, killing and maiming, slavery, intimidating displays of martial power, and the policing presence and actions of imperial agents, as well as through economic redistribution achieved through ordinary systems of taxation and tribute and extraordinary acts of plunder. . . . These forms of *dominio* were oppressive, to be sure, and, as noted above, they occasioned a critical response in the Book of Watchers. But they did not seek overtly to negate Jewish theological claims for the sovereignty of their God. By contrast, Antiochus IV's persecution of the Jews made a totalitarian claim on his Judean subjects that not only denied God's sovereignty but, as some Jews perceived (Dan. 8:11–12; 11:36), directly attacked it" (24). See also Leo G. Perdue and Warren Carter, *Israel and Empire: A Postcolonial History of Israel and Early Judaism* (London: Bloomsbury, 2015), 190–98.

25. Hindy Najman, "The Inheritance of Prophecy in Apocalypse," in Collins, *The Oxford Handbook of Apocalyptic Literature*, 40.

26. "The turbulent sea is familiar from the OT, both as the abode of mythical chaos monsters and as an embodiment of chaos in its own right." John J. Collins, *The Apocalyptic Vision of the Book of Daniel* (Ann Arbor, MI: Scholars Press, 1977), 96.

other. The first was like a lion and had eagles' wings. Then, as I watched, its wings were plucked off, and it was lifted up from the ground and made to stand on two feet like a human being; and a human mind was given to it. Another beast appeared, a second one, that looked like a bear. It was raised up on one side, had three tusks in its mouth among its teeth and was told, "Arise, devour many bodies!" After this, as I watched, another appeared, like a leopard. The beast had four wings of a bird on its back and four heads; and dominion was given to it. After this I saw in the visions by night a fourth beast, terrifying and dreadful and exceedingly strong. It had great iron teeth and was devouring, breaking in pieces, and stamping what was left with its feet. It was different from all the beasts that preceded it, and it had ten horns. I was considering the horns, when another horn appeared, a little one coming up among them; to make room for it, three of the earlier horns were plucked up by the roots. There were eyes like human eyes in this horn, and a mouth speaking arrogantly. (vv. 1–8)

Each of the kingdoms is portrayed in the form of unnatural or hideous beasts that are arrogant and violent, indicating that their rule is fundamentally "bestial." The final beast, in particular, referring to the Seleucid empire and the reign of Antiochus IV Epiphanes (215-164 BCE), is interpreted to Daniel as the most violent and ruthless of all the kingdoms (cf. 7:15–25). Already in chapter 7, the final defeat of these powers is announced in the context of the throne room of the Ancient of Days and the enthronement of the Son of Man (7:9–14, 22, 26–27), a figure to whom we will return below. Chapters 8, 9, and 10–12 offer even more descriptive accounts of the confrontation, which is described in compact form in chapter 7. The point, however, is the same: "the meaning of history lies in its vertical dimension, in the revolt of the world-kingdoms, embodied by Antiochus, against the kingship of God."[27]

YHWH's confrontation with the regime of Antiochus IV is nothing less than a confrontation with the demonic powers of chaos and death. This point is highlighted both by the mythological origin of Antiochus IV's reign (i.e., it arises from out of the primordial sea of chaos) and by the final outcome, which is not only the overthrow of the "powers and principalities" embodied on earth but also YHWH's promise of resurrection (12:1–3), effectively declaring that God's sovereignty extends even over death.[28]

---

27. Collins, *The Apocalyptic Vision*, 161.

28. Perdue and Carter describe this as a clash of metanarratives. See *Israel and Empire*, 199–203.

Daniel 9:20–27 envisions the confrontation and victory of YHWH over Antiochus IV and the powers of chaos as tantamount to the inauguration of the Great Jubilee, a theme we have already encountered in the prophets and one that will continue as we turn to the New Testament.

When combined with the vision given to us in Isaiah 24–27, the so-called Isaiah Apocalypse, it is clear that the apocalyptic tradition envisions a cosmic confrontation wherein the true powers that stand behind earthly oppression and violence will be dealt with by YHWH, giving way to the great cosmic Jubilee of God's reign.

Cosmological Soteriology and Apocalyptic Epistemology

The language and imagery of confrontation between God and the powers leading to a subsequent liberation resemble the themes of release and reversal that we have already seen in the Jubilee traditions, bringing us into the orbit of soteriology, or salvation. This soteriological perspective has rightly been named "cosmological" by Martinus C. de Boer, because of the ways in which it conceives of both the plight of humanity and the divine solution for that plight.[29] Human beings are enslaved by death-dealing powers that have revolted against God, with the result being the despoliation of creation and the physical and eschatological death of humanity, or its total and ultimate separation from God. What is more, human beings are fundamentally incapable of standing against these powers.[30] Only God can act to liberate. "Only God has the power to defeat and overthrow the angelic powers that have subjugated and perverted the earth."[31] From this perspective, salvation, as Lorenzo DiTommaso notes, "transcends covenant fidelity and divine reciprocity,"[32] focusing exclusively on divine action.

This leads to two interrelated elements in Daniel's apocalyptic outlook, first, the deep commitment to the supremacy and priority of divine action, and second, a way of seeing the world that is given as a divine gift, enabling one to truly see and behold the meaning and final goal of history.[33]

---

29. See Martinus C. de Boer, *The Defeat of Death: Apocalyptic Eschatology in 1 Corinthians 15 and Romans 5* (Sheffield: Sheffield Academic Press, 1988), 47–50, 85–86.

30. "By definition, death (physical, moral, eschatological) is not remediable through human effort." Boer, *The Defeat of Death*, 84.

31. Boer, *The Defeat of Death*, 85.

32. DiTommaso, "Deliverance and Justice," 77.

33. There is an extensive discussion of the difference between "historical" and "otherworldly" apocalyptic texts in the secondary literature. Our engagement here is concerned

In continuity with the prophets, but in an intensified fashion, apocalyptic texts emphasize the supremacy and priority of divine action. It was divine, not human, action that would bring about the end of the rule of tyranny.[34] Johannes Weiss's pithy remark regarding the sole efficacy of divine action in relation to the coming of the kingdom of God captures well this tenet of apocalyptic eschatology: "God himself must come and make everything new."[35] For the apocalyptic writers of the Second Temple period, the plight of Israel (and the plight of humanity) would only be resolved by divine intervention and the divine establishment of a divine kingdom.

In the apocalyptic tradition, there is a pronounced emphasis on the divine nature and the priority of divine action in the bringing of the reign of *God*. Only divine action could liberate the community from its foes. The deadly "powers and principalities" that stand behind the violent and repressive ways of empire are ultimately beyond the capacity of human beings to deal with. Rather, it is only YHWH who can and will vanquish them. The final denouement will happen when YHWH "will swallow up death forever" (Isa. 25:8), implying that the confrontation of God with the powers of chaos is ultimately meant to be for the salvation of creation. "Then all the redeemed (human and nonhuman alike) will enjoy the flourishing and blessing that God intended; then God's salvation will indeed be as wide as creation itself."[36] As we shall consider below, emphasis upon the priority of divine action in apocalyptic does not empty out or make human resistance to such powers futile. Rather, it makes it provisional and penultimate.

Likewise, and in significant agreement with the prophets, the apocalyptists were also concerned with *seeing*, or rather, *perceiving*. In the context of the New Testament, J. Louis Martyn has argued that Paul functioned with an "apocalyptic epistemology," or a way of viewing the world that prioritizes the decisive efficacy and initiative inherent in the divine engagement with creation.[37] As Fleming Rutledge describes it, "Seeing the world

---

primarily with the "historical" form of apocalyptic texts because of their relevance for understanding the New Testament. For a discussion of the differences between "historical" and "otherworldly" forms of apocalyptic texts, see Collins, *The Apocalyptic Imagination*, 3–15.

34. Portier-Young, *Apocalypse against Empire*, 262–65, 278.

35. Johannes Weiss, *Jesus' Proclamation of the Kingdom of God* (Philadelphia: Fortress, 1971), 108.

36. J. Richard Middleton, *A New Heaven and a New Earth* (Grand Rapids: Baker Academic, 2014), 128.

37. See J. Louis Martyn, "Epistemology at the Turn of the Ages" and "Apocalyptic Antinomies," in *Theological Issues in the Letters of Paul*, by J. Louis Martyn (Nashville: Abing-

through the lens of biblical apocalyptic is *a transformative way of seeing*."[38]
From this vantage, apocalyptic refers to a way of seeing the world, and
especially God's past, present, and coming intervention in the world to
end the rule of sin and death. This also held true in Jewish apocalyptic.[39]
Almost all apocalyptic texts deal with the divine communication of hith-
erto hidden knowledge, or "mysteries."[40] The term "mystery" appears for
the first time in the canonical texts of the Old Testament in the apocalyptic
book of Daniel. The term has a prehistory in Persian religion but is closely
related to wisdom.

One of the central elements in Daniel, and other apocalyptic literature,
is that despite evidence to the contrary, God is in fact still at work in the life
and history of God's people. As D. S. Russell describes it: "Contemporary
experience was to be seen, not in isolation, but as part of that wholeness
of human history which declared, on the authority of God himself, that
despite all appearances to the contrary he was in complete control. . . . The
'mystery' now disclosed to these visionaries was that the God who reigned
in glory 'above' was the same God who reigned in power 'below.'"[41] Apocalyptic literature was often produced by communities under duress, overrun
by events and overpowered by stronger foes. In the midst of this situation,
however, the message was not to despair but to trust that God had not and
would not abandon the people, nor utterly forsake the covenant.

To summarize, apocalyptic as a mode of thought further widened the
already broad gaze of the prophets, by configuring God's coming judgment
and rescue as a cosmic event. As an event of cosmic consequence, apocalyptic modes of discourse emphasized the priority of divine action and
transfigured historical events through an appeal to be mindful of God's
salvific struggle on behalf of creation. Such a transfiguration or revelation

don, 1997), 89–110, 111–24. For a programmatic sketch of the theological relevance of apocalyptic for Christian theology, see Philip G. Ziegler, *Militant Grace: The Apocalyptic Turn
and the Future of Christian Theology* (Grand Rapids: Baker Academic, 2018).

38. Fleming Rutledge, *The Crucifixion: Understanding the Death of Jesus Christ* (Grand
Rapids: Eerdmans, 2015), 351.

39. Here I am following Loren Stuckenbruck's correction of Martyn on this issue. See
Loren Stuckenbruck, "Overlapping Ages at Qumran and 'Apocalyptic' in Pauline Theology," in *The Dead Sea Scrolls and Pauline Literature*, ed. Jean-Sébastien Rey (Leiden: Brill,
2014), 309–26.

40. In fact, Christopher Rowland argues that the conveyance of knowledge is the real
essence of apocalyptic literature. See his *The Open Heaven*.

41. D. S. Russell, *Divine Disclosure: An Introduction to Jewish Apocalyptic* (Minneapolis:
Fortress, 1992), 87–88. See also Rutledge, *The Crucifixion*, 352.

dislodged an epistemology of mere human observation and calculation, in favor of seeing the world differently, and therefore seeing the situation in which the community found itself differently.

The Two Ages

In the context of apocalyptic literature, to speak of a new way of seeing the world is to speak of a division of ages. From an apocalyptic perspective, the impending confrontation between YHWH and the powers establishes a temporal and, in some sense, spatial contrast between "this age" and the "age to come."

Speaking in regard to the apocalyptic text 4 Ezra, Jörg Frey describes the dynamic as follows: "The programmatic phrase is: 'God has created not one aeon but two' (*4 Ezra* 7:50), but the two aeons or worlds meant here are not parallel . . . but in a temporal sequence: 'this aeon' (4:2, 27; 6:9; 7:12; 8:1), 'this time' (7:113), 'this world' (9:19) or also 'the great aeon' (7:13). At the appointed time, at the end of days (12:32), the present world will come to an end, and the new world will appear."[42] The present age is marked by the overthrow of the just rule of God by which all of creation lives, and thus the very possibility of human and creaturely existence is threatened. It is "'full of sorrow and impotence' (II Esd. 4.27); it is corruptible (II Esd. 4.11) and a 'world of sickness' (II Enoch 66.6) so that men's hearts fail them when they think of it (II Esd. 4.2)."[43] In apocalyptic perspective, the world "lay in the hands of evil cosmic forces which were bent on the destruction of mankind and of the world itself."[44] The present age is dominated by the powers of death, which are the root of the violence, oppression, and destruction that human beings and communities suffer.

This age of suffering and violence is contrasted with the age to come, which is the realm and aeon dominated by life with God—a genuine age of liberation. As the later pseudepigraphic apocalyptic text of 2 Enoch describes: "the great aeon will begin, and they will live eternally, and then too there will be amongst them neither labor, nor sickness, nor humiliation, nor anxiety, nor need, nor brutality, nor night, nor darkness, but great light. . . . For all corruptible things shall pass away, and there will be eternal

---

42. Jörg Frey, "Apocalyptic Dualism," in Collins, *The Oxford Handbook of Apocalyptic Literature*, 288.

43. Russell, *The Method and Message*, 267.

44. Russell, *The Method and Message*, 267.

life" (65:6-7). Though the present age will pass away, this future age will never pass away.

In the midst of the radical discontinuity between the present evil age and the age to come is an even more profound continuity rooted in the determination of YHWH to re-create the heavens and the earth. God's will that creation exist in covenant with God will not finally be undermined. Rather, "The usurped creation will be restored; the corrupted universe will be cleansed; the created world will be re-created."[45] Resurrection, which, as we have noted, is a mark of God's divine sovereignty over death in relation to the people Israel and the individual Israelite, is now extended to the creation of a new heaven and a new earth. Though some apocalyptic texts imagine this new life to be angelic in nature, a significant number of texts imagine a re-created, physically embodied form of life lived under a new heaven and upon a new earth.[46]

THE TRIBULATION OF PURGATION

Though the two ages are radically distinct, there is some permeability, though in an asymmetrical relationship. That is, the new age does indeed begin to press into the old. In the apocalyptic tradition, this permeability is characterized most notably under the heading of tribulation. The transition between the two ages, which implies a period of overlap in which the new age invades the old, will be marked by tribulation, affliction, or what are sometimes called the "messianic woes." It will be "a time of unprecedented woes when the powers of evil will make their last desperate attempt to overthrow the powers of good."[47] Daniel 12:1 describes it as follows: "There shall be a time of anguish, such as has never occurred since nations first came into existence." Importantly, not only do the tribulations point to the permeability of the old and the new, but they function much like the purgation that the Day of Atonement was meant to achieve. Tribulation is tantamount to testing, and testing is meant to bring out that which is pure. As in the Jubilee legislation in Leviticus 25, so here: an old form of life must pass away for a new one to emerge; purgation/conversion is constitutive of the new world (cf. Dan. 9:24).

---

45. Russell, *The Method and Message*, 280.
46. See Russell, *The Method and Message*, 281-84.
47. Russell, *Divine Disclosure*, 92-93.

In Daniel, tribulation leading to purgation and conversion is lodged within the larger theo-political context of the confrontation between YHWH and the nations, specifically Antiochus IV Epiphanes. Other apocalypses portray the tribulations and woes as cosmic events that shake heaven and earth.[48] As Russell notes, "Even the physical universe itself will be affected; the very stars of heaven will change their course; the earth will be stricken by earthquake, famine and fire; there will be mysterious portents on the earth and in the heavens reminding men that the End is near."[49] This is not an unusual development, given the wide-ranging belief that events within the social-political sphere were thought to be mirrored in the realm of nature, and vice versa. This is also evidenced in various political theologies in the ancient Near East, from the Assyrians up into the Roman period.[50] The rule of the king, endowed with divine sanction, was supposed to result in fertility in the land, blessing for the people, and the defeat of rivals. Consequently, natural disasters were not only events in nature but were signs to be read, as they spoke either of current corruption or of future upheaval in the social and divine realm.[51] Thus, confrontations between different rulers were events that shook heaven and earth. Such a connection is already evidenced in the royal ideology of Israel herself, where the just rule of the king results in blessing on the land.

In the context of exile or oppression (i.e., Daniel's context), the divine-human-nature theo-political complex is deployed as an act of resistance. The royal ideologies of Assyrian, Babylonian, Persian, and Hellenistic empires all assumed that their kingdoms had brought order and peace to the cosmos. On the contrary, the prophets and apocalyptists proclaimed that an age of upheaval such as these kingdoms could not possibly imagine was about to be unleashed upon them as a sign of their failure to secure peace, as well as a sign of their impending end. The messianic woes would mark the end of all human pretension, as well as the violence and death that accompanied it, and would finally give way to God's reign of compassionate justice, righteousness, and *shalom*. YHWH would redeem the people.

In the face of the oncoming catastrophe, there was only one response: faithfulness. Attempts by earthly rulers to appease their gods through sac-

---

48. See Rowland, *The Open Heaven*, 156–57.

49. Russell, *Divine Disclosure*, 93.

50. See Perdue and Carter, *Israel and Empire*, 40–44, 72–74, 111–14, 138–43, 162–66, 172–74, 190–98, 227–34.

51. See Allen Brent, *A Political History of Early Christianity* (Edinburgh: T&T Clark, 2009), 117–28.

rifice, war, arrogance, etc., would prove useless. However, faithfulness to YHWH—a faithfulness unto death—would result in vindication through resurrection (cf. Dan. 12:3).

THE SON OF MAN

Of great importance for understanding the connection between the apocalyptic tradition and Jesus's preaching of the reign of God is the enigmatic figure of the Son of Man.[52] Though the roots of the image are complex and include passages from the writings of Ezekiel (1:5), the Son of Man appears first in Daniel 7 in the context of divine rule:

> As I watched in the night visions,
> I saw one like a human being
>   coming with the clouds of heaven.
> And he came to the Ancient One
>   and was presented before him.
> To him was given dominion
>   and glory and kingship,
> that all peoples, nations, and languages
>   should serve him.
> His dominion is an everlasting dominion
>   that shall not pass away,
> and his kingship is one
>   that shall never be destroyed. (7:13–14)

As translated above, the phrase simply means "one like a human being."[53] In the context of Daniel, the image of the Son of Man is undeniably connected to kingship, as this figure is contrasted with earlier representations of the rule of Nebuchadnezzar (cf. 2:37; 5:18). This is not only self-evident, as the figure is endowed by YHWH with an everlasting rule, but the figure is also described as arriving "with the clouds of heaven," an unmistakable

---

52. For a recent survey of the origins of the phrase, see Lester L. Grabbe, "'Son of Man': Its Origin and Meaning in Second Temple Judaism," in *Enoch and the Synoptic Gospels: Reminiscences, Allusions, Intertextuality*, ed. Loren T. Stuckenbruck and Gabriele Boccaccini (Atlanta: SBL Press, 2016), 169–97.

53. See John J. Collins, *Daniel: A Commentary on the Book of Daniel* (Minneapolis: Fortress, 1993), 304.

reference to the Old Testament theophany in which YHWH is revealed as sovereign. The image of the "storm-cloud theophany," which is found throughout the Old Testament and other ancient Near Eastern texts, indicates the nearness and transcendence of God, as well as the royal splendor of the divine presence.[54] By being placed in such a context, the Son of Man is being identified with, even if he remains subordinate to, the Great King, the Ancient of Days.[55]

The New Testament background for the Son of Man moves beyond the boundaries of the canon,[56] as the Son of Man plays an especially conspicuous role in the so-called Similitudes of Enoch (also called the Book of Parables), which constitutes chapters 37-71 of the apocalyptic text 1 Enoch. "In a number of places throughout the Similitudes the expression 'Son of Man' or simply 'Man' is used (cf. 46.1-6; 48.2-7; 62.5-9, 14; 63.11; 69.26-29; 70.1; 71.17) to describe a being who is elsewhere in the same book designated 'the Elect One' (cf. 40.5; 45.3; 49.2; 51.3; 61.8; 62.9, cf. also Luke 9.35; Acts 3.14) or 'the Righteous One' (cf. 38.2) or 'his Anointed' (cf. 48.19)."[57] In keeping with Daniel, the Son of Man in the Similitudes is associated with divine rule, though he also stands in as a representative figure of all the elect (cf. 1 En. 49:7).[58] The Son of Man was, in some sense, preexistent, having been "chosen and hidden before him before the world was created, and forever" (1 En. 48:6).[59] His appearing marks the beginning of God's reign on earth. As described by Mowinckel:

54. See Frank Moore Cross, *Canaanite Myth and Hebrew Epic: Essays in the History of the Religion of Israel* (Cambridge, MA: Harvard University Press, 1996), 145-94.

55. See Collins, *Daniel*, 289-91. Interpreters are divided over the identity of the figure the author of Daniel might have intended. Is this a single individual? Is he a corporate figure, meant to represent the "holy ones" mentioned in Dan. 7:27? Notwithstanding later developments, especially the appropriation of this title by Jesus and the early Christian community, Collins notes three different options for the identity of the son of man within the context of Daniel: "(1) an exalted human being, (2) a collective symbol, and (3) a heavenly being" (308).

56. This is entirely understandable, since the concept of a canon did not exist at the time of the writing of the New Testament.

57. Russell, *The Method and Message*, 327-28.

58. See Thomas Kazen, "Son of Man as Kingdom Imagery: Jesus between Corporate Symbol and Individual Redeemer Figure," in *Jesus from Judaism to Christianity: Continuum Approaches to the Historical Jesus*, ed. Tom Holmén (Edinburgh: T&T Clark, 2007), 87-108; see also Shirley Lucass, *The Concept of the Messiah in the Scriptures of Judaism and Christianity* (London: T&T Clark International, 2011), 144-57.

59. Translation is found in Mitchell G. Reddish, ed., *Apocalyptic Literature: A Reader* (Peabody, MA: Hendrickson, 1995), 166-87.

When he is enthroned, they kneel and pay him homage (1En. xlviii, 5); and he is hailed with praise not only by "all who dwell above in heaven" (lxi, 6ff), but also by all the living; "and the kings and the mighty and all who possess the earth shall bless and glorify and extol him (i.e., the Son of Man) who rules over all, who was hidden."

This means that his enthronement is not only something which is visible in heaven. It is the great change of the ages, inaugurating the judgment and the new aeon.[60]

In effect, the revelation of the Son of Man is equivalent to the revelation of the reign of God. As in Daniel, the Son of Man sits on or near God's throne, and God's judgment or rectification of the world is enacted through him. Keeping with this theme, 4 Ezra 13, another important apocalyptic text dealing with the Son of Man, depicts the figure as opposing the violence of the world with the law and word of God.[61] Through simple speech—the text literally says "without effort" (4 Ezra 13:38)[62]—evil is removed. Endowed with royal power, the reign of the Son of Man is marked by *shalom* and a people of *shalom*.

Having divine characteristics, he "accompanies God."[63] He is intimately associated with YHWH's saving work, "for in his name they are saved, and he is the one who will require their lives" (1 En. 48:7). He reveals "all the secrets of wisdom" (51:3) and is identified with the Messiah (48:10; 52:4). The references from Daniel and 4 Ezra 13 intimate that there are even some oblique allusions to suffering.[64] What is certain is that the Son of Man is an apocalyptic figure, representing the human face of God's coming reign. He is endowed with God's justice, righteousness, and wisdom, and his appearance marks the beginning of the reign of God and the triumph of God's *shalom*.

An Apocalyptic Politics

Scholars have long noticed the political dimensions of apocalyptic, describing it as a form of resistance literature.[65] In this regard, Anathea E. Portier-

---

60. Sigmund Mowinckel, *He That Cometh: The Messiah Concept in the Old Testament and Later Judaism* (Grand Rapids: Eerdmans, 2005), 389.

61. See Mowinckel, *He That Cometh*, 393-99.

62. Translation is found in Reddish, *Apocalyptic Literature*, 92-94.

63. Mowinckel, *He That Cometh*, 373.

64. See Mowinckel, *He That Cometh*, 410-15; Russell, *The Method and Message*, 334-40; and Portier-Young, *Apocalypse against Empire*, 272-76.

65. See Anathea E. Portier-Young, "Jewish Apocalyptic Literature as Resistance Liter-

Young's description of the book of Daniel is apt: "No book of the Hebrew Bible so plainly engages and opposes the project of empire as Daniel."[66] Produced by people in situations of duress, apocalyptic is not simply the fantasy literature of end-times scenarios, but neither is it meant as a simple valve to release pent-up frustration, or to express feelings of revenge or rage. Rather, it imagines a political praxis that can be lived in the here and now.

In the book of Daniel, wisdom and the wise teacher assume great importance in the context of the impending apocalyptic crisis. The wise person or "wise teacher" (*maskil*) understands the real direction of history and the final outcome as the triumph of God's rule and is faithful in imparting this knowledge to others.[67] Wisdom here is connected to teleology, or the ends toward which all things move. It is another way of describing an apocalyptic epistemology, or way of viewing history. In Daniel, though Babylon/Antiochus claims unlimited power and authority, demanding absolute obedience and loyalty, it is God's reign that will triumph (cf. Dan. 3–5), for the empire's feet are made of clay (cf. Dan. 2). Attending to the ways of God is how wisdom is found, and as such the true end of wisdom is doxology.[68]

In Daniel 9, wisdom comes through attending especially to Scripture's witness. Daniel reads Jeremiah 25 and 29, which speak about the duration of the exile. He then turns to offer a prayer of confession, a petition for forgiveness, and praise. Portier-Young notes that Daniel's act of prayer is a refusal of Babylonian or Seleucid myths of invincibility and the presumption that the imperial actors are really the cause of Israel's downfall. The real being and identity of Israel is found in the history of covenant with YHWH, and therefore, Daniel recognizes that the fate of Israel is, and has always been, in the hands of YHWH. "Praise and petition affirm that their deliverance can come only from God."[69] Judgment and forgiveness do not flow from the emperor, but from YHWH, to whom "belong mercy and forgiveness" (Dan. 9:9).

According to Portier-Young, there are also parallels with Isaiah's suffering servant. The "wise teachers" are called to make righteous the many[70]

---

ature," in Collins, *The Oxford Handbook of Apocalyptic Literature*, 145–62. See also Collins, *The Apocalyptic Vision*, 191–218.

66. Portier-Young, *Apocalypse against Empire*, 223. See also Richard H. Horsley, *Scribes, Visionaries, and the Politics of Second Temple Judea* (Louisville: Westminster John Knox, 2007), passim, esp. 173–91.

67. Portier-Young, "Jewish Apocalyptic Literature," 151.

68. See Walter Brueggemann, "Praise to God Is the End of Wisdom—What Is the Beginning?" *Journal for Preachers* 12, no. 3 (Easter 1989): 30–40.

69. Portier-Young, *Apocalypse against Empire*, 253.

70. Cf. Isa. 53:11; Dan. 12:3.

through their knowledge[71] and their atoning humility.[72] Furthermore, the "wise teachers" were called to be faithful unto death and were promised vindication through resurrection.[73] These parallels, when coupled with the earlier stories in the book of Daniel (chaps. 1–6), offer a sense that the political practice envisioned moves in the direction of creative nonviolence. "So the six beautiful stories of the book of Daniel show how he and his friends Shadrak, Mishak, and Abednego were saved repeatedly, not by the power of the sword but by prayer and loyalty to God."[74] Daniel's refusal to eat the food of the king (Dan. 1), his refusal to worship the idol made by Nebuchadnezzar (Dan. 3), and his refusal to cease from offering prayer (Dan. 6) were all nonviolent provocations of the ways of empire, which carried the potential of the death penalty.[75] Each provocation refused a specific claim of the empire over the body and mind.

The way of wisdom is life and peace (Prov. 3:17). Daniel's understanding of wisdom refers not only to the final end toward which all things move, but also the path that the faithful are called to traverse to get there. It is the way of God's *shalom*; the peaceable provocation in the face of the ways of empire. And though their path leads to a "witness unto death," nevertheless, God is sovereign even over death, for resurrection is the true end of this way.

Apocalypse and Jubilee have both been prominent and potent in modern political movements. One of the most important sites where these two themes have been entangled in hopes for liberation and a flourishing life can be found in the Black freedom movements in the United States. In the nineteenth century, alongside other images and narratives like exodus and the Sabbath,[76] apocalypse and Jubilee were central categories for people who were struggling to free themselves from the oppression of white supremacy and its many manifestations, whether in the form of chattel

71. Cf. Isa. 52:15; Dan. 11:33.

72. Cf. Isa. 53:4, 6, 10–12; Dan. 9:24; 10:12; 11:33, 35; 12:10. See Portier-Young, *Apocalypse against Empire*, 273–74.

73. Cf. Dan. 12:1–3; Isa. 53:10–12.

74. Naim Stifan Ateek, *A Palestinian Christian Cry for Reconciliation* (Maryknoll, NY: Orbis, 2008), 135.

75. See Portier-Young, *Apocalypse against Empire*, 223–79.

76. See Albert J. Raboteau, *Slave Religion: The "Invisible Institution" in the Antebellum South* (Oxford: Oxford University Press, 2004), 311–12, and Emerson B. Powery and Rodney S. Sadler Jr., *The Genesis of Liberation: Biblical Interpretation in the Antebellum Narratives of the Enslaved* (Louisville: Westminster John Knox, 2016), chap. 3.

slavery, Jim Crow segregation, or the more ubiquitous and decentralized forms we see today. In the spirituals, slave narratives, abolitionist pamphlets, sermons, and circular newspapers, the "Biblical narratives offered more than inspiration; they offered real political strategies."[77]

In the works of abolitionists like David Walker, one can detect an apocalyptic mind-set.[78] In his 1829 "Appeal," Walker urged Americans—especially white Americans—to immediately end slavery or "God Almighty will tear up the very face of the earth!!!!"[79] Walker's call to repentance was predicated on the truth that chattel slavery was an affront to God's justice and righteousness. Abolitionist freedmen like Walker and the enslaved alike "anticipated emancipation as a divinely inspired event, an apocalyptic event when God would break in on human history."[80] It was not only the odiousness of slavery and the concomitant desires for freedom and judgment that drew African Americans to apocalyptic modes of thought, it was also the sheer insurmountable character of the slavocracy in the United States. To have believed in the 1850s that within only a few years the slave system would be ended, and what is more, the vote would be given to Black men, was literally unthinkable. As David Roediger states, "If anything seemed impossible in the 1850s political universe, it was the immediate, unplanned, and uncompensated emancipation of four million slaves."[81] When these realities did come, apocalyptic offered a constellation of images and themes that could help to make sense of the seismic changes that occurred in a compressed period of time, which has rightly been named "revolutionary time."[82]

Of great significance is the fact that the images of apocalyptic and Jubilee were not used primarily to motivate white Americans but to fire the imagination and underwrite the agency of enslaved and freedmen alike. "The exciting vision of what was to come released the power of the future into

77. Matthew Harper, *The End of Days: African American Religion and Politics in the Age of Emancipation* (Chapel Hill: University of North Carolina Press, 2016), 46.

78. For a detailed discussion of the multiracial history of abolitionism, see Manisha Sinha, *The Slave's Cause: A History of Abolition* (New Haven: Yale University Press, 2016).

79. David Walker, "Walker's Appeal, in Four Articles; Together with a Preamble, to the Coloured Citizens of the World, but in Particular, and Very Expressly, to Those of the United States of America, Written in Boston, State of Massachusetts, September 28, 1829," accessed January 27, 2022, https://docsouth.unc.edu/nc/walker/walker.html.

80. Harper, *The End of Days*, 20.

81. David Roediger, *Seizing Freedom: Slave Emancipation and Liberty for All* (London: Verso, 2015), 17.

82. Roediger, *Seizing Freedom*, 9.

their lives, bringing not only the strength to survive but also the courage to strive toward freedom. The eschaton was not an opiate; it functioned proleptically. The transcendent future was also the present."[83] This was especially the case as the former moved to emancipate themselves in what W. E. B. Du Bois called the "general strike of the slaves," which refers to the close to one million formerly enslaved who simply walked away from their bondage prior to the Emancipation Proclamation.[84] Interpreting the events of this remarkable period in such a manner was indeed "an impressive act of mass theology performed by a people denied literacy and kept from the Bible."[85]

Though an apocalyptic hermeneutic and epistemology undoubtedly included the notion of judgment, it was above all the positive images of freedom, festivity, and reversal that resonated among the newly freed. Like others seeking a changed world, they "jubilated."[86] In the form of public festivals and pageants, with music, "heard as strange, wild, and moving," formerly enslaved and freedmen alike celebrated emancipation, and even dared hope that a radical redistribution of the land—as prescribed in Leviticus 25—might begin to bring healing, restoration, and a future marked by flourishing rather than degradation.[87]

Matthew Harper documents an especially potent example of how General Sherman's so-called forty acres and a mule[88] proposal was interpreted through the lens of apocalypse and Jubilee:

> One group of African Americans in Mississippi put a precise date on the coming Jubilee and millennium. They heard a story that the Freedman's Bureau had a "Great Document" sealed with four seals, which would be broken on New Year's Day 1866, when the federal government would deliver its "final orders" for land confiscation and redistribution. This was a

83. George C. L. Cummings, "The Slave Narratives as a Source of Black Theological Discourse: The Spirit and Eschatology," in *Cut Loose Your Stammering Tongue: Black Theology in the Slave Narratives*, ed. Dwight N. Hopkins and George Cummings (Maryknoll, NY: Orbis, 1991), 58.

84. See W. E. B. Du Bois, *Black Reconstruction in America: 1860–1880* (New York: Free Press, 1992), 55–83; see also Roediger, *Seizing Freedom*, 25–43.

85. Roediger, *Seizing Freedom*, 17.

86. See Peter Linebaugh, "Jubilating; or, How the Atlantic Working Class Used the Biblical Jubilee against Capitalism, with Some Success," *Radical History Review* 50 (1991): 143–80.

87. See Roediger, *Seizing Freedom*, 44–45. See also Harper, *The End of Days*, 41–44.

88. For an extended discussion of the "forty acres and a mule" scheme, its relation to workers' rights, and Jubilee, see Roediger, *Seizing Freedom*, 59–65.

dramatic retelling of St. John's vision in the Book of Revelation of a great document with seven seals, each broken seal releasing new terrors such as the four horsemen of the apocalypse. In the freed people's vision, the opening of the document paralleled the apocalypse, even if the contents of the document sounded more like Jubilee.[89]

These expectations were repeated as rumors of a broad land redistribution appeared again in 1867, 1868, and 1873.[90]

Apocalypse and Jubilee even remained significant in the postemancipation era of Reconstruction, as African American communities strategized together for economic and racial justice in an era when neither would easily occur. As white supremacy reformulated and reorganized itself, bringing about the collapse of Reconstruction and, with it, new forms of enslavement like debt peonage, sharecropping, and legal and extralegal forms of racial terror, African American communities did not totally give up on the possibility of Jubilee. They reimagined it, though now in tandem with themes like exodus and exile, as the Great Migrations of the late nineteenth century led many to flee the southern United States, heading north and west.[91] These themes, and others, continue to have purchase even as Black theology has reformulated itself in the twentieth and twenty-first century under the guidance of figures like James Cone, J. Deotis Roberts, Gayraud Wilmore, Katie Cannon, Delores Williams, and others.

Conclusion

Before moving on to consider the New Testament witness, it seems worthwhile to stop and take stock of the dynamics and themes that we have encountered in our study thus far. We have not sought to offer a comprehensive picture of all the dimensions attached to notions of kingship and the reign of God in the psalms, prophets, and apocalyptic traditions. Rather, we have attempted to pick up on the various threads of key elements in these earlier texts as they feed into the New Testament. At the same time, we should also note that we are not attempting to offer a kind of "salvation history" approach in our descriptive work, as if the New Testament's wit-

89. Harper, *The End of Days*, 72.
90. Harper, *The End of Days*, 74.
91. Harper, *The End of Days*, chap. 3.

ness to the reign of God in Jesus was simply the logical outflow of earlier insights. On the contrary, our assumption is that the life history of Jesus determines the meaning and substance of the earlier themes, rather than the other way around. Nevertheless, in these earlier texts and traditions we have begun to discern some of the key building blocks for our argument that the reign of God is embodied in Jesus. Our job in this short concluding section is to gather those insights into a loosely coherent picture.

In our discussion of the psalms, we noted the correlation between human and divine kingship, with the preference of subordinating the human to the divine. Though there are significant exceptions, the real emphasis is on the fact that "YHWH has become king." This statement was not so much an ontological claim about divine sovereignty as a way of pointing to a living history, which in the psalms focused especially on creation, exodus, and covenant. Importantly, these events were not understood as simply past occurrences but were conceptualized as present living events, such that, when the psalmist makes proclamations regarding these events, YHWH is understood to step forth as the living Lord who has liberated and is liberating the people of God, taming the chaos of creation, and establishing covenant with the people. Thus, they disclose to the hearer or reader what it means both in the past and in the present that YHWH rules. The result of this is the impression that the reign of God is a present and living reality—a history that impinges on the here and now—even if the core events are located in the remote past.

Second, we noted the fact that the psalms describe God's rule as fundamentally different from all human rule. God's reign is distinct from all other "gods" and from human rule in general, in that it is marked by compassionate justice and righteousness. The divine righteousness that comes against human unrighteousness refers to God's faithfulness to the divine decision that creation should live a flourishing life in fellowship with God. In this regard, we discussed the significant image of the Jubilee Year, which serves as a kind of subterranean resource for the psalms. The Jubilee justice outlined in Leviticus 25 and alluded to in the psalms imagines a community set right through judgment and new life.

Finally, we briefly noted that though there is a definite ambivalence and even hostility toward human rule, the psalms do nevertheless enact a kind of politics of praise that opens up a space in which to imagine a political or social life and action that does not conform to the dominant mode of politics or political realities. Rather, it recalls or anticipates events of liberation, healing, restoration, and the establishment of God's compassionate justice. To ground this somewhat allusive claim, we turned to the Black musical tradition in North America, specifically the spirituals, which offered to those struggling against the dehumanizing reality of white supremacy and chattel slavery an outlet for resistance, calling on the God who liberates to act. These were not just furtive cries, but in the very act of singing, swaying, shouting, and dancing, those who were captive experienced a taste of a freedom that they longed to come toward them from the future.

The psalms, then, offer three key insights. The first is that God's reign has an event character and is rooted in a history of God with the people of God. The second refers to the character of God's reign. The reason that God's reign is not only different but also victorious has to do with its liberative character. God rules through righteousness and justice, or Jubilee. Finally, God's reign is capacious enough to provide space for human cooperation in the form of a kind of politics of praise.

These insights are taken up in the prophets and apocalyptists. A significant difference is that in the prophets and the apocalyptists, YHWH's rule is spoken of primarily as future or eschatological. The impending rule of God is understood to come forth from the future into the present, marking an end of the current state of affairs and the inauguration of a new reality. As such, God's rule is marked by both judgment and new life. Both exile (judgment) and restoration (new life) are expressions of God's rule in the prophets. In the apocalyptic writers, the event of YHWH's appearing will be cataclysmic and marked by tribulation and upheaval, and they describe it as a transition from the old age to the new. Judgment and new life are given cosmic scope, as death itself is judged and removed from creation. The old state of affairs is one marked by the ways of death, seen especially in the unfaithfulness of Israel and the lawlessness of the nations, while the new state of affairs is characterized by God's Jubilee justice and *shalom*.

Both the prophets and the apocalyptic tradition emphasize divine agency in the coming of the kingdom. The coming reign of God is initiated by God and is rooted in YHWH's faithfulness. YHWH comes to the rescue of God's people, and through them, to the nations. At the same time, it is not as though YHWH has not been present with Israel as they have been sent into exile. Rather, God is with Israel in their suffering, depicted by the prophet Isaiah as suffering alongside the people—even bearing the judgment of exile—in the figure of the servant whose representative action brings about the repentance and conversion of the people.

Human agency, though significantly relativized and subordinated to divine agency, still plays an important role in relation to the reign of God.

First, in the prophetic and apocalyptic literature we encounter a litany of human figures that are depicted as the human face of God's rule. The Davidic Messiah, the suffering servant, and the Son of Man are all traditions that appear in various ways in the prophetic and apocalyptic literature. All three are eschatological figures, associated with the appearing of YHWH, and all three are subordinated to YHWH, depicted as faithful servants and instruments through which God rules Israel and the nations. Though they share significant overlap in the writings of the prophets and apocalyptic writings, for the most part they remain separate traditions.

Second, both the prophetic and the apocalyptic traditions call for human response in the here and now. Fueled by the notion that YHWH's cosmic rule comes from the future into the present, these writings imagine ways of life that reject exploitation and injustice, and that embrace life-giving forms of community (i.e., they echo God's Jubilee justice). The theo-politics of the psalms, prophets, and apocalyptic traditions share two commonalities: (1) they all refuse to acknowledge the ultimate authority of any other power but God, and (2) they are all rooted in the vision of compassionate justice depicted in the Jubilee legislation of Leviticus 25 with its prophetic and apocalyptic expansions. God's coming will be marked by Jubilee and *shalom*; in the meantime, the community is called to humbly live and act in the light of that coming. That is, to live in such a way that the logic of Jubilee and *shalom* is more determinative for life than scarcity and violence.

As an illustration of this, we considered the Black freedom movements during the nineteenth century. As we noted, Africans and African Americans were drawn to the images of apocalypse and Jubilee because they gave both the free and the enslaved a way of conceptualizing the dehumanizing and overwhelming forces arrayed against them, as well as the belief that it would take a divine act to break into history to end slavery and legalized oppression. Their work was more than interpretative, however, as both apocalypse and Jubilee motivated, underwrote, and gave direction to their agency in self-emancipation and later in attempts to imagine and establish a flourishing life.

Chapter Four

"THE KINGDOM OF GOD IS IN YOUR MIDST"

In our previous chapters we highlighted the theme of the coming reign of God as found in the psalms, the prophets, and the apocalyptic traditions. As we have seen, the theme of YHWH's rule was depicted in multifaceted ways and with multiple associations. Though the psalms speak of God's reign in connection with past events, the primary orientation of the prophets and apocalyptic writers is eschatological: the reign of God is coming toward us from the future. God's epiphany will result in the twin phenomena of judgment and new life and will be marked by a tumultuous transition from the old age to the new. Importantly, the justice and righteousness that characterizes God's reign, and therefore the new age, is the compassionate justice embodied in the image of Jubilee, rooted especially in Leviticus 25, but further radicalized and expanded in the prophets and apocalyptic visionaries. Finally, God is the sole agent in bringing the divine reign to fruition, though space is made for human participation both in the form of representative figures (i.e., Son of Man, etc.) and in the theo-politics that the promised future calls for in the here and now.

Our next three chapters turn to the New Testament and especially to the figure of Jesus, for it is in Jesus that God's reign has now come into the midst of history. These chapters constitute the heart of our argument that the person and work of Jesus are effectively the reign of God. The present chapter offers a sketch of Jesus's life, tracing the themes associated with God's rule. To this end we selectively explore passages on the inauguration of Jesus's life and ministry, his teaching, and his works of healing and exorcism. In chapters 5 and 6 we will focus on the death and resurrection of Jesus, which together constitute the climax of Jesus's life history. Chapter 6 concludes with a consideration of the Spirit of Jesus.

Before we begin our discussion of the New Testament witness to Jesus, however, a critical qualification regarding the relationship between Jesus and the witness of the Hebrew Scriptures must be made. Though Jesus was certainly influenced by the ideas and traditions that preceded him, and though in a certain sense he fulfilled those traditions, they do not ultimately define him. Rather, it is Jesus—in both his words and deeds—that defines the reign of God.

THE DIFFERENCE THAT JESUS MAKES

Christian confession begins with Jesus.[1] "At the centre of Christian faith is the history of Christ."[2] He is the central fact around which Christian theology cannot get.[3] The documents of the New Testament are best understood as literary expressions of the earliest communities' attempts to grapple with the event of Jesus Christ. As James Cone puts it, "The New Testament is the early Church's response to the history of Jesus Christ."[4] In all their diversity, these documents crystallize around the conviction that the events that transpire in the history of the man Jesus coincide "with the history of God Himself."[5] Thus, "what occurs in the history of Jesus Christ is unsurpassed and unsurpassable; there is no reality, no historical or mythical figure, no system, framework, idea, or anything else that transcends the reality of Jesus Christ, for in the strongest possible sense, God's action and the history of Jesus Christ are both one and singular."[6] The whole of the witness of the New Testament turns on this axis.

The book of Hebrews puts it as follows: "Long ago God spoke to our ancestors in many and various ways by the prophets, but in these last days he has spoken to us by a Son, whom he appointed heir of all things, through

1. "It began with Jesus—'it' being Christianity." James D. G. Dunn, *Christianity in the Making*, vol. 1, *Jesus Remembered* (Grand Rapids: Eerdmans, 2003), 11.

2. Jürgen Moltmann, *The Way of Jesus Christ: Christology in Messianic Dimensions* (Minneapolis: Fortress, 1993), 151.

3. "Christian theology begins and ends with Jesus Christ. He is the point of departure for everything to be said about God, humankind, and the world." James H. Cone, *A Black Theology of Liberation*, fortieth anniversary ed. (Maryknoll, NY: Orbis, 2016), 116.

4. James H. Cone, *God of the Oppressed*, rev. ed. (Maryknoll, NY: Orbis, 1997), 102.

5. Karl Barth, *Church Dogmatics* IV/2 (Edinburgh: T&T Clark, 1958), 336.

6. Douglas Harink, *Paul among the Postliberals: Pauline Theology beyond Christendom and Modernity* (Grand Rapids: Brazos, 2003), 68-69.

whom he also created the worlds. He is the reflection of God's glory and the exact imprint of God's very being, and he sustains all things by his powerful word" (1:1-3). In the New Testament witness, though there is a profound continuity between the history of Jesus Christ and God's history with Israel, Jesus is nevertheless understood as the determinative key by which we understand who God is. "What God is, the Son is: they share the same 'imprint of being.'"[7] He bears God's glory, which refers both to the Shekinah, or presence of YHWH, and the royal splendor that attends the divine presence.[8] He is superior to the angels (Heb. 1:4). Though Jesus comes in the flow of the history of Israel, he is also understood to precede it (cf. John 8:58). He is the one through whom God created the universe, and he is also the goal of creation (Col. 1:16-17). He is the *telos*, or goal, of the law (Rom. 10:4), the one to whom the law and the prophets point (Luke 24:27). He is the Word (John 1:1, 14) and very wisdom of God (1 Cor. 1:24). Such New Testament acclamations are the basis for the statement that "The story of Jesus is not a mere illustration of the divine identity; Jesus himself and his story are intrinsic to the divine identity."[9] The conceptual implication of the early Christian confession that "Jesus is Lord" (Rom. 10:9), then, is that the history that the name Jesus of Nazareth denotes reveals to us the identity of God in a decisive fashion.

The principal reason that the New Testament witness as a whole converges on this affirmation is itself rooted in the reality of Jesus's resurrection. It is because Jesus, a human being who was executed by the Roman authorities, is raised from the dead that the New Testament authors are compelled to speak about him in this way. As Jürgen Moltmann puts it: "without the event which the first Christians called 'God's raising of Jesus from the dead' there would be no New Testament, no church, no Christianity—and no knowledge about Jesus of Nazareth."[10] This is what we mean when we say that the various documents in the New Testament are

---

7. Luke Timothy Johnson, *Hebrews: A Commentary* (Louisville: Westminster John Knox, 2006), 70.

8. See Richard Bauckham, *Gospel of Glory: Major Themes in Johannine Theology* (Grand Rapids: Baker Academic, 2015), 43-62.

9. Richard Bauckham, *Jesus and the God of Israel: God Crucified and Other Studies on the New Testament's Christology of Divine Identity* (Grand Rapids: Eerdmans, 2008), 51. See also Charles B. Cousar, *A Theology of the Cross: The Death of Jesus in the Pauline Letters* (Minneapolis: Fortress, 1990), 25-51.

10. Jürgen Moltmann, *Sun of Righteousness, Arise! God's Future for Humanity and the Earth* (Minneapolis: Fortress, 2010), 39.

attempts to reckon with the event of Jesus. It is not simply the identity and life history of the Jesus who lived and died with whom the authors of these documents are attempting to grapple. Rather, it is this person as seen in the light of his livingness, his resurrection.[11]

If the history of Jesus can be said to define the divine identity, then it stands to reason that the history of Jesus can be said to define the reign of God. Identifying God's reign with Jesus in this way is captured in the passage from which we have taken our present chapter title. In a conversation with the teachers of the law, Jesus answers a question about the time of the kingdom's coming by telling his interlocutors, "The kingdom of God is not coming with things that can be observed; nor will they say, 'Look, here it is!' or 'There it is!' For, in fact, the kingdom of God is among you" (Luke 17:20b-21). Though long mistranslated as the "kingdom of God is within you," the better rendering of the Greek text here is "the kingdom of God is in your midst" or "among you."[12] Such a translation, as offered in the NRSV, captures the deeper point of the New Testament witness as a whole, which is that Jesus's person and work are to be identified with the person and work of the God who reigns. In other words, it is in Jesus—and more specifically in the path he treads, or in his life, death, resurrection, and presence in the Spirit—that the reign of God is present. Jesus is the *autobasileia*, or "the kingdom itself," as the third-century North African theologian Origen once called him.[13]

Thus, though drawing on earlier traditions and ideas, it is nevertheless the life history of Jesus that molds, shapes, and reveals to us the reign of God, such that we are compelled to say that Jesus *is* the reign of God, and that by attending to the narrative of Jesus's life, death, and resurrection we come to see the concrete *way* in which God reigns. From the perspective of the New Testament, then, the various traditions that we have outlined in our previous chapters are themselves subject to redefinition, amplifica-

---

11. See Robert W. Jenson, *Systematic Theology*, vol. 1, *The Triune God* (Oxford: Oxford University Press, 1997), 44.

12. See I. Howard Marshall, *Commentary on Luke* (Grand Rapids: Eerdmans, 1978), 655-56; Joseph A. Fitzmyer, *The Gospel according to Luke X–XXIV* (Garden City, NY: Doubleday, 1985), 1157-62; Luke Timothy Johnson, *The Gospel of Luke* (Collegeville, MN: Liturgical Press, 1991), 263; Sharon H. Ringe, *Luke* (Louisville: Westminster John Knox, 1995), 221-22; Joel B. Green, *The Gospel of Luke* (Grand Rapids: Eerdmans, 1997), 628-30.

13. Origen, *Commentary on Matthew* 14.7, as cited in Hans Urs von Balthasar, ed., *Origen, Spirit and Fire: A Thematic Anthology of His Writings* (Washington, DC: Catholic University of America Press, 1984), 362.

on, or transfiguration under the impress of the history of Jesus. This is the critical qualification of our portrait of God's rule as recounted in the witness of the psalms, the prophets, and the apocalyptic writings. This is the difference that Jesus makes.

THE ANTICIPATION OF GOD'S JUBILEE REIGN

In the Gospel of Mark, Jesus inaugurates his public ministry with the following proclamation: "The time is fulfilled, and the kingdom of God has come near; repent, and believe in the good news" (1:15). The Gospels of Matthew and Luke place Jesus's initial declaration of the nearness of God's reign in a somewhat larger frame and on the heels of a history of anticipation. They include a number of figures in this history of anticipation: Mary and Joseph, the parents of Jesus; Elizabeth and Zechariah, the parents of John the Baptist; the devout Simeon and Anna the prophetess; and a host of shepherds, wise men, angels, and wicked rulers.

In recounting this history, we will confine ourselves to Mary, the mother of Jesus, and John the Baptist. Their anticipations of God's coming reign are broadly in keeping with the prophetic and apocalyptic expectations that we outlined in our previous two chapters, with the important caveat that the coming of Jesus stands at the center of their expectations. In different though complementary ways, these two figures anticipate the apocalypse of God's Jubilee reign that is Jesus the Christ.

The Magnificat

We begin with the song of Mary, often called the Magnificat, a title taken from "the first word of its Latin translation."[14] Mary, a young, vulnerable woman, pledged to be married to the older Joseph, has received an unsettling visitation from the angel Gabriel, which included the startling declaration that she would give birth to "the Son of the Most High" (Luke 1:32), whose reign would have no end. After receiving this declaration, Mary is understandably unnerved, and leaving the town of Nazareth, perhaps to avoid the scandal of a premarital pregnancy (cf. Matt. 1:19), she "went with haste" to visit her relative Elizabeth, "herself swelling with a pregnancy

---

14. Ringe, *Luke*, 34.

95

in her old age."[15] Elizabeth, the mother of John the Baptist, greets the younger Mary in the power of the Spirit: "Blessed are you among women, and blessed is the fruit of your womb" (Luke 1:42), exulting in the one Mary will bring into the world, who will bring the blessings of God's reign. After this remarkable greeting from Elizabeth, Mary bursts into a song of her own, a song of praise and liberation:

> "My soul magnifies the Lord,
>> and my spirit rejoices in God my Savior,
> for he has looked with favor on the lowliness of his servant.
>> Surely, from now on all generations will call me blessed;
> for the Mighty One has done great things for me,
>> and holy is his name.
> His mercy is for those who fear him
>> from generation to generation.
> He has shown strength with his arm;
>> he has scattered the proud in the thoughts of their hearts.
> He has brought down the powerful from their thrones,
>> and lifted up the lowly;
> he has filled the hungry with good things,
>> and sent the rich away empty.
> He has helped his servant Israel,
>> in remembrance of his mercy,
> according to the promise he made to our ancestors,
>> to Abraham and to his descendants forever." (Luke 1:46-55)

Appropriating a range of images and allusions scattered throughout the Old Testament, Mary's song anticipates the approach of God's revolution.[16] The one to whom she will give birth comes to abolish the bonds that hold his people down.

In her song, Mary speaks of YHWH as the "Mighty One" who does "great things," the kingly warrior who fights on behalf of the lowly, whose

---

15. Elizabeth Johnson, *Truly Our Sister: A Theology of Mary in the Communion of Saints* (New York: Continuum, 2003), 258.

16. See Richard A. Horsley, *The Liberation of Christmas* (New York: Continuum, 1993), 110-14; Raymond E. Brown, *The Birth of the Messiah: A Commentary on the Infancy Narratives in the Gospels of Matthew and Luke*, rev. ed. (New York: Doubleday, 1993), 355-65; Stephen Farris, *The Hymns of Luke's Infancy Narratives: Their Origin, Meaning, and Significance* (Sheffield: JSNT, 1985), 108-26.

aim is release from bondage. Influenced by Hannah's Song in 1 Samuel (2:1–10), her anticipations are structured along the line of the eschatological drama that the prophets and apocalyptic writings also recounted: the revelation of YHWH's kingship is a confrontation between God and the powers and principalities. This confrontation will result in their overthrow through judgment, and will simultaneously liberate and save Israel. She anticipates that judgment and new life will characterize the appearing of the one who sits on "the throne of his ancestor David" (Luke 1:32).

In her song, Mary describes herself as lowly. This is not a remark about her psychology. "Low estate is used throughout the Old Testament (LXX) to refer primarily to the objective state of the poor, not to humility. It is used to describe both personal (e.g., Gen. 31:42, 1 Sam. 1:11) and national (e.g., Dt. 26:7) distress, and occurs frequently in the psalms of the poor and afflicted (LXX Pss. 21:22, 27; 24:18; 30:6–8; 118:50; 132:23). Mary's reference to her own low estate is a statement of solidarity with the poor and oppressed, not a statement of her personality type."[17] Mary is one of the poor and oppressed on whose behalf God is about to act. To be clear, Mary's vulnerability has to do not only with her economic status but also with her status as a woman. "As a woman, specifically a woman from among the poorer classes of a colonized people under the mighty empire of Rome, she represents the oppressed community that is to be lifted up and filled with good things in the messianic revolution."[18] Indeed, in Luke's Gospel, Mary's act of proclamation itself is an initial sign of the coming liberation, as this young, vulnerable, poor woman living in a patriarchal society becomes the first herald of the dawning of God's reign. Her words serve as anticipatory performances of the coming apocalyptic reversal when the great will be made low and the low will be lifted up.[19]

In the Jewish tradition, YHWH was understood to have sojourned and suffered with the people in exile. As present among the people in their distress, it was implicit that YHWH would arise from within the midst of the downtrodden people of Israel to liberate and restore them. Likewise, in the Gospels, the confrontation arises from among the lowly. The redemption

---

17. Gail O'Day, "Singing Woman's Song: A Hermeneutic of Liberation," *Currents in Theology and Mission* 12, no. 4 (August 1985): 207.

18. Rosemary Radford Ruether, *Sexism and God-Talk* (London: SCM, 1983), 132.

19. This is especially typical of Luke's Gospel. See Karl Allen Kuhn, *The Kingdom according to Luke and Acts: A Social, Literary, and Theological Introduction* (Grand Rapids: Baker Academic, 2015), 130, 131–35. See also John O. York, *The Last Shall Be First: The Rhetoric of Reversal in Luke* (London: JSOT Press, 1991).

and reversal by which the lowly will be raised up comes under the guise of its opposite: from among the least of these.

From the very beginning, Jesus is numbered among the lowly. As with all poor, his life is placed in jeopardy by the great political powers. We see this in both of the infancy accounts in the New Testament. In Luke the birth of Jesus is placed in the context of empire, as the family is forced to relocate to Bethlehem to fulfill the imperial mandate for a census (Luke 2:1-7). "The purpose of the census is to count heads for tax purposes. The Roman emperor can command tribute; the colonized villagers must hustle and obey."[20] Marginalized transients, the family of Jesus arrives in Bethlehem with no place to stay;[21] they are literally outsiders forced to lodge with the animals (2:7). Likewise, the Gospel of Matthew recounts the "slaughter of the innocents" (Matt. 2:16-18), an act of terrifying hubris in which the poor are clearly displayed as powerless and worthless in the face of imperial ambitions. Herod, after hearing of the birth of the "king of the Jews" from Persian "wise men," has all children two years old or under murdered. This catastrophe flushes out Jesus's family, and they become illegal immigrants, exiled and forced to travel under cover of night to Egypt.

Together, these two vignettes place Jesus—the one whose birth will mark the beginning of the history of God's reign—squarely among the oppressed about whom Mary speaks in her song. Karl Barth's observation that "Christ was born in poverty in the stable at Bethlehem, and He died in extreme poverty, nailed naked to the Cross"[22] is apposite here. Jesus doesn't just go to the poor and lowly, he *is* poor and lowly. He is from among the "wretched of the earth," to use Frantz Fanon's phrase.[23] And as Mary has said yes to the coming of God's reign (cf. Luke 1:38), which will occur in and through her with the birth of Jesus,[24] so also will her son be one who is faithful unto death.

Of course, Jesus is distinct from Mary, in that he is eventually identified as the one who will save the people. In the context of Mary's song, however, the distinction between Mary and Jesus only helps to reinforce YHWH's

---

20. Elizabeth Johnson, *Truly Our Sister*, 275.

21. See Elizabeth Johnson, *Truly Our Sister*, 275.

22. "Poverty," in *Against the Stream: Shorter Post-War Writings, 1946-52*, by Karl Barth (London: SCM, 1954), 246.

23. See Frantz Fanon, *The Wretched of the Earth* (New York: Grove, 2004).

24. "Mary is exalted because, through her, God will work this revolution in history. Or, to be more accurate, she herself is both subject and object of this liberating action. She makes it possible through her act of faith, but the liberating action of God in history liberates her." Ruether, *Sexism and God-Talk*, 130.

solidarity with the poor and lowly. For if Jesus is the instrument of YHWH's salvation, and he himself is poor and lowly, then this means that YHWH is indeed with the people in their precarious and perilous situation.

At the same time, YHWH is not in solidarity with the oppressed to leave them in their oppression. Rather, from the position of the underside, God will effect redemption: "for it is from here that the power comes which will overthrow the world, the wretched, *unhappy* world."[25] As Karl Allen Kuhn puts it, "the Israelite infant lying in a feedbox among sheep, goats, cattle, and fowl undermines the significance of Caesar and Rome, because in his humility and lowliness this one named 'Savior' and 'Messiah Lord' manifests the identity and power of Yahweh. For this reason, his birthday, not Caesar's, is truly good news for all humankind. He, not Caesar, is Lord and Savior of the world. His reign, not Caesar's, will lead the heavens to erupt in praise of God and the celebration of enduring peace."[26] According to Mary, in the coming of the lowly Jesus, God has "shown strength with his arm" and "lifted up the lowly," filling them with good things and liberating the people of God.

The identification of Mary and Jesus with the poor and oppressed, and the coming liberation that Mary's song portends, evokes the theme of Jubilee that we have already encountered. In this case, however, YHWH's place among those in distress is made even more palpable and concrete. The Song of Zechariah, the father of John the Baptist, is often read alongside Mary's song because of its proximity and shared themes (Luke 1:68–79). For Zechariah, the history of liberation that is about to begin is nothing less than an act of compassion (cf. 1:78), done by the God of Israel on behalf of God's people, and by extension the nations, as the gospel accounts will attest. The events about to unfold will make possible not only freedom from oppression but will enact forgiveness and the ability to be a holy people who live by the compassionate justice of God (cf. 1:73). The Jubilee themes of compassion, righteousness, and liberation for the oppressed are all central elements of Mary's and Zechariah's anticipation of the reign of God.

The Forerunner

The anticipation of and proper response to the coming reign of God is also the content of the preaching of John the Baptist. In the Synoptic Gospels,

25. Christoph Blumhardt, *Christoph Blumhardt and His Message*, ed. R. Lejeune (Woodcrest, NY: Plough, 1963), 190.

26. Kuhn, *The Kingdom*, 227.

John appears on the scene as a fierce, wild-eyed prophet, whose diet and clothing characterize him as an ascetic (cf. Matt. 3:1-6; Mark 1:2-6). He is commissioned as the "voice of one crying out in the wilderness" (Mark 1:3), saying, "Prepare the way for the Lord" (Luke 3:4). He comes as the latter-day Elijah (Mal. 4:4-6), and his preaching is characterized by a single image: apocalyptic fire. He appears "as a prophet denouncing the sin of the people, announcing the coming of God, and his radical judgment."[27] Even in the Gospel of John, where the Baptist is seemingly less abrasive, he is still a figure associated with judgment—his appearing raises the question of whether the hearer will respond rightly to the approaching "light of the world."[28]

For John the Baptist, the coming of God's reign is marked especially by judgment and wrath—it is the great and terrible Day of YHWH (cf. Joel 2:1-3; Obad. 18; Mal. 4:1), which comes to purify the people of Israel. Employing images from the Torah and the writings of the prophets, he speaks of the vineyard about to be cleansed and the winnowing of the threshing floor (cf. Matt. 3:12; Luke 3:9, 17). Both are images of judgment. In the former, the vineyard is the people Israel about to be cleansed of blight, an event John says is imminent: "As close as the first blow of the woodcutter after the axe has been laid on the point where the cut will begin—that is how close God's wrathful judgment is."[29] The image of the winnowing fork evokes the agricultural practice of removing the less valuable chaff, stubble, and stem from the more valuable grain. The message is clear: the apocalyptic judgment of the Day of YHWH, long ago proclaimed by the prophets and apocalyptic writers, is now upon us. For John, the Day of YHWH is placed in the hands of one who comes after him, who is more powerful than he (Luke 3:16). Thus, John's expectation is for a coming purgation to be enacted by the one who comes after him.

Anticipation of this appearing, however, is not only marked by terror and fear. Rather, John offers a "baptism of repentance for the forgiveness of sins" (Mark 1:4). The only response to the onrush of judgment is a genuine turning round or repentance, symbolically displayed in baptism. The practice of baptism itself picks up on images of divine cleansing (Zech. 13:1). The precise relation between the baptism of John and the baptism, and even death,

27. Jon Sobrino, *Jesus the Liberator: A Historical-Theological View* (Maryknoll, NY: Orbis, 1993), 73.

28. In the Gospel of John, confrontation with Jesus, the "light of the world," is no less apocalyptic, as it is described as that event that moves one from "death to life." See John 5:24.

29. Marius Reiser, *Jesus and Judgment: The Eschatological Proclamation in Its Jewish Context* (Minneapolis: Fortress, 1997), 175.

of Jesus has been a subject of some debate for scholars.[30] How could the Baptist offer a baptism for the forgiveness of sins when only God can forgive sins? The answer may lie in the idea that the baptism offered by John will be made efficacious by a later eschatological act of God.[31] That is, John's baptism will be made efficacious through a later act of divine compassion.

The shape of the repentance that God demands, which must accompany baptism, is outlined in Luke: "And the crowds asked him, 'What then should we do?' In reply he said to them, 'Whoever has two coats must share with anyone who has none; and whoever has food must do likewise.' Even tax collectors came to be baptized, and they asked him, 'Teacher, what should we do?' He said to them, 'Collect no more than the amount prescribed for you.' Soldiers also asked him, 'And we, what should we do?' He said to them, 'Do not extort money from anyone by threats or false accusations, and be satisfied with your wages'" (Luke 3:10-14). John's first response echoes the themes of equity and compassionate justice we have found in the Jubilee vision of the law and the prophets, while response two and three extend these images to address specific issues of corruption that would have afflicted Judean society at that time. Stanley Hauerwas describes the parallel text in Matthew 3 as follows: "The repentance for which John calls, the same repentance that Jesus preaches in Matt. 4:17, is the call for Israel to again live as God's holy people, a holiness embodied in the law, requiring Israel to live by gift, making possible justice restored."[32] The shape of the repentance John calls for suggests that the coming judgment is meant to prepare the people to move into a new reality, the reality of God's Jubilee reign.

What, then, is the act of God that will make the acts of cleansing and repentance efficacious? Although there are similarities between Jesus and John—most notably their preaching about the kingdom of God—one of the key differences is that John preached a coming judgment, which fell upon Jesus (e.g., Mark 12:38; Luke 12:49). This, in fact, is also the key to understanding John's baptism: the act to which John's baptism points, which would make his baptism efficacious, is the event of Jesus himself.[33] In John's own words, his baptism points to one who comes, who will baptize

---

30. See, for example, Walter Wink, *John the Baptist in the Gospel Tradition* (Eugene, OR: Wipf & Stock, 2000), and Joan Taylor, *The Immerser: John the Baptist within Second Temple Judaism* (Grand Rapids: Eerdmans, 1997).

31. See W. D. Davies and Dale C. Allison, *A Critical and Exegetical Commentary on the Gospel according to Saint Matthew*, vol. 1 (Edinburgh: T&T Clark, 1988), 300.

32. Stanley Hauerwas, *Matthew* (Grand Rapids: Brazos, 2006), 45.

33. "With his demand for repentance John did in fact, implicitly, summon the people

with the Spirit and with fire. John and Jesus did not seem to have the same understanding of these terms, given his questioning of Jesus's identity in the synoptic tradition (cf. Luke 7:18-30). As Karl Barth puts it, "The future wrath of God (Mt. 3:7) had become present. . . . The hour of judgment on Israel and the world had struck. This had all taken place, of course, in a way far different from any that those who were called to repentance and baptized with water at the Jordan, however serious they might have been, could ever have imagined. He who had come as Judge allowed Himself to be judged and executed as the One condemned and rejected in place of all the rest."[34] The event of Jesus, his life, death, and resurrection, is that act of God to which John's baptism points, for he is "the Lamb of God who takes away the sin of the world!" (John 1:29).

INAUGURATING THE REIGN OF THE ANOINTED

That events that would transpire over the course of Jesus's life history were those to which John pointed also makes sense of another key difference between John and Jesus: John spoke of a reality that was coming, while Jesus spoke of a reality that was "at hand" (cf. Mark 1:15). Though certainly initiated and anticipated in the birth and infancy narratives, it is with the baptism of Jesus and the public inauguration of his ministry that the Gospels understand God's reign to be present in the midst of history.

Jesus's baptism with water and the Spirit points to two realities. First is the complex double identification of Jesus: he is one of us, and we are one with him. All of Israel, and by extension all of humanity, is included in his life. Thus, he submits to the baptism of repentance, identifying himself as a son of Israel, a human being in need of divine grace and mercy. Initially, John was horrified by this prospect: "I need to be baptized by you, and do you come to me?" (Matt. 3:14). Jesus's answer is instructive; his baptism was to fulfill all "righteousness" (3:15). This does not refer to the obligation to fulfill a mere cultic requirement, but is connected to the dawning of God's righteous reign and the repentance required of humanity in the light of its coming. The coming reality envisions a transformation not only of the cosmos but also of human community and human beings—a great

---

to faith in Jesus, who was to come after him. His baptism was in fact baptism in the name of Jesus." Karl Barth, *Church Dogmatics* IV/4 (Edinburgh: T&T Clark, 1969), 75.

34. Barth, *Church Dogmatics* IV/4, 78.

turning or conversion.[35] John's baptism, pointing forward to an act of divine grace, symbolized conversion and judgment: the waters washed away the old reality and signified a new cleansed reality. But it is important to remember that the event toward which John's baptism points is Jesus himself, his life, death, and resurrection. Therefore, the conversion of Israel and the nations happens in Jesus, for in him God's name is hallowed, God's kingdom has come, and God's will is done on earth as in heaven. As the book of Hebrews provocatively puts it, "he learned obedience through what he suffered" (5:8) and was "made perfect" (5:9).[36] In Jesus God finds the one true covenant partner in whom the conversion of the whole heart is effected and effective.

At the same time, the repentance embodied in Jesus, though done by a human being, is also the act of God, and is thus an expression of God's righteousness, God's compassionate justice that seeks the least and the lost—categories into which the whole of Israel and the world fall from the perspective of the Gospels. The descent of the Spirit and the divine proclamation that Jesus is the beloved Son point to his divine commission and identity as God's royal representative. Thus, the second reality to which Jesus's baptism with water and the Spirit points is nothing less than an eschatological coronation.

Mark's Gospel relays it as follows: "And just as he was coming up out of the water, he saw the heavens torn apart and the Spirit descending like a dove on him. And a voice came from heaven, 'You are my Son, the Beloved; with you I am well pleased'" (Mark 1:10-11). The scene is filled with the imagery of apocalyptic kingship. Corresponding to the plea of Isaiah (64:1), the heavens are "torn apart" as a sign of God's apocalyptic grace.[37] The open heaven and downpour of the Spirit indicate God's definitive act of judgment and rescue. That the Spirit alights and "remains" on Jesus, as in John's Gospel (cf. John 1:32), indicates the locus of God's action and its permanence. The Spirit will not come and go; rather, it resides in the history

---

35. See Barth, *Church Dogmatics* IV/4, 62-64.

36. For a discussion of the theme of faithfulness and obedience in Hebrews, see Todd D. Still, "*CHRISTOS* as *PISTOS*: The Faith(fullness) of Jesus in the Epistle to the Hebrews," in *A Cloud of Witnesses: The Theology of Hebrews in Its Ancient Contexts*, ed. Richard Bauckham et al. (London: T&T Clark, 2008), 40-50.

37. "In Mark, then, God has ripped the heavens irrevocably apart at Jesus' baptism, never to shut them again. Through this gracious gash in the universe, he has poured forth his Spirit into the earthly realm." Joel Marcus, *Mark 1-8: A New Translation with Introduction and Commentary* (New York: Doubleday, 2000), 165.

of Jesus. What is about to unfold is *also* God's history with Israel—and by extension the nations—but now in a way that is definitive and permanent. As the Spirit was present at the beginning of creation in Genesis 1, so now too the Spirit is present in a definitive act of re-creation.[38]

The Beloved Son is the anointed; the king, in and through whom God's kingly rule is expressed.[39] In the Synoptic Gospels, the heavenly declaration combines phrases from two sources, both of which deal with kingship. The first clause, "You are my son, the Beloved," comes from the LXX version of Psalm 2:9 (2:7 in NRSV), a royal psalm, wherein YHWH endows the enthroned king with authority and power, identifying the reign of the king with the reign of YHWH. "In the psalm, moreover, the kingship of the 'anointed one' is congruent with that of God, and it is against *both* of their kingships that the evil rulers array themselves, only to be swiftly destroyed."[40] The second clause comes from the first Servant Song, Isaiah 42:1. In the context of Isaiah, the servant is the one in whom YHWH has taken delight. He is the one on whom YHWH has placed the Spirit, YHWH's chosen instrument through which YHWH's compassionate justice will come forth.[41]

Bringing Jesus's divine commissioning together with his identification with unfaithful humanity in the one event of his baptism means that he "humbly accepts from God both the good portion and the portion of the chastised, and he meekly sides with the weak and powerless while being delivered over into the hands of the mighty and powerful.... From this we learn that sonship largely consists in choosing to take up the ministry of the suffering servant."[42] In all of the Synoptic Gospels, Jesus's baptism is immediately followed by temptation and the public inauguration of his ministry.

The divine Spirit, or commissioning by which Jesus is coronated and identified as God's royal representative, and the sign John the Baptist be-

---

38. Marcus, *Mark 1–8*, 165.

39. See Joel Marcus, *The Way of the Lord: Christological Exegesis of the Old Testament in the Gospel of Mark* (Louisville: Westminster John Knox, 1992), 72.

40. Marcus, *Mark 1–8*, 166. See also Robert D. Rowe, *God's Kingdom and God's Son: The Background to Mark's Christology from Concepts of Kingship in the Psalms* (Leiden: Brill, 2002), 242.

41. "This is the enthronement pronouncement and the theological legitimation of Israel's kings which we find in Psalm 2:7. Jesus is uniquely endowed with the Spirit, his anointing is 'without measure' (John 3.34), and the Spirit 'rested' on him—that is to say, in him the Shekinah found its abiding dwelling place." Moltmann, *Way of Jesus Christ*, 90.

42. Davies and Allison, *Critical and Exegetical Commentary*, 344.

lieved would mark the messianic judgment, drives Jesus into the wilderness to face the tribulation of temptation. "On the old view the wilderness was a place which, like the sea, had a close affinity with the underworld, a place which belonged in a particular sense to demons."[43] Like the suffering servant, anointed by God (Isa. 42:1–4; 49:4; 50:6; 52:13–53:12), temptation and confrontation will beset the ministry of Jesus on every side. His testing illumines the struggle in which God's kingly rule is involved, and we are given a glimpse of the real peril in which Jesus and the reign that he embodies will find itself—a peril that ends in Jesus's own death.

The temptation narrative certainly recapitulates the testing of Israel, as Jesus is said to sojourn in the desert for forty days just as Israel had sojourned for forty years. But it is also a form of apocalyptic tribulation, as Jesus faces the "powers" embodied in his central protagonist—the accuser, or Satan. The temptations of "the son of God" (a royal title, evoking kingship) of miraculous food, of instantaneous kingly rule, and the miraculous aversion of a suicidal leap are all variations on the theme of the refusal to obediently walk the path of the suffering servant. Will Jesus prove faithful, or will he take the easy way out? Will he feed himself with bread, meeting his basic needs, or will he feed on the Word of God, which has placed him on the path of obedient service (cf. Mark 1:10–11)? Will he short-circuit the difficult way of obedient repentance and judgment that John's baptism called for, by capitulating to the claims to power of earthly kingdoms, all of which are under the sway of death (i.e., Satan)? Will Jesus prove to himself—and perhaps to others—that he is indeed God's Messiah by risking the offering that his life is meant to be, through a suicidal testing of God's miraculous power? To each of these temptations, none of which is overtly "satanic" in the popular sense of that word, Jesus responds with Scripture and the resolve of the Spirit. He is genuinely and really tempted and tested (cf. Heb. 4:14–5:10), and yet he genuinely and really remains obedient and resists these temptations—and many others besides (cf. Matt. 16:23; 26:39; Mark 14:34–36; Luke 22:39–44).[44]

The temptation narratives function like the opening chapter of the Gospel of John, wherein Jesus is described as the Word or Light of God, come into the world to wrestle with darkness (cf. John 1:1–14). They establish the overarching context within which his ministry will unfold: apocalyptic confrontation, rejection, and eventually death. "The temptation is then

43. Karl Barth, *Church Dogmatics* IV/1 (Edinburgh: T&T Clark, 1956), 260.
44. I am guided in these reflections by Barth. See Barth, *Church Dogmatics* IV/1, 260–64.

the first battle in Jesus' effort to make God's rule effective."[45] This conflict is on narrative display during Jesus's inaugural sermon in the Gospel of Luke. Visiting his hometown of Nazareth, Jesus is invited to read a passage of Scripture in the context of a synagogue service, which Luke relays to us as the following:

> "The Spirit of the Lord is upon me,
>   because he has anointed me
>   to bring good news to the poor.
> He has sent me to proclaim release to the captives
>   and recovery of sight to the blind,
>   to let the oppressed go free,
>   to proclaim the year of the Lord's favor." (Luke 4:18-19)

Adapted from Isaiah 61,[46] the passage speaks of the eschatological inauguration of God's Jubilee reign. Jesus, however, "did not merely proclaim *a* year of liberation. He evidently announced *the* messianic year of liberation. . . . What he announces is the messianic sabbath without end."[47] The history of Jesus's ministry is the fulfilled time in which God's Jubilee reign will appear in the midst of history (cf. Luke 4:21).

The far-reaching radicality of this proclamation is evidenced in the response of the townspeople. The Jubilee envisions an apocalyptic reversal. The poor, the destitute, the outsider, the sojourner, all those whom societies from across history and across the world deem unclean, useless, and to be feared will in fact be lifted up. The captives, those imprisoned both because of human justice and because of injustice, will be released. In other words, in a Jubilee world the normal patterns of acceptance and belonging will be transcended or laid aside. André Trocmé describes the Jubilee proclaimed by Jesus as nothing short of a social revolution, because of the radical reversal and social reorganization that it calls for: "Was this good news or bad? That depended on who you were. The Jubilee demanded, among other things, expropriating the lands of the wealthy and liquidating

---

45. John Thomas Fitzgerald, "The Temptation of Jesus: The Testing of the Messiah in Matthew," *Restoration Quarterly* 15, no. 3-4 (1972): 154.

46. For a discussion of the textual peculiarities of the passage, see Sharon H. Ringe, *Jesus, Liberation, and the Biblical Jubilee: Images for Ethics and Christology* (Philadelphia: Fortress, 1985), 38-39.

47. Moltmann, *Way of Jesus Christ*, 121.

the usurious system by which the ruling class prospered."[48] The eventual response of the townspeople—their attempt to throw Jesus off a cliff—to this vision is therefore understandable in this context. As Sharon Ringe describes it: "The Nazareth pericope itself thus becomes the enactment of the message of the Isaiah text in which the release from old sovereignties, such as those undergirding notions of privilege and election, is effected in the message of God's reign. In that pericope it is the 'in-group' whose reaction to the message is recorded, as they in effect declare their exclusion from the announced kingdom by clinging to the old order."[49] The kingdom that Jesus announces challenges the normal modes of social organization and belonging, and the citizens of Nazareth are aware of this fact.

Jesus's appeal to the prophets Elijah and Elisha and to episodes in their ministry wherein gentiles (cf. Luke 4:25-27), rather than Israelites, were given divine grace, indicates a deepening of the radical inversion of normal protocol. In Isaiah 61, the Jubilee proclamation occurs as an event of God's vengeance on the nations. But Jesus's understanding of the Jubilee aligns more clearly with the universal hopes of the prophets, as found especially in Isaiah 25, wherein God's Jubilee will mean the inclusion of the gentiles. In fact, in the version that appears in Luke, those portions of Isaiah 61 that promise judgment on the nations have actually been left out.

The stories of Elijah and Elisha also make clear that Jesus stands within a more inclusive vision of the Jubilee tradition, as "God's grace [is] poured out not only upon Gentiles, but upon the lowliest of the low class among the Gentiles, a widow and a leper."[50] This vision is clearly offensive to the audience, for "when Jesus challenges his fellow Nazarenes' sense of entitlement based on ethnic prejudice or pedigree, they are so enraged that they attempt to cast him off a precipice (Luke 4:23-30)."[51] The judgment that was to fall upon sinners and the enemies of God's people appears here to be set aside—though, as we follow the gospel story, it will eventually fall upon Jesus himself. God's blessings, however, which were to come to faithful Israel alone, will be extended to those considered unworthy and unwanted.[52]

---

48. André Trocmé, *Jesus and the Nonviolent Revolution* (Maryknoll, NY: Orbis, 2003), 17.

49. Sharon H. Ringe, "Luke 4:16-44: A Portrait of Jesus as Herald of God's Jubilee," *Proceedings* 1 (1981): 79.

50. Paul Hertig, "The Jubilee Mission of Jesus in the Gospel of Luke: Reversals of Fortune," *Missiology* 26, no. 2 (April 1998): 170.

51. Kuhn, *The Kingdom*, 241.

52. See Darrin W. Snyder Belousek, *Atonement, Justice, and Peace: The Message of the Cross and the Mission of the Church* (Grand Rapids: Eerdmans, 2012), 418-19.

Jesus's temptation and the Nazareth episode set the tone for the larger context of Jesus's ministry, as they highlight the consistent opposition and misunderstanding that he will face. These tribulations will eventuate in his total rejection, through crucifixion. These episodes also tell us that rejection of Jesus as God's anointed is bound up with the rejection of God's coming Jubilee reign. They obliquely raise the question of who, among the people that Jesus meets, will respond faithfully to his message. Of course, there are many who respond positively, even becoming his followers; nevertheless, at the end Jesus is deserted, with only a few women witnessing his death. From the perspective of the Gospels, then, Jesus alone is faithful unto death; Jesus alone resists temptation and carries through the repentance and conversion that God's Jubilee reign demands. This is the mystery of the kingdom of God.

With the anointing of the king, the kingdom itself is announced as one characterized by the preaching of "good news to the poor" and proclaiming "release" to those in bondage. Establishing a trajectory for the reign of God as embodied in Jesus, "the Jubilee traditions point to what happens whenever humankind encounters the fact of God's sovereignty."[53] In what follows we sketch these trajectories across the ministry of Jesus, by organizing them according to the themes of release and reversal. Jesus both proclaimed and enacted the release and reversal of the Jubilee and revealed in his person and work that he was in fact the obedient servant of YHWH; the reign of God enfleshed.

RELEASE FROM BONDAGE

Central to Jesus's message of the nearness of God's reign was the proclamation of "release to the captives" (Luke 4:18). *Aphiēmi*, the Greek verb for "release" or "forgive," has several interlocking references in the biblical witness. "In the NT the verb *aphiēmi* is found with monetary debts (Matt. 18:27, 32), 'captives' (Luke 4:18), and 'sin' (Matt. 6:14-15; Mark 2:5-10; 3:28; Luke 7:47-50) as its objects."[54] In the gospel witness, these different applications are not meant to be pulled apart. They imagine an entwining of

---

53. Ringe, *Jesus, Liberation*, 36.
54. Ringe, *Jesus, Liberation*, 65-66.

the so-called "spiritual" and material—a corporeal or bodily release that is productive of an economy of forgiveness. Jesus proclaims a release that is inclusive of body and soul; it is spiritual, embodied, and political.

Healing Forgiveness

One such example of the corporeal forgiveness that Jesus proclaimed and embodied is described in Mark 2:1-12:

> When he returned to Capernaum after some days, it was reported that he was at home. So many gathered around that there was no longer room for them, not even in front of the door; and he was speaking the word to them. Then some people came, bringing to him a paralyzed man, carried by four of them. And when they could not bring him to Jesus because of the crowd, they removed the roof above him; and after having dug through it, they let down the mat on which the paralytic lay. When Jesus saw their faith, he said to the paralytic, "Son, your sins are forgiven." Now some of the scribes were sitting there, questioning in their hearts, "Why does this fellow speak in this way? It is blasphemy! Who can forgive sins but God alone?" At once Jesus perceived in his spirit that they were discussing these questions among themselves; and he said to them, "Why do you raise such questions in your hearts? Which is easier, to say to the paralytic, 'Your sins are forgiven,' or to say, 'Stand up and take your mat and walk'? But so that you may know that the Son of Man has authority on earth to forgive sins"—he said to the paralytic—"I say to you, stand up, take your mat and go to your home." And he stood up, and immediately took the mat and went out before all of them; so that they were all amazed and glorified God, saying, "We have never seen anything like this!"

The connection between forgiveness of sins and a physical and embodied release is striking. In Mark, Jesus begins his ministry with the announcement, "The time is fulfilled, and the kingdom of God has come near; repent, and believe in the good news" (Mark 1:14). This parallels his announcement in Luke, that the Jubilee reign of God is present in his ministry (cf. Luke 4:18-19). Immediately in Mark, Jesus initiates a ministry of exorcism and healing (cf. Mark 1:21-45), both characteristic markers of the release/forgiveness of the Jubilee. Our present passage continues along this line, as Jesus authoritatively pronounces a forgiveness that is radical, even apocalyptic. A paralyzed man, borne along by friends, is placed at the feet of Jesus, who declares him released. But this good word is not well received by all. As with the townspeople of Nazareth (cf. Luke 4:28–29), Jesus's words cause conflict and controversy, as members of the scribal elite question the theological propriety of Jesus's claims. From the perspective of the scribes, Jesus has trespassed on the domain of God. But Jesus is no mere teacher; rather, he is the Son of Man.

For the first time in Mark's Gospel we encounter Jesus's favorite,[55] and most enigmatic, self-descriptor, the Son of Man. In the book of Daniel and other Jewish apocalyptic texts (i.e., 1 Enoch, 4 Ezra, etc.), the appearing of the Son of Man was to mark the end of the ages and the dawning of God's Jubilee reign.[56] Jesus has already proclaimed the presence of God's reign (Mark 1:14), a proclamation bound up with his person and work (Luke 17:21); now he identifies himself as the eschatological figure, the Son of Man. His proclamation of forgiveness/release to this man, therefore, is in keeping with his calling as the one in whom the eschatological kingdom is dawning. Wherever the reign of God is present, humanity and creation will be set at liberty. To press this point, Jesus commands the paralyzed man to stand and walk; the man, finding himself whole and wholly set free, obediently responds to Jesus's commanding word. The crowd—presumably including the scribes—is left in utter disbelief, exclaiming that they have never before witnessed anything like this.

The crowd's stunned amazement further highlights the apocalyptic nature of Jesus's commanding word of release/forgiveness. His words overthrow the powers and principalities that bind human beings and communities. This is a theo-political confrontation. In this vein, the objection of the scribes can be described as no mere theological nicety, nor is the identity of the man an indifferent factor. Both details illumine the theo-political character of the forgiveness that Jesus pronounces. The scribes object that only God can forgive sins. This is a claim about power. Where is forgiveness found? Presumably, it is found with the God ensconced in the temple, access to whom is carefully guarded by the scribal and temple elite. Thus, the forgiveness that Jesus so carelessly pronounces was in fact

---

55. "Son of man is the only title used by Jesus of himself whose authenticity is to be taken seriously." Joachim Jeremias, *New Testament Theology* (New York: Macmillan, 1971), 258.

56. See Sigmund Mowinckel, *He That Cometh: The Messiah Concept in the Old Testament and Later Judaism* (Grand Rapids: Eerdmans, 2005), 389.

available through participation in the temple cult, but it could only be accessed through the prescribed channels, which were controlled by scribes and priests.[57] Seen from this angle, the objection against Jesus is both that he presumes on the prerogative of God by pronouncing forgiveness of sins *and* that he does so with no recourse or connection to the temple and its cultic operations. As Myers notes, "their complaint that none but God can remit debt (2:7b) is not a defense of the sovereignty of Yahweh, but of their own social power."[58]

The identity of the man adds an additional layer. As an outcast, the physical afflictions of this man would have carried real social and political ramifications. Furthermore, the man was probably poverty-stricken and "simply could not afford the outlay of either time or money/goods involved in ritual cleansing processes."[59] For Jesus to declare his "sins forgiven" was tantamount to removing the barriers that kept him from full standing in the social order. It was a genuine release from bondage.

Liberation by "the Finger of God"

The release/forgiveness that comes from Jesus sets human beings and communities free from powerful forces that bind and deform. In the case of the paralytic, sin, illness, and social ostracism all coordinate together to form a complex matrix of forces that enslave. The Jubilee reign that Jesus inaugurates confronts these powers, judging, overthrowing, and ultimately liberating the community and the individual, leaving them speechless.

The apocalyptic and confrontational character of Jesus's declaration of release/forgiveness is even more powerfully displayed in Jesus's work as an exorcist. In Luke, Jesus is described as casting out demonic powers by "the finger of God" (Luke 11:20), a reference to the work of YHWH in the events of exodus and the establishing of the covenant at Sinai.[60] The release effected through exorcism is a liberation and expression of God's reign (cf. Luke 11:20). "This is how Jesus acts in His exorcisms. He does not put new patches on old clothes. He goes to the root of the evil."[61] Through

---

57. See Ched Myers, *Binding the Strong Man: A Political Reading of Mark's Story of Jesus* (Maryknoll, NY: Orbis, 1997), 78-80.

58. Myers, *Binding the Strong Man*, 155.

59. Myers, *Binding the Strong Man*, 76.

60. See Edward J. Woods, *The "Finger of God" and Pneumatology in Luke-Acts* (Sheffield: Sheffield Academic, 2001), 87-98.

61. Barth, *Church Dogmatics* IV/2, 230.

Jesus God overpowers the demonic powers, binding them and plundering their abode (cf. Mark 3:27; Luke 11:21–22). "And this total war and victory can be followed by the plundering of the house of the strong man, the dividing of the spoils, the forgiving of man's sins, the comforting of the sad and the healing of the sick."[62] As with the psalms, the prophets, and apocalyptic literature, this is a confrontation between the compassionate justice of YHWH and the powers and principalities that oppress humanity. Exorcism was nothing short of an eschatological form of God's rescue of the oppressed.[63]

One of the most theo-politically potent episodes in which the declaration of release/forgiveness is placed on a collision course with cosmic powers is found in Mark 5:

They came to the other side of the sea, to the country of the Gerasenes. And when he had stepped out of the boat, immediately a man out of the tombs with an unclean spirit met him. He lived among the tombs; and no one could restrain him any more, even with a chain; for he had often been restrained with shackles and chains, but the chains he wrenched apart, and the shackles he broke in pieces; and no one had the strength to subdue him. Night and day among the tombs and on the mountains he was always howling and bruising himself with stones. When he saw Jesus from a distance, he ran and bowed down before him; and he shouted at the top of his voice, "What have you to do with me, Jesus, Son of the Most High God? I adjure you by God, do not torment me." For he had said to him, "Come out of the man, you unclean spirit!" Then Jesus asked him, "What is your name?" He replied, "My name is Legion; for we are many." He begged him earnestly not to send them out of the country. Now there on the hillside a great herd of swine was feeding; and the unclean spirits begged him, "Send us into the swine; let us enter them." So he gave them permission. And the unclean spirits came out and entered the swine; and the herd, numbering about two thousand, rushed down the steep bank into the sea, and were drowned in the sea.

The swineherds ran off and told it in the city and in the country. Then people came to see what it was that had happened. They came to Jesus and saw the demoniac sitting there, clothed and in his right mind, the very

---

62. Barth, *Church Dogmatics* IV/2, 230–31.
63. See Cheryl S. Pero, *Liberation from Empire: Demonic Possession and Exorcism in the Gospel of Mark* (New York: Lang, 2013), 151.

man who had had the legion; and they were afraid. Those who had seen what had happened to the demoniac and to the swine reported it. Then they began to beg Jesus to leave their neighborhood. As he was getting into the boat, the man who had been possessed by demons begged him that he might be with him. But Jesus refused, and said to him, "Go home to your friends, and tell them how much the Lord has done for you, and what mercy he has shown you." And he went away and began to proclaim in the Decapolis how much Jesus had done for him; and everyone was amazed. (5:1–20)

The first part of the narrative pits Jesus against the demonic powers. Having left the predominantly Jewish side of the Sea of Galilee, Jesus is immediately accosted by the powers in the pitiful figure of a man possessed. The demonic powers have taken possession, rendering the man helpless in the face of that which enslaves him; he wanders around torturing himself, being literally overpowered by a "legion" (Mark 5:9). "The overall impression is of a person who has lost control of himself and is at the mercy of destructive outside forces; his neighbors, too, are unable to help him."[64] Alienated both from himself and the human community around him, the man is forced to wander among the tombs as a dead man.

Upon the appearance of Jesus, the demonic powers perform an act of obeisance, bowing before the "Son of the Most High God" (cf. 5:6–7). The mere presence of Jesus has overpowered them (cf. 1:27).[65] The arrival of God's reign in Jesus produces a crisis that terrorizes the powers of evil. "The inspirer of fear in others"[66] is now itself afraid. Having shown no mercy, they beg for mercy; having exiled the man to wander among the tombs, they now beg not to be exiled. Jesus, determined to liberate the man by the "finger of God" and restore him to life with God and others, enters into a game of wits, allowing the demonic powers to determine their fate. Opting for a nearby herd of swine, "Legion"—the self-given name of the demonic powers—enters into them. The fear by which the demonic powers controlled living flesh becomes the instrument of their own undoing; the swine immediately go out of control and rush headlong into the nearby sea and drown, presumably taking the demonic powers with them.

64. Marcus, *Mark 1–8*, 350.
65. See Amanda Witmer, *Jesus, the Galilean Exorcist: His Exorcisms in Social and Political Context* (London: T&T Clark, 2012), 178.
66. Barth, *Church Dogmatics* IV/2, 231.

The second portion of the story recounts the amazement, and then fear and opposition, of the local townspeople. Marcus describes the parallels between the opposition of the demons and the opposition of the townspeople: "Like the demons, they are initially drawn to Jesus, almost against their will (5:6, 14–15). Like the demons, however, their overriding reaction is one of fear (5:7, 15 end), which causes them to plead (*parakalein*) that Jesus depart or leave them alone (5:7, 10, 17). The demons desire to stay in possession of the territory (5:10), and so their human agents evict Jesus from it (5:17)."[67] By freeing the man of his torment, Jesus's actions have upset the normal state of affairs. The villagers beg him to leave. Perhaps the man was not the only one possessed by demonic powers?

The powers of oppression at work in the man and the community—and especially the theo-political dimension of the exorcism—become apparent when one notes the imagery of uncleanness with its attendant dynamics of insider/outsider found throughout the episode. Jesus has entered gentile territory, identified as located near Gerasa and the Decapolis. In this "unclean" region, Jesus is confronted by a man who wanders among the tombs—a site that would have also been considered unclean—one who is possessed by an "unclean spirit" (5:2). "Thus, the combination of his possession by an unclean spirit and his abode in the cave tombs indicates that the man is seen as marginal to society and cannot be civilized."[68] The cumulative effect of these details is meant to lead one to see that Jesus's act of release through exorcism is a challenge to the symbolic order controlled by notions of clean/unclean, insider/outsider. "The reaction of the townspeople revealed Jesus' ministry acts to be dangerous to average people because Jesus' exorcism of the Gerasene demoniac disrupted the normal social order."[69] This may also explain why the man begged to go with Jesus—he knew that, though he had been liberated, he would nevertheless not be taken back into the community, since it had not yet been freed from its own oppressive patterns of social life.

Since this was a predominantly gentile area, however, the source of the symbolic structures that organized the community came from a direction other than Jewish purity codes, and this is where the name of the demonic powers becomes important. "My name is Legion; for we are many" (5:9). The insertion of this Latin term here is conspicuous, as it would have im-

67. Marcus, *Mark 1–8*, 353.
68. Witmer, *Jesus, the Galilean Exorcist*, 176.
69. Pero, *Liberation from Empire*, 161.

mediately been associated with the Roman garrisons that oppressed the people and assured foreign possession of the land.[70] "The name 'Legion' signifies power and control and is an allusion to Hellenistic culture's intrusion in the region and Rome's demonic incursion."[71] Joshua Garroway notes that the use of this term to only convey the sense of "numerousness" is not in keeping with its usage elsewhere. "A review of the term's usage in ancient texts confirms this expectation, for in no Greek text prior to Mark is 'legion' used solely in the sense of a legion's worth."[72] Sending the demonic power to its death through entrance into the swine also bears symbolic meaning, as pigs were not only unclean animals but the wild boar was "the emblem of the Roman legion stationed in Palestine."[73] The drowning of the swine, much like the drowning of Pharaoh's army during the exodus event, indicated the judgment/exorcism of Roman pretensions by the "finger of God" (Luke 11:20).[74] In view of these symbolic resonances, it is not necessary to collapse the episode of the Gerasene demoniac into a commentary on the oppressive realities of Galilean peasant life, whether Jewish or gentile, in order to see that the gospel stories associate the demonic powers that enslaved the man—and presumably the village—with the oppressive rule of the pagan Romans.

Associated spiritual, embodied, and political liberation fits with the overall claims that the dawning of God's reign is also the dawning of Jubilee, a conception that has unmistakable systemic ramifications, as the downtrodden, oppressed, and dispossessed—social outcasts of all kinds—are set at liberty. The context of exorcism highlights the inherently conflictual nature of Jesus's proclamation—the kingdom of God comes against the kingdom of Satan, undoing the latter in the form of judgment, in order that humanity might be set free. "Jesus' liberating actions are acts of justice against Satan's usurped dominion; by destroying satanic forces, he reorders power in the world."[75] The response of the villagers to Jesus's act of forgiveness/release

---

70. See Witmer, *Jesus, the Galilean Exorcist*, 170-73.

71. Witmer, *Jesus, the Galilean Exorcist*, 170-75. See also Myers, *Binding the Strong Man*, 190-94; Marcus, *Mark 1-8*, 351-52.

72. Joshua Garroway, "The Invasion of a Mustard Seed: A Reading of Mark 5.1-20," *Journal for the Study of the New Testament* 32, no. 1 (2009): 62.

73. Marcus, *Mark 1-8*, 351.

74. See Pero, *Liberation from Empire*, 161.

75. Enrique Nardoni, *Rise Up, O Judge: A Study of Justice in the Biblical World* (Peabody, MA: Hendrickson, 2004), 206-7

is an unfortunate expression of the "colonization of the mind."[76] As Stanley Hauerwas, commenting on the parallel text in Matthew, notes: "If we have to choose between a life we know, even a life possessed by demons and ruled by death, and a life of uncertainty to which Jesus calls us, a life that may well expose us to dangers in Jesus' name, we too may ask Jesus to leave our neighborhood."[77] The refusal to receive Jesus is tantamount to a refusal to receive the liberation that Jesus brings. "Jesus annoyed the townspeople—liberation is not an easy mantle to wear!"[78]

The refusal to receive Jesus, however, is not the end of the story or of the graciousness of the reign of God that has dawned with him. The liberated man, who had begged to accompany Jesus, is instead commissioned to proclaim the good news of what God has done for him. "Jesus' actions against Satan, though brief and occasional, symbolize and anticipate the liberation from dehumanizing forces of evil."[79] This recipient of God's gracious release/forgiveness is now commissioned to preach the good news of God's reign among his fellow gentiles, becoming a parable of God's coming Jubilee reign in and for the nations. As so commissioned, the man becomes a nonidentical repetition of Jesus, who with the word of his mouth vanquished the demonic powers (cf. Mark 1:27). In contrast to the violence displayed in the rule of the demonic powers, the man's ministry of witness will be like the mustard seed; though small and seemingly insignificant, his witness will nevertheless contribute to God's work of reclamation.[80]

Economy of Forgiveness

Jesus's confrontation with the powers sets at liberty those who have been in bondage. The forgiveness/release from sin, debt, and the powers that enslave initiate what can be described as an economy of forgiveness in spiritual, embodied, and political dimensions. The Lord's Prayer, and in particular the fifth petition found in Matthew 6:12, is illustrative of this: "And forgive us our debts, / as we also have forgiven our debtors" (Matt. 6:12).

---

76. Myers, *Binding the Strong Man*, 193. Myers takes this from Frantz Fanon via Paul W. Hollenbach. See Paul W. Hollenbach, "Jesus, Demoniacs, and Public Authorities: A Socio-Historical Study," *Journal of the American Academy of Religion* 49, no. 4 (December 1981): 567–88, and Fanon, *The Wretched of the Earth*.

77. Hauerwas, *Matthew*, 98.

78. Pero, *Liberation from Empire*, 161–62.

79. Nardoni, *Rise Up, O Judge*, 271.

80. See Garroway, "Invasion," 70–71.

Luke's parallel text intensifies the interconnection of the spiritual, em-bodied, and political forgiveness enjoined on followers of Jesus: "And forgive us our sins, / for we ourselves forgive everyone indebted to us" (Luke 11:4). The prayer is set within an eschatological context, as disciples are instructed to pray for the hallowing of God's name, the will of God to be done, and the kingdom to come, on earth as in heaven. "Since the Lord's Prayer is a prayer for God's reign to be established, the petition concerning forgiveness needs to be seen in relationship to that reign."[81] To be more precise, it is the context of the Jubilee reign of God for which the disciple is instructed to pray in the third petition (Matt. 6:10).

The language of the forgiveness of debts is the key that "Jesus' proc-lamation of the jubilee year is unmistakably present in the prayer he is teaching us to pray."[82] As we outlined in chapter 2, the ground or basis for the Jubilee legislation was the fact that YHWH owned the land and was the redeemer of the people. The people as a whole were commissioned to be "servants" of YHWH, and therefore permanent ownership of the land and internal slavery were simply unthinkable. In addition, the Jubilee legisla-tion was aimed specifically at righting wrongs done to the most vulnerable by mitigating or dismantling systems and structures of oppression. Those structures bound individuals in cycles of debt and eventually slavery.

In the context of the Lord's Prayer, the disciples are reminded that they owe God everything—they are in debt to God. "We are God's debtors. We owe him not something, whether it be little or much, but, quite simply, our person in its totality; we owe him ourselves, since we are his creatures, sustained and nourished by his goodness."[83] The petition for daily bread has both a present and an eschatological connotation as the disciple asks not only for the messianic bread of the final eschatological banquet but also for the bread necessary to sustain life in the present.[84] The very life of the disciple, both in the form of physical sustenance—which the preceding petition for "daily bread" underlines—and in the form of release from the bondage of sin, is a gift of God.[85] As such, the disciple is to enter into the unending labor of the forgiveness of debts (cf. Matt. 18:21-22). The condi-

---

81. Ringe, *Jesus, Liberation*, 79.

82. Hauerwas, *Matthew*, 78. See also Ringe, *Jesus, Liberation*, 83.

83. Karl Barth, *Prayer*, fiftieth anniversary ed. (Louisville: Westminster John Knox, 2002), 53.

84. See Ringe, *Jesus, Liberation*, 82-83.

85. See Leonardo Boff, *The Lord's Prayer: The Prayer of Integral Liberation* (Maryknoll, NY: Orbis, 1983), 88.

tional clause in the petition establishes the expectation that forgiveness/ release by God is to be reproduced in our relations toward others. "In the petition we ask God to exercise on our behalf a permanent jubilee of forgiveness toward others."[86] Furthermore, the interchanging language of "sins" and "debts" in the Lukan version makes clear the embodied and social implications of forgiveness. As Hauerwas notes: "The forgiveness of debts signals that nothing is quite so political as the prayer that Jesus teaches us. To have debts forgiven certainly challenges our normal economic and political assumption. But the forgiveness of debts is also at the heart of truthful memory. No people are free from a past or present that is not constituted by injustices so horrific nothing can be done to make them right."[87] In regard to the truthful memory mentioned by Hauerwas, Jan Milič Lochman draws attention to the fact that the daily bread for which the disciple prays in the fourth petition does not miraculously appear, but rather, it comes to us through social and political practices that are thoroughly compromised. "Much more often than we think, we eat daily bread and struggle for it at the expense of others. . . . We are thus entangled in a nexus and relationship of guilt even when we are not aware of it and do not want to be aware of it."[88] Jacob Milgrom has established that the principal forms of sin that defiled the temple cult and thus polluted the people's relationship with YHWH—the forms of sin with which the rites of atonement and purgation were meant to deal—were acts of injustice committed against the neighbor, and were thus social sins.[89] Thus, to recognize the sin/debt forgiven by God and to likewise extend that same forgiveness to others was to invariably engage in a social and political act.

This is powerfully illustrated in Jesus's parable of the unmerciful servant. After having instructed Peter that forgiveness was to be unending (i.e., Matt. 18:21–22), he then goes on to describe the obligations that God's forgiveness/release enjoins on the disciple:

> "For this reason the kingdom of heaven may be compared to a king who wished to settle accounts with his slaves. When he began the reckoning, one who owed him ten thousand talents was brought to him; and, as he

86. Nardoni, *Rise Up, O Judge*, 230.

87. Hauerwas, *Matthew*, 79.

88. Jan Milič Lochman, *The Lord's Prayer* (Grand Rapids: Eerdmans, 1990), 108.

89. See Jacob Milgrom, "Israel's Sanctuary: The Priestly 'Picture of Dorian Gray,'" *Revue biblique* 83, no. 3 (July 1976): 390-99.

could not pay, his lord ordered him to be sold, together with his wife and children and all his possessions, and payment to be made. So the slave fell on his knees before him, saying, 'Have patience with me, and I will pay you everything.' And out of pity for him, the lord of that slave released him and forgave him the debt. But that same slave, as he went out, came upon one of his fellow slaves who owed him a hundred denarii; and seizing him by the throat, he said, 'Pay what you owe.' Then his fellow slave fell down and pleaded with him, 'Have patience with me, and I will pay you.' But he refused; then he went and threw him into prison until he would pay the debt. When his fellow slaves saw what had happened, they were greatly distressed, and they went and reported to their lord all that had taken place. Then his lord summoned him and said to him, 'You wicked slave! I forgave you all that debt because you pleaded with me. Should you not have had mercy on your fellow slave, as I had mercy on you?' And in anger his lord handed him over to be tortured until he would pay his entire debt. So my heavenly Father will also do to every one of you, if you do not forgive your brother or sister from your heart." (18:23-35)

The gift of release from a debt that is far too large to repay is meant to produce in the servant a similar graciousness toward others. The point is clear: "We cannot maintain two attitudes, one toward God and the other toward our neighbor. Both are subject to a single motivation, that of love."[90] The Jubilee reign that comes with Jesus's person by which those in bondage are set free enables a new possibility. The parable portrays "the choices now possible concerning the rules by which one's life is to be governed, and the consequences of choosing the old order over the new."[91]

The social and political dimensions become clearer in light of the larger context in Matthew's Gospel. Having just been instructed on how someone wronged should respond to a perpetrator of sin (i.e., Matt. 18:15-20), the disciples are now instructed on unending forgiveness. Without setting aside the demands placed on an offender, the parable places such demands under the sign of God's mercy. The declaration of God's Jubilee envisions a new form of intercommunal and intracommunal Jubilee politics. "Accordingly, the forgiveness that marks the church is a politics that offers an alternative to the politics based on envy, hatred, and revenge."[92] To be

90. Boff, *The Lord's Prayer*, 95.
91. Ringe, *Jesus, Liberation*, 76.
92. Hauerwas, *Matthew*, 166.

sure, Matthew 18:15–20 does not imagine forgiveness willy-nilly. Genuine repentance and restitution, with the hope for restoration, are required. But an alternative economy of the release/forgiveness of debts/sins establishes a new context for life together.

The economy of forgiveness is an expression of God's reign come in Jesus. To refuse to act along the axis of release laid down by Jesus was "in effect to deny the new economy of mercy in favor of the old one in which the bonds and obligations leading to indebtedness still hold sway."[93]

THE GREAT REVERSAL

The second major theme in Jesus's proclamation of the arrival of God's Jubilee reign is reversal. The vision of apocalyptic reversal that the Jubilee reign of God announces is enshrined in the so-called beatitudes found in the Gospels of Matthew (5:3–12) and Luke (6:20–26). It is worked out through everyday practices like the extension of table fellowship and through remarkable events of embodied care as seen in Jesus's works of healing.

The Beatitudes

The word "beatitude" derives from Latin *beatus*, which in turn translates the Greek word *makarios*, "blessed."[94] Both the Matthew and Luke versions appear at the beginning of significant teaching sections—the Sermon on the Mount (Matthew) and the Sermon on the Plain (Luke)—and should be understood as "eschatological blessings"[95] that speak of consolation and the reversal that God's reign will bring and is bringing in Jesus's person and ministry. "Jesus is himself the promise to the poor that they are not forgotten by God and that their day of vindication is coming."[96] Luke's version, in particular, brings out the apocalyptic flavor of the text by including corresponding woes (cf. 6:24–26).

93. Ringe, *Jesus, Liberation*, 76.

94. See Robert Guelich, *An Introduction for Understanding the Sermon on the Mount* (Dallas: Word, 1982), 66.

95. W. D. Davies and Dale C. Allison, *Matthew: A Shorter Commentary* (London: T&T Clark International, 2004), 65.

96. George Hunsinger, *The Beatitudes* (Mahwah, NJ: Paulist, 2015), 10.

The beatitudes are addressed to the very poor to whom Jesus was commissioned to announce good news. "Blessed are the poor in spirit . . . Blessed are those who mourn . . . Blessed are the meek" (Matt. 5:3, 4, 5), "Blessed are you who are hungry now . . . you who weep now" (Luke 6:21). In Matthew, the beatitudes are preceded by an allusion to the Isaiah passage read at Nazareth, as recounted by Luke (i.e., Luke 4:18-19). Jesus is described as "proclaiming the good news of the kingdom" (Matt. 4:23). Thus, the "poor in spirit" are not simply the humble, but they are those who have been crushed by the powerful, those who live on the underside of history, those with their backs against the wall.[97] They are indeed materially poor, but their poverty extends to a crushed spirit (cf. Ps. 34:18). The connection between material and spiritual poverty is made clearer when one attends to the sociology of Judea at that time. The poor to whom such promises were addressed, making up around 97 percent of the population,[98] were widely considered accursed by the elite, not simply because they were poor, but because they were too ignorant and poverty-stricken to keep the Torah.[99] Thus, these were the nonobservant, the accursed.

That they are blessed, or endowed with life-giving power, however, does not have to do with something inherent in their situation. "In neither case should the blessing be seen as a reward either for particular moral behavior or attitudes, as Matthew's version has often been understood, or for some qualification inherent in the condition of economic poverty, as Luke's version might seem to suggest."[100] The point, rather, is the coming apocalyptic reversal; it is an act of divine grace that saves and makes right. In other words, it is neither their nonobservant status nor their poverty that makes them blessed, *but God's action.* Jesus's address to the poor that they are to be blessed underlines that God alone is the one who rescues. The poor "are those close to the slow death poverty brings, those for whom surviving is a heavy burden and their chief task, and those who are also deprived of social dignity and sometimes also of religious dignity for not complying"[101] with religious authorities. All people are in need of divine grace, but it is the poor who know this most explicitly and intimately. God's action on their

97. See Howard Thurman, *Jesus and the Disinherited* (Boston: Beacon, 1996).
98. See Warren Carter, "Matthew's Gospel: An Anti-Imperial/Imperial Reading," *Currents in Theology and Mission* 34, no. 6 (December 2007): 426.
99. See Moltmann, *Way of Jesus Christ*, 100-102, 113-14.
100. Ringe, *Jesus, Liberation*, 52-53.
101. Sobrino, *Jesus the Liberator*, 81.

behalf signals the setting right of the world's wrongs, for "when the poor are redeemed, then the world will be redeemed."[102] When those whom the world has rejected and forgotten are remembered and lifted up, then indeed compassionate justice for all has arisen.

The reversal proclaimed by Jesus comes against the very structures that have made them poor. In neither Matthew nor Luke are they promised that they will simply exchange places with the rich. Rather, the reversal that God's reign envisions is the undoing of the very violence and exploitation that create such categories in the first place; as such it is potentially inclusive of all, with the caveat that the wealthy and the powerful are especially subject to the terrifying judgment that brings new life. They are being called into the company of Jesus's followers. Already Jesus has called disciples to himself (cf. Matt. 4:18-22), but the Sermon on the Mount will further describe a social order marked by sharing and community (cf. 6:25-34). The blessing of land—a key theme in the Jubilee and a vital element for a thriving life in an agricultural society—comes to the meek (cf. 5:5), and a "culture of sharing" will displace the violence and greed of the current social order.[103]

Those who "hunger and thirst for righteousness" (5:6) are those who long for the appearing of God's compassionate justice. "They hunger and thirst for righteousness, which simply means justice according to Yahweh's dictates, a justice that is not blindly objective but looks out especially for orphans, widows, and aliens and seeks to reorder unjust structures."[104] These ones are not the materially satiated or religiously self-satisfied, but those who long for an end to systems of exploitation and oppression that deform human communities and a right relationship with God. "To *hunger and thirst for righteousness* describes the dire need of a right relationship with God and others."[105] The appearing of God's compassionate justice as announced in the prophets looked toward a new form of existence for Israel, one wherein the Spirit would be poured into the people, enabling them to live according to the compassionate justice that God demands. This is the longing that Jesus addresses. Again, it is not as though those who hunger and thirst for righteousness are themselves righteous in their

102. Christoph Blumhardt, *Ansprachen, Predigten, Reden, Briefe, 1865-1917*, vol. 2, *1890-1906*, ed. Johannes Harder (Neukirchen-Vluyn: Neukirchener Verlag, 1978), 272.

103. See Moltmann, *Way of Jesus Christ*, 101.

104. Ross Kinsler and Gloria Kinsler, *The Biblical Jubilee and the Struggle for Life: An Invitation to Personal, Ecclesial, and Social Transformation* (Maryknoll, NY: Orbis, 1999), 99.

105. Guelich, *Sermon on the Mount*, 87.

dealings with others or with God. Rather, they long for God's appearing, which will set all things right. To these Jesus says: "You will be filled."

That their longing implies also a doing can be seen in the "second table" of Matthew's account of the beatitudes. Here the merciful, the pure in heart, and the peacemakers are all addressed (cf. Matt. 5:7-9). These are all descriptions having to do with the coming of YHWH's Jubilee reign. In this context, "purity of heart" refers to an absolute and unbending loyalty in one's desire that God's kingdom come. Such an absolute commitment ensures that one will be able to stand before God when God appears—that is, one will be able to "see God" (Matt. 5:8).

When God's justice arrives, it will be an event of mercy and compassion, even in the midst of judgment, for it heralds the removal of the powers and principalities that oppress humankind and the earth. Death, that power that shapes human actions in the here and now, will be overthrown and all will be set free (cf. Isa. 25:6-9). In the light of this coming, the community of the Messiah is called to exercise this same mercy. Those who hunger for the appearing of God's righteousness cannot long only for their vindication, nor are they to nurse grudges against those who have done them wrong. Rather, "one is declared *blessed* who exercises mercy towards those who are in the wrong."[106] To live in the light of such mercy requires love of one's enemies in the here and now (cf. Matt. 5:43-48; Luke 6:27-29). This requires the ongoing attempt to sow peace. And, as in the apocalyptic tradition (cf. 4 Ezra 13:39-40), so in Matthew, the peace or *shalom* of God will characterize the people or "children of God" (Matt. 5:9).

The beatitudes portend a coming cosmic reversal, but they also assume a people who will live differently in the light of that coming. Such a way of life will surely provoke outrage, as Jesus anticipates: "Blessed are those who are persecuted for righteousness' sake, for theirs is the kingdom of heaven" (Matt. 5:10). This concluding beatitude and its amplification in verses 11-12 assume that the shape of the life of the community of disciples will mirror that of the one they seek to follow. The opposition and sufferings of the community express the community's "concrete fellowship with him."[107] Jesus's own ministry began under the sign of tribulation and testing, as he was taken out into the desert to face the wiles of the evil one. He was then rejected by members of his home community of Nazareth when he proclaimed a general Jubilee, inclusive of everyone, not merely those

106. Guelich, *Sermon on the Mount*, 89.
107. Hunsinger, *The Beatitudes*, 112.

deemed respectable or even faithful. Those who follow the kingdom way of Jesus can expect the same kind of response.

In the face of all unfaithfulness, even among the disciples, the New Testament portrays Jesus as the one who most fully and truly embodies the beatitudes, thereby fulfilling and receiving their blessings on behalf of all those with whom he identified himself in John's baptism. As George Hunsinger notes, "Jesus is the secret center of the Beatitudes as a whole and, therefore, of each one in particular. He is finally their subject matter, and in them he points to his own person. It is he who embodies each personal attribute, he who is truly blessing, and he who is always the promise."[108] He is the poor one (cf. Luke 2:7), who mourns (cf. Luke 19:41-44; John 11:28-37); the lowly and meek one (cf. 2 Cor. 10:1), who hungers and thirsts for God's righteousness (cf. Matt. 3:15; 4:34), who shows mercy even to his enemies (cf. Luke 23:34), resolute in his calling (cf. Matt. 16:22-23), and a genuine and effective peacemaker (cf. Luke 24:36; John 16:25-33). Again, as Hunsinger puts it: "He himself is the defining instance of what it means to be poor in spirit, what it means to mourn, what it means to be meek, and what it means to hunger and thirst for righteousness."[109] As such, the true blessing that hearers of the beatitudes receive is nothing other than Jesus himself and the mission of his upending the powers and principalities.[110]

Table Fellowship

Alongside Jesus's proclamation and teaching should be placed his practice of table fellowship, which offered an initial glimpse of the great reversal enacted. For example, in Luke 14 Jesus has been invited to the house of a Pharisee for a Sabbath meal. Having already caused controversy by an act of healing on the Sabbath, Jesus offers instruction on table fellowship and inclusion that imagines a humble and radically inclusive community.

> [7]When he noticed how the guests chose the places of honor, he told them a parable. [8]"When you are invited by someone to a wedding banquet, do not sit down at the place of honor, in case someone more distinguished

---

108. Hunsinger, *The Beatitudes*, xix.
109. Hunsinger, *The Beatitudes*, 119.
110. See Barth, *Church Dogmatics* IV/2, 188-91.

than you has been invited by your host; [9]and the host who invited both of you may come and say to you, 'Give this person your place,' and then in disgrace you would start to take the lowest place. [10]But when you are invited, go and sit down at the lowest place, so that when your host comes, he may say to you, 'Friend, move up higher'; then you will be honored in the presence of all who sit at the table with you. [11]For all who exalt themselves will be humbled, and those who humble themselves will be exalted."

[12]He said also to the one who had invited him, "When you give a luncheon or a dinner, do not invite your friends or your brothers or your relatives or rich neighbors, in case they may invite you in return, and you would be repaid. [13]But when you give a banquet, invite the poor, the crippled, the lame, and the blind. [14]And you will be blessed, because they cannot repay you, for you will be repaid at the resurrection of the righteous."

[15]One of the dinner guests, on hearing this, said to him, "Blessed is anyone who will eat bread in the kingdom of God!" [16]Then Jesus said to him, "Someone gave a great dinner and invited many. [17]At the time for the dinner he sent his slave to say to those who had been invited, 'Come; for everything is ready now.' [18]But they all alike began to make excuses. The first said to him, 'I have bought a piece of land, and I must go out and see it; please accept my regrets.' [19]Another said, 'I have bought five yoke of oxen, and I am going to try them out; please accept my regrets.' [20]Another said, 'I have just been married, and therefore I cannot come.' [21]So the slave returned and reported this to his master. Then the owner of the house became angry and said to his slave, 'Go out at once into the streets and lanes of the town and bring in the poor, the crippled, the blind, and the lame.' [22]And the slave said, 'Sir, what you ordered has been done, and there is still room.' [23]Then the master said to the slave, 'Go out into the roads and lanes, and compel people to come in, so that my house may be filled. [24]For I tell you, none of those who were invited will taste my dinner.'" (Luke 14:7-24)

This scene is one of several to which we could turn, wherein Jesus turns the tables on his hosts in more ways than one. In the context of reversal, verses 11, 13, and 21 are especially important, as they speak of the pattern of reversal—"all who exalt themselves will be humbled, and those who humble themselves will be exalted" (v. 11)—and provide characteristic lists of those on the underside and outside. Jesus's teaching and encouragement—as well as his examples (see Mark 2:15-17; Luke 7:36-50; 19:1-10)—fly in the face of general practice at the time. As Craig Evans has remarked, "If shared meals in the OT typically marked off close friends or co-religionists from outsiders, even while acknowledging an ideal age in which the ground rules would differ, the period between the two testaments saw Judaism assign a large swath of teaching to the category of avoiding ritual impurity, including that which accrued through table fellowship with those who did not follow the laws of *kashrut*."[111]

Throughout the Gospels, Jesus is portrayed as eating with tax collectors, sinners, and prostitutes:

> Those concerned with their own possessions and honor are outside; those without possessions and honor are inside. In the setting of a banquet, the two oppositions repeatedly seen in the bi-polar reversal are used to demonstrate proper ethical behavior in the present and attitudes that will likewise lead to eschatological inclusion or exclusion. The self-seeking, self-interested pursuit of honor and possessions, as exemplified by the Pharisees, is contrasted with the decision to act in humility, sacrificing honor in the present for future honor. By associating with the poor and maimed and lame and blind—the people in society without honor—one may be included in the eschatological banquet.[112]

His concern is with those normally deemed beyond the pale: "I have come to call not the righteous but sinners" (Mark 2:17). Such table fellowship enacts a radical form of community—one that mirrors the Jubilee vision of God's compassionate justice, wherein the poor, the imprisoned, and the captives are all set at liberty. Fully embraced and honored, with their person and dignity affirmed.

Not to be forgotten is the real material difference that table fellowship makes in the life of the poor. "In poverty, God's creation is vitiated and annihilated."[113] The gift of table fellowship is the gift of life; it is an initial reversal of the status quo, a sign that points beyond itself to the great banquet where all those who hunger will be filled (Luke 5:21).

---

111. Craig Evans, "Jesus, Sinners, and Table Fellowship," *Bulletin for Biblical Research* 19, no. 1 (2009): 41-42.

112. York, *Last Shall Be First*, 144.

113. Sobrino, *Jesus the Liberator*, 84.

Healing Reversal

The movement of reversal also marks many of the healing narratives found in the Gospels. The healing of the hemorrhagic woman is one such example. The account is placed within another story, the healing of the daughter of Jairus, the synagogue ruler.

> When Jesus had crossed again in the boat to the other side, a great crowd gathered around him; and he was by the sea. Then one of the leaders of the synagogue named Jairus came and, when he saw him, fell at his feet and begged him repeatedly, "My little daughter is at the point of death. Come and lay your hands on her, so that she may be made well, and live." So he went with him.
>
> And a large crowd followed him and pressed in on him. Now there was a woman who had been suffering from hemorrhages for twelve years. She had endured much under many physicians, and had spent all that she had; and she was no better, but rather grew worse. She had heard about Jesus, and came up behind him in the crowd and touched his cloak, for she said, "If I but touch his clothes, I will be made well." Immediately her hemorrhage stopped; and she felt in her body that she was healed of her disease. Immediately aware that power had gone forth from him, Jesus turned about in the crowd and said, "Who touched my clothes?" And his disciples said to him, "You see the crowd pressing in on you; how can you say, 'Who touched me?'" He looked all around to see who had done it. But the woman, knowing what had happened to her, came in fear and trembling, fell down before him, and told him the whole truth. He said to her, "Daughter, your faith has made you well; go in peace, and be healed of your disease."
>
> While he was still speaking, some people came from the leader's house to say, "Your daughter is dead. Why trouble the teacher any further?" But overhearing what they said, Jesus said to the leader of the synagogue, "Do not fear, only believe." He allowed no one to follow him except Peter, James, and John, the brother of James. When they came to the house of the leader of the synagogue, he saw a commotion, people weeping and wailing loudly. When he had entered, he said to them, "Why do you make a commotion and weep? The child is not dead but sleeping." And they laughed at him. Then he put them all outside, and took the child's father and mother and those who were with him, and went in where the child was. He took her by the hand and said to her, "Talitha cum," which means, "Little girl, get up!" And immediately

the girl got up and began to walk about (she was twelve years of age). At this they were overcome with amazement. He strictly ordered them that no one should know this, and told them to give her something to eat. (Mark 5:21-43)

The text is somewhat opaque as to the nature of the woman's ailment, though most commentators agree that it is probably of a gynecological nature, rendering the woman unclean, her touch impure, and her ability to produce offspring at risk.[114] The text is also not forthcoming as to the woman's ethnicity—we do not know if she is Jewish or gentile, unlike the daughter of Jairus, the synagogue ruler. Nevertheless, as Marie-Eloise Rosenblatt points out, "It was not just a Jewish view that menstruation, ejaculation and sexual intercourse involved pollution and the need for purification, especially in relation to worship. Greek, Roman, and Jewish texts all made references to pollution in association with menstruation."[115] Whether the woman was Jewish or gentile, her position in her community is precarious—she is an outsider considered unclean and unproductive.

Sandwiched, as it were, within the story of the healing of Jairus's daughter, the woman is positioned in a web of contrasts that highlight her lack of social status. Marcus enumerates the differences as follows: "This woman is at the opposite end of the social, economic, and religious spectrum from Jairus. While he is a male leader, she is a nameless woman; while he is a synagogue official, she is ritually unclean and thus excluded from the religious community; while he has a family and a large household, she must presumably live in isolation because of her condition; while he is rich, she is impoverished by payment of doctors' fees."[116] Narratively and symbolically linked,[117] both women have crossed from the realm of the living into

114. See Myers, *Binding the Strong Man*, 200-203; Hisako Kinukawa, "The Story of the Hemorrhaging Woman (Mark 5:25-34) Read from a Japanese Feminist Context," *Biblical Interpretation* 2, no. 3 (1994): 283-93; Marcus, *Mark 1-8*, 366-69; Susan Haber, "A Woman's Touch: Feminist Encounters with the Hemorrhaging Woman in Mark 5.24-34," *Journal for the Study of the New Testament* 26, no. 2 (2003): 171-92; Shelly Rambo, "Trauma and Faith: Reading the Narrative of the Hemorrhaging Woman," *International Journal of Practical Theology* 13 (2009): 233-57; and Candida R. Moss, "The Man with the Flow of Power: Porous Bodies in Mark 5:25-34," *Journal of Biblical Literature* 129, no. 3 (2010): 507-19.

115. Marie-Eloise Rosenblatt, "Gender, Ethnicity, and Legal Considerations in the Haemorrhaging Woman's Story Mark 5:25-34," in *Transformative Encounters: Jesus and Women Re-viewed*, ed. Ingrid Rosa Kitzberger (Leiden: Brill, 2000), 150.

116. Marcus, *Mark 1-8*, 366.

117. Both women are connected symbolically through the number twelve—the number of years the woman struggled with her ailment (v. 25) and the age of the young girl (v. 42).

the realm of the dead.[118] The woman is poor, ill, and rejected, with no one to advocate for her, in contrast to Jairus's daughter. All of these factors make the account of her healing all the more striking. Rather than Jesus laying hands on her, it is she who lays hands on Jesus.

Her action is risky and audacious, for "she is unclean, and her touch defiles, and therefore there is a danger that any physical contact she may have with the healer will annul his miracle working power and wreck the whole effort."[119] As soon as she touches him, power flows out from Jesus, releasing and restoring the woman. Demanding to know who touched him, Jesus is strangely configured as one not in control of his own power. He is not, however, as dense as the disciples, whose response Jesus ignores (vv. 31-32). Rather, he is a witness to the power of God's Spirit: "He witnesses the woman's spirit infused with the divine."[120] For the woman, the experience of healing is instantaneous and overwhelming. In fear and trembling—terms associated with the experience of divine power and the presence of God[121]—the woman comes to Jesus to tell him "the whole truth" (v. 33). Jesus seals his witness with the restorative address "daughter." "She is no longer the 'woman' with a flow of blood, but has been transformed into a 'daughter' within the community."[122] The nameless woman, a transgressive figure who reaches out for Jesus, is liberated and affirmed as a member of the community, declared a faithful daughter. As Myers notes, a profound reversal has occurred: "From the bottom of the honor scale she intrudes upon an important mission on behalf of the daughter of someone on the top of the honor scale—but by the story's conclusion, *she* herself has become the 'daughter' at the center of the story!"[123] Though Jesus will also go on to heal the synagogue ruler's daughter, in contrast to the woman, Jesus has to reprimand Jairus for his lack of faith (i.e., v. 36). The destitute and unclean woman is the model of faith, while the disciples and Jairus are configured as ambivalent figures in regard to trusting in the emergence of God's reign in Jesus.

Another contrast within the story also highlights how the flow of power from Jesus effects a reversal. As Candida Moss points out, the woman's action establishes a connection between the woman and Jesus, in that,

---

118. Haber, "A Woman's Touch," 187.

119. Marcus, *Mark 1-8*, 366.

120. Rambo, "Trauma and Faith," 249.

121. See Rambo, "Trauma and Faith," 247, and Moss, "Man with the Flow," 518.

122. Haber, "A Woman's Touch," 184.

123. Myers, *Binding the Strong Man*, 201-2.

like the woman, Jesus also leaks in an unnatural way: "In the narrative, the flow of power from Jesus mirrors the flow of blood from the woman. Like the woman, Jesus is unable to control the flow that emanates from his body. Like the flow of blood, the flow of power is something embodied and physical; just as the woman feels the flow of blood dry up, so Jesus feels—physically—the flow of power leave his body. Both the diseased woman with the flow of blood and the divine protagonist of Mark are porous, leaky creatures."[124] In Greco-Roman thought, such porosity was a negative characteristic associated with weakness, inferiority, and women: "Porous bodies are vulnerable to external attack and threaten the subjects and those around them with contagion. . . . What are the characteristics of a healthy body in the ancient world? We find that it is impermeable, dry, hot, hard, regulated, and masculine. Conversely, a sickly body is drippy, leaky, moist, uncontrolled, feminine, soft, and porous."[125] Women were explicitly associated with such porosity and were thus considered inferior to men, in need of male policing.

The observation that Jesus's body takes on the same characteristics as the woman's, then, heightens the sense of reversal. Jesus switches places with the woman, taking up the position of the outsider; he becomes vulnerable. Because of the woman's "impure touch" and because of the flow of power, he becomes like the impure and unclean, one whose body leaks unnaturally, in order that the woman may be released and restored to her community. At the same time, by becoming a porous body, one that would have been feared and despised in the ancient world, Jesus identifies with this woman, undermining the gender politics operative in the social order by enacting a reversal that leads to liberation and restoration.

CONCLUSION

Jesus preached the gospel of God's reign, and in word and deed he made it present. Both Mary and John anticipate the appearance of God's Jubilee reign, which consists of judgment and new life, and both associate this appearing with the coming of Jesus. Anointed and tested, Jesus announces the fulfilled time of the kingdom's appearance, appealing to the prophetic tradition of God's Jubilee, which is inclusive and salvific, moving beyond the

124. Moss, "Man with the Flow," 516.
125. Moss, "Man with the Flow," 514.

normal boundaries of religious and social expectations. In keeping with the prophets and apocalyptic traditions, the rule of God is associated with the in-breaking of God's Jubilee reign. This is good news for the outcast, for the poor, for the oppressed, for women, but also for gentiles as well as Jews. In keeping with certain strands of the prophetic tradition, then, the horizon of the kingdom Jesus preached and enacted is universal and cosmic.

The inbreaking of God's Jubilee reign means release and reversal. As in the earlier Jubilee traditions where the declaration of the year of the Lord's favor meant the release of the captives, the forgiveness of debts, and the lifting up of the lowly, so with Jesus the time is fulfilled and the hour of release and reversal is at hand. These two themes shape much of the ministry of Jesus as displayed in the Gospels. Jesus confronts social, physical, political, and cosmic powers by declaring and enacting the release of those held in bondage. Release is forgiveness and forgiveness is release; the forgiveness of debt and forgiveness of sins are entwined in the preaching and practice of Jesus, as are release from physical, social, and spiritual bondage. God's reign means good news for all because it means good news for the poor. Good news for the poor means release from the oppressive and systemic forces in which all are entrapped, and by which *all* are dehumanized, *especially* the poor. The gospel proclaimed and enacted by Jesus is not the resentment of the peasantry, but the proclamation that all will be set at liberty.

As such, the proclamation of God's reign means the world is turned upside down, as the lowly are lifted up, and everything that counts for power in this world is laid low. Already in the ministry of Jesus, the normal social boundaries that keep people "in their place" are transgressed and even overthrown. Jesus embraces the lowly, the sick, the unclean, outsiders, and women—all figures considered beyond the boundaries of God's grace in the context of the ancient world. This embrace indicates that there is no one and nothing beyond God's reach. Furthermore, enfolded in Jesus's proclamation of release and reversal is a call to those who follow him to engage in the unending labor of forgiveness/release, to pursue peace and practice mercy toward both friends and enemies.

The good news that Jesus proclaims, however, is disturbing. In the preaching and practice of this lowly peasant is the revolution of God, which means the overthrow of the powers and principalities that organize a world bound to death. Everyone with a vested interest is therefore aroused to resistance, and in a world governed by cosmic powers, *everyone*, in fact, is roused to resistance. In other words, though Jesus seeks to elicit faithfulness in response to his own faithfulness, he also elicits conflict and opposition; and that conflict and opposition ultimately overcome even those who would be faithful (i.e., the disciples) as they join in rejecting and abandoning him. Jesus alone is the faithful one; Jesus alone is faithful unto death.

According to the gospel narratives, however, though tragic, this turn against Jesus, even by his own disciples, is not unanticipated. In fact, woven into the appearance of God's reign in the life of Jesus *is his death*. This is because the ultimate conflict is not between the faithful and the faithless, nor between Jews and gentiles, nor men and women, nor any other merely human powers. Rather, the conflict is cosmic. The conflict is between the God of life who wills that creation live in fellowship with its Creator, and the powers of sin and death that seek ultimately to destroy and undo creation itself. In Jesus, therefore, the reign of God confronts the powers and principalities of sin and, above all, death. The apocalyptic sufferings of Jesus on the cross are nothing less than the crescendo of the conflict between God and the lordless powers,[126] chief among whom is death. That conflict ends in the defeat of death and the revelation of the true nature and final goal of God's rule. To see the *way* in which God rules and the *goal* toward which that rule moves, one must look to the active suffering of the living God in the midst of the suffering and death of the Jew from Nazareth, and to his resurrection from the dead. To this we now turn.

---

126. See Karl Barth, *The Christian Life: Church Dogmatics* IV/4; *Lecture Fragments* (Grand Rapids: Eerdmans, 1981), 214-33.

Chapter Five

THE WAY OF THE KINGDOM

The central theme of the preaching and ministry of Jesus was the radical presence of the reign of God. As we showed in earlier chapters, the theme of God's kingship was intimately related to expectations regarding the dawning of God's Jubilee reign, which also coincided with the end of exile and the liberation of the people of God. In his life and ministry, Jesus proclaimed and embodied the realities of release and reversal that characterized the earlier hopes found in the prophets and the apocalyptic traditions. Through acts of healing and exorcism, through the extension of table fellowship, and in the proclamation of forgiveness and release, the reign of God present in Jesus meant good news for the outcast, the poor, the oppressed, women, and gentiles as well as Jews. Jesus's life and ministry enacted and pointed toward the overthrow of the powers and principalities that enslave all of humanity.

There is, however, a dialectic at work in the gospel witness, for though his life and ministry reveal a deep commitment to the life-giving presence of the reign of God, nevertheless, the specter of rejection and death haunts Jesus's every step. Though the coming of God's Jubilee reign means freedom, it also means suffering, and as we have already noted, Jesus's ministry, from its very beginning, is marked by conflict, suffering, and rejection. Does his ultimate rejection by means of crucifixion mean his failure? Not according to the witness of the New Testament. Rather, the gospel proclaims the resurrection of the crucified. But what then is the purpose of Jesus's suffering? What does it tell us about the reign of God he proclaimed and embodied? How are the crucifixion and the theme of the reign of God connected?

The theme of the kingdom and the reality of Jesus's cross have often been pitted against one another. As Jeremy Treat puts it, "Some champion the kingdom and others cling to the cross, usually one to the exclusion of the other."[1] As will become clear, the present chapter attempts to avoid this bifurcation. We do so by drawing special attention to the prevalence of apocalyptic motifs that are found in New Testament accounts of Jesus's passion. Our discussion of apocalyptic in chapter 3 highlighted the ways in which kingdom language and motifs are embedded in apocalyptic discourse. In our last chapter we found ourselves especially drawn to the Jubilee content of God's reign, which Jesus proclaimed and embodied in his ministry, preaching, and practice. In this chapter, apocalyptic motifs are more prominent because the death of Jesus is placed within an apocalyptic context across the four Gospels and in many of the epistles found in the New Testament. The great Jubilee, however, is never far away, as it is God's compassionate justice and righteousness that confront the powers that enslave humanity in the event of the cross, where, in Jesus, God hazards death that creation might be free to live a truly flourishing life in fellowship with God and the whole of creation.

THE DEATH-DEALING ADVERSARIES OF YHWH

Jesus's ministry and proclamation were marked by conflict and struggle from the very beginning. As recounted in the Gospel of Luke (4:16-30), the inauguration of his ministry was first welcomed by modest approbation and then quickly violent rejection, as the people of Nazareth—those with whom he grew up!—sought to throw Jesus from a cliff. Likewise, the opening chapter of the Gospel of John, using the imagery of light, describes the coming of Jesus in conflictual terms—the entry of the light of God into the world precipitates a conflict with the darkness in the world (cf. 1:1-5). A central dynamic of that gospel is the unrelenting crisis that Jesus's every word and action produces among hearers and onlookers. How will those who encounter Jesus respond? Will they accept the faithful witness of Jesus? Or

---

1. Jeremy R. Treat, *The Crucified King: Atonement and Kingdom in Biblical and Systematic Theology* (Grand Rapids: Zondervan, 2004), 25. Treat assumes that "cross" necessarily means "substitutionary atonement." We will not follow this line of thought, though we will attempt to bring together the kingdom and the cross, as the way of the Crucified is understood here as the "way of the kingdom."

will they reject him? This dynamic culminates with the final miracle performed by Jesus in the Gospel of John, the raising of Lazarus from the dead. In the flow of the narrative, the raising of Lazarus—a miracle that displays the life-giving power of Jesus—becomes the event that seals his fate, as the authorities decide that Jesus must die, rather than the whole nation.

Jesus's Religious and Political Adversaries

From a historical perspective, Jesus was executed by people in power—religious, political, and economic.[2] His message and ministry, his commitment to a life shaped by God's love, by God's compassionate justice elicited the only "logical" response that could be expected from the world "as it is": death. As such, his death reveals the depth of human antipathy to God's justice and surfaces human sin in all of its sinfulness.

From the perspective of the religious authorities, the ostensible reason for Jesus's arrest was probably his remarks about the temple, while his messianic "confession" was decisive in his execution, or this appears to be the case in the synoptic accounts.[3] Though sharing some concern over the temple (cf. John 2:12–25), the Gospel of John alludes more directly to political expediency, when the high priest ominously intones that it is better that "one man die for the people than to have the whole nation destroyed" (11:50).

Whatever the role of the religious authorities in Jerusalem, the New Testament clearly contends that Jesus's execution was secured in collusion with Rome.[4] Under the watchful eye of the Roman prefect Pontius Pilate, Jesus was mocked, tortured, and crucified, one of the most heinous forms of execution ever devised. Thus, it was Roman authority and justice that ultimately oversaw the unjust act of condemning an innocent man to death.

The Gospel of John offers the most expansive version of Jesus's trial before Pilate, with seven different scenes (18:28–19:16). Pilate is often seen as a weak and sympathetic figure by interpreters, but I agree with David Rens-

---

2. See Jon Sobrino, *Jesus the Liberator: A Historical-Theological View* (Maryknoll, NY: Orbis, 1993), 199.

3. E.g., Mark 14:58, 61–64; Matt. 26:60–61, 63–67; Luke 22:67–71. Jürgen Moltmann offers a plausible historical reconstruction that places Jesus's comments about the temple front and center in his arrest, while his admission of his messianic status became decisive in his execution. See *The Way of Jesus Christ: Christology in Messianic Dimensions* (Minneapolis: Fortress, 1993), 160–64.

4. See Roy A. Harrisville, *Fracture: The Cross as Irreconcilable in the Language and Thought of the Biblical Writers* (Grand Rapids: Eerdmans, 2006), 4–16.

berger's assessment that though he is undeniably hostile to the religious authorities, "that does not make him friendly to Jesus, for whose innocence he is not really concerned. Rather, his aim is to humiliate 'the Jews' and to ridicule their national hopes by means of Jesus."[5] In other words, much like the story of the woman caught in adultery (John 7:53–8:11), from this angle the innocent Jesus is but a pawn in a larger game; his fate is an afterthought. The irony (or revelation, if you will) is that in both cases those who would seem to represent the interests of the law (whether Roman or Jewish) are shown to be calloused and fundamentally uninterested in human life, thereby revealing themselves as, at base, lawbreakers and death dealers. This becomes especially clear as the trial unfolds.

After an initial interchange between Jesus and Pilate, in which Pilate's hostile interrogation leads to Jesus's acceptance of the appellation "king of the Jews," Pilate's cruel intentions become clear. He declares Jesus innocent, but rather than releasing him, as would be proper protocol, he toys with his real opponents, the Jewish authorities, by merely offering to release Jesus in honor of the impending Passover festival. The crowd rejects this, opting instead for the revolutionary Barabbas. Mark tells us that this choice was made at the urging of the religious authorities (Mark 15:11). Pilate then has a man whom he has just declared to be innocent (John 18:38) scourged and mockingly attired as the "king of the Jews," not intending to placate the religious leadership "but to humiliate them."[6] In a scene that inverts Daniel 7, wherein the Son of Man is presented before the divine throne as YHWH's servant and co-regent whose appearance at the end of the ages marks the end of the powers arrayed against YHWH, Jesus is brought out dressed in mocking royal attire, complete with a robe and crown of thorns, with the double acclamation "behold the man," the "king of the Jews."[7] From the perspective of the Gospel of John, this mocking scene turns Pilate into an unwitting witness to the truth (cf. John 18:37–38) that Jesus is in fact the royal Son of Man.[8]

---

5. David Rensberger, *Johannine Faith and Liberating Community* (Philadelphia: Westminster, 1988), 92.

6. Rensberger, *Johannine Faith*, 93.

7. I am inspired in this reading of the scene before Pilate by Daniel Boyarin's provocative suggestion that the passion narrative should be understood as a midrash on Dan. 7. Though Boyarin limits his reading to Mark's Gospel, I believe this approach can also be applied to other gospels, particular some key sections of John. See Daniel Boyarin, *The Jewish Gospels: The Story of the Jewish Christ* (New York: New Press, 2012), esp. chap. 4.

8. See Rensberger, *Johannine Faith*, 94.

Only after he is told that Jesus claimed to be a "son of God" (also a political title in the ancient world)[9] does Pilate seem to seriously attempt to release Jesus. But even as he attempts to free him, Pilate still taunts the Jewish authorities and their own national aspirations, which ultimately pays off, as the religious powerbrokers align themselves with Pilate in declaring that they have "no king but the emperor" (John 19:15).[10] We will return to John's account of the trial of Jesus later, but for now, the point is simply that Pilate has colluded with the religious authorities to execute an innocent man, one who was viewed as a threat to both political and religious power.[11]

The Powers and Principalities

At the same time, however, the crucifixion of Jesus is not only the calculated response of politico-religious leaders to a charismatic figure. Notwithstanding the religious, political, and social dynamics at play in the events that led to the death of Jesus, from the perspective of the New Testament, these figures are but the historical representatives or expressions of larger cosmic forces, which are often described as the "powers and principalities." Since the middle of the twentieth century, a great deal of scholarly energy has been devoted to considering the nature of the powers and principalities and the relationship between these larger cosmic powers and the various historical actors driven by them.[12] Walter Wink has offered one of the most complete discussions of the so-called powers in English-language scholarship, mapping the technical, though unsystematic, terminology in the New Testament.

Wink's extensive investigations helpfully cleared away the notion that the New Testament imagined "a variety of invisible demonic beings flap-

---

9. See Michael Peppard, *The Son of God in the Roman World: Divine Sonship in Its Social and Political Context* (Oxford: Oxford University Press, 2011).

10. "Surely their final exclamation in 19:15 ('We have no king by Caesar!') is precisely in accord with Roman desires, so that in the end it is Pilate, not 'the Jews,' who emerges triumphant." Rensberger, *Johannine Faith*, 92.

11. See Rensberger, *Johannine Faith*, 94-95.

12. One thinks here especially of the work of Hendrik Berkhof and especially Walter Wink. See Hendrik Berkhof, *Christ and the Powers*, trans. John Howard Yoder (Scottdale, PA: Herald, 1977); Walter Wink, *Naming the Powers: The Language of Power in the New Testament* (Philadelphia: Fortress, 1984); Walter Wink, *Unmasking the Powers: The Invisible Powers That Determine Human Existence* (Philadelphia: Fortress, 1986); and Walter Wink, *Engaging the Powers: Discernment and Resistance in a World of Domination* (Minneapolis: Fortress, 1992).

ping around in the sky, occasionally targeting some luckless mortal with their malignant payload of disease, lust, possession, or death."[13] He argued instead that "the 'powers and principalities' are the inner and outer aspects of any given manifestation of power. . . . Every Power tends to have a visible pole, an outer form—be it a church, a nation, or an economy—and an invisible pole, an inner spirit or driving force that animates, legitimates, and regulates its physical manifestation in the world."[14] In other words, at one level, the "powers and principalities" refers to the reigning ideologies, structures, institutions, and even cultural assumptions that form the everyday existence of human beings.

These ideologies organize and are often an attempt to make sense of the world in which human beings live. They "show us the world, the human and society, what is proper and how we should be."[15] As Dick Boer notes, we human beings are born into such ideologies and therefore "can only poorly defend ourselves against these images because they take effect before we are even conscious of it."[16] Thus, to return to the language of "powers and principalities," whenever "a particular Power becomes idolatrous, placing itself above God's purposes for the good of the whole, then that Power becomes demonic."[17] From this perspective, the forces arrayed against Jesus are not simply the human personalities of Pilate or the religious authorities, but the larger social, political, and religious interests that they represent; interests that seem to have a life of their own. The world as currently structured cannot and will not abide the compassionate justice of God proclaimed and enacted in the life and ministry of Jesus. Rather, Jesus was on a collision course with the regnant powers of the world.[18]

Our contemporary world is also marked by such realities. Though there are many ideologies at work in our age, white supremacy has proven to be virtually unchallenged in catastrophic consequences for human life, insidious in its deployment as a legal regime and expression of "common-sense" wisdom, and far-reaching and penetrating in its ability to convince both the willing and the unwilling to engage in acts of collusion. Described

13. Wink, Naming the Powers, 4.

14. Wink, Naming the Powers, 5

15. Dick Boer, Deliverance from Slavery: Attempting a Biblical Theology in the Service of Liberation (Chicago: Haymarket Books, 2015), 25.

16. Boer, Deliverance from Slavery, 25.

17. Wink, Naming the Powers, 5.

18. See Martin Hengel, Christ and Power (Dublin: Christian Journals, 1977), 15–22.

variously as "racism,"[19] "whiteness," "white privilege," and "racial capi-talism"[20]—the latter being much closer to the truth because it names the deep entanglement of racial regimes with the political economy of capi-talism—"white supremacy" does not refer to the organizing of personal or in-group predilections regarding phenotype, as if "race" were a natu-ral category rooted in biology. Rather, the terminology of "race" and the subsidiary terms "white," "black," etc., are all social constructions loaded with social, economic, moral, and political assumptions. As Jennifer Har-vey helpfully explains regarding the category "race":

> To say that race is a social construction is to suggest that even though we hold "common sense" notions about what race is—for example, we just know it or think we know it when we see it—race isn't something pre-wired into the human body. It's not something already there that we can then point to or take note of in a second act. It is not an essential reality that exists before or outside of human social activity. Instead, in a real way, race actually comes to exist in the act of pointing and taking note. Race is very real. But it becomes real only in the interactions between different bodies and laws, economics, education, the criminal justice system, and a nearly infinite number of other institutions and processes.[21]

Harvey's dynamic intersectional analysis of "race" illumines the socially constructed nature of a category that has become central to the way in which the world has been organized. The descriptor "white supremacy"

19. One of the most influential descriptions of "racism" is offered by Ruth Wilson Gilmore: "Racism is a practice of abstraction, a death-dealing displacement into hierar-chies that organize relations within and between the planet's sovereign political territories. Racism functions as a limiting force that pushes disproportionate costs of participating in an increasingly monetized and profit-driven world onto those who, due to the frictions of *political* distance, cannot reach the variable levers of power that might relieve them of those costs. Indeed, the process of abstraction that signifies racism produces effects at the most intimately 'sovereign' scale, insofar as particular kinds of bodies, one by one, are materially (if not always visibly) configured by racism into a hierarchy of human and inhuman persons that in sum form the category 'human being' (Agamben 1999)." Ruth Wilson Gilmore, "Fatal Couplings of Power and Difference: Notes on Racism and Geography," *Professional Geographer* 54, no. 1 (2002): 16.

20. See Cedric J. Robinson, *Black Marxism: The Making of the Black Radical Tradition* (Chapel Hill: University of North Carolina Press, 2000), 9–28.

21. Jennifer Harvey, *Dear White Christians: For Those Still Longing for Racial Reconcili-ation*, 2nd ed. (Grand Rapids: Eerdmans, 2020), 44–45.

expands on this by naming the real material relations that over the course of the last five hundred years have been constructed, perpetuated, and maintained to structure the material relations between different human communities and individuals to the detriment and destruction of those deemed "not white."

"White supremacy," then, names the ideology and organizing logic of power that structures our contemporary era and is "pervasive, systemic, and multifaceted."[22] Because of its connection to the reigning order of power, "white supremacy" is not the same thing as "Black power," etc., precisely because it names the dominant and real material organization of power in our time that places those deemed "white" on top, while placing all others on the bottom in the position of exploitable subhuman labor. "White supremacy" names the flow of power that continues to shape the political and material economic relations that make up what is often called "modernity." As Gerald Horne has pointed out, the seventeenth-century material economic realities that gave birth to our contemporary age were "marked with the indelible stain of what might be termed the Three Horsemen of the Apocalypse: Slavery, White Supremacy, and Capitalism, with the bloody process of human bondage being the driving and animating force of this abject horror."[23] And though slavery itself has ended in the United States, as has the legal regime of Jim Crow, nevertheless, there are numerous myths that continue to prop up "white supremacy" and to sustain the basic patterns of organization it was meant to police.[24]

Conversely, "blackness" also names a way of seeing the world. As James Cone eloquently puts it:

Being Black in America has very little to do with skin color. To be black means that your heart, your soul, your mind, and your body are where

22. Jennifer Harvey, Karin A. Case, and Robin Hawley Gorsline, introduction to *Disrupting White Supremacy from Within: White People on What We Need to Do*, ed. Jennifer Harvey et al. (Cleveland: Pilgrim, 2004), 23.

23. Gerald Horne, *The Apocalypse of Settler Colonialism: The Roots of Slavery, White Supremacy, and Capitalism in Seventeenth-Century North America and the Caribbean* (New York: Monthly Review Press, 2018), 9.

24. For a discussion of these myths, see Kelly Brown Douglas, *Stand Your Ground: Black Bodies and the Justice of God* (Maryknoll, NY: Orbis, 2015). For a recent discussion of the potent and ongoing dynamics of "white supremacy," see Michelle Alexander, *The New Jim Crow: Mass Incarceration in the Age of Colorblindness* (New York: New Press, 2012).

the dispossessed are. We all know that a racist structure will reject and threaten a black man in white skin as quickly as a black man in black skin. It accepts and rewards whites in black skins nearly as well as whites in white skins. Therefore, being reconciled to God does not mean that one's skin is physically black. It essentially depends on the color of your heart, soul, and mind.[25]

"Blackness" can be described as the "underside of modernity,"[26] as it refers to the place of the oppressed and dispossessed "wretched of the earth."[27] However, it also correlates almost precisely with the posture of Jesus in the Greco-Roman world, and therefore one can and must say, with Cone and others, that Jesus was indeed "Black" and affirm that "the blackness of God means that God has made the oppressed condition God's own condition. . . . By electing Israelite slaves as the people of God and by becoming the Oppressed One in Jesus Christ, the human race is made to understand that God is known where human beings experience humiliation and suffering."[28]

We highlight the ideology of "white supremacy" to offer a concrete description of what the New Testament labels as "powers and principalities" when it is considered as a reigning ideology which is enacted by human beings, but which also has a power greater than the sum of its parts. Though we will return to this later, of additional significance is the fact that our description of these concrete realities with which we are all daily threatened makes plain that the confrontation between Jesus and the powers and principalities in his own day has not ended. Indeed the Spirit of Jesus presses, pushes, and more often than not cajoles disciples to be faithful unto death in the face of the reigning ideology of "white supremacy"; to be a "protest people of hope,"[29] who seek a foretaste of God's promised liberation in the here and now.

25. James H. Cone, *Black Theology and Black Power*, rev. ed. (Maryknoll, NY: Orbis, 1997), 151.

26. See Enrique Dussel, *The Underside of Modernity: Apel, Ricoeur, Rorty, Taylor, and the Philosophy of Liberation* (Atlantic Highlands, NJ: Humanities, 1996).

27. See Frantz Fanon, *The Wretched of the Earth* (New York: Grove, 2004).

28. James H. Cone, *A Black Theology of Liberation*, fortieth anniversary ed. (Maryknoll, NY: Orbis, 2016), 67.

29. Jürgen Moltmann, *Sun of Righteousness, Arise! God's Future for Humanity and the Earth* (Minneapolis: Fortress, 2010), 77.

The Powers of Sin and Death

As should be obvious in light of chapter 3, the language of "powers" also places us squarely in the realm of apocalyptic and the expectation of a cosmic confrontation, not merely between human ideas, institutions, structures, practices, and personalities but between God and the powers of sin and death. These are the real powers that organize our world, from the ways in which political entities organize themselves along the lines of insider/outsider, with fear of death as a driving force, to the ways in which human bodies are regulated through various sociopolitical, religious, gender, ethnic, sexual, and other identities (cf. Gal. 3:28),[30] determining who is or is not acceptable, worthy of love, belonging, or care.

From a theological perspective, it is the powers of sin and death that exercise a distorting and dehumanizing rule, and any who cross them will be confronted by their death-dealing lackeys. As we outlined in chapter 4, the proclamation and enactment of release and reversal embodied in Jesus were a tour de force in challenging the reigning ideologies, structures, and powers. Furthermore, Jesus did not simply challenge the human constructs (i.e., ideologies, institutions, etc.), but he dared even to forgive sin and to call forth the dead from the grave. Jesus's ministry was nothing less than the reign of God invading the territory of the rule of sin and death. As such, the life of Jesus was a provocation.[31]

Theologically speaking, the couplet "sin and death" speaks to the fundamentally incoherent nature of these powers. It quite simply refers to the power of negation. Sin is at its base the creature's refusal of its Creator, and is therefore an irrational attempt at self-negation. To refuse the Creator is to refuse to be a creature of God. Sin is the creature's incomprehensible attempt to will its own nonbeing through its refusal to be a creature in covenant relationship with God, or to will the nonbeing of fellow creatures as though they did not belong to God.[32] It is the attempt to undo the will of

---

30. See J. Louis Martyn, *Theological Issues in the Letters of Paul* (Nashville: Abingdon, 1997), 125-40.

31. "In other words, the fate of Jesus was neither an accident nor suicide, but the result of action against him by *others*, who had been provoked by actions of his own. In order to obey the God he believed in, he had entered into conflict; and he died both as victim to those who contradicted him, and in consequence of his own opposition to them." Alan E. Lewis, *Between Cross and Resurrection: A Theology of Holy Saturday* (Grand Rapids: Eerdmans, 2001), 46.

32. See Karl Barth, *Church Dogmatics* III/3 (Edinburgh: T&T Clark, 2000), 302-48, 363-64.

God that there should *be* a creature and a creation (cf. Rom. 8:19-23), and thus death—and its association with the meaninglessness of the abyss—is always the partner of sin. Though, as Paul says, "sin entered the world" through human disobedience (Rom. 5:12-21), in the New Testament sin is not merely a human action but refers to a power to which humanity is enslaved, an enemy that can only be defeated by a greater power.[33] As Fleming Rutledge puts it: "Sin is not so much a collection of individual misdeeds as it is an active, malevolent agency bent upon despoiling, imprisonment, and death—the utter undoing of God's purposes. Misdeeds are signs of that agency at work; they are not the thing itself. It is 'the thing itself' that is our cosmic Enemy."[34] In Paul's language, sin and death are described as powers that rule over humanity, that make human beings into "sinners" (Rom. 5:19), enslaving and distorting humanity and creation as a whole (Rom. 8:19-23).

A similar thematic can be discerned in the Gospels, though in more mythopoetic language. The Accuser, or Satan, and other demonic powers are depicted at almost every turn as actors behind the scenes. Whether as the one who tempts Jesus to turn from his calling as the servant of YHWH (e.g., Luke 4:1-13), or in the misunderstanding of the disciples (e.g., Matt. 16:23; Luke 22:31), or as one of the sources behind debilitating disease (e.g., Luke 13:10-17), or in the possession and defilement of human beings leading to their exclusion from community (e.g., Mark 5:1-20), or as the motivating force that leads to Jesus's betrayal (John 13:21-30), powers that are well beyond human control have arrayed themselves against Jesus.

An important caveat here is that from the perspective of the New Testament, and especially Paul, the situation of enslavement in all its horrible depths is not fully known or understood until the powers and principalities reveal their full intentions, a revelation that is tied especially to their confrontation with God and God's anointed. In 1 Corinthians 15, Paul speaks of the reign of God at work in Jesus as an event in which these powers are subdued, and death itself is destroyed (15:26). In the opposition to Jesus, and ultimately in his death and resurrection, though human culpability in the act of executing the innocent man Jesus is not removed (cf. Acts 2:22-23),

33. See Beverly Roberts Gaventa, *Our Mother Saint Paul* (Louisville: Westminster John Knox, 2007), 128-32. See also Beverly Roberts Gaventa, *When in Romans: An Invitation to Linger with the Gospel according to Paul* (Grand Rapids: Baker Academic, 2016), 38-43.

34. Fleming Rutledge, *The Crucifixion: Understanding the Death of Jesus Christ* (Grand Rapids: Eerdmans, 2015), 175.

it is the cosmic powers of sin and death who are revealed as the tyrannical forces that stand against God and God's anointed.[35]

THE APOCALYPTIC SUFFERINGS OF THE SERVANT OF YHWH

The conflict between the powers and principalities, in all of their complexity, and Jesus results in a final confrontation which is described in the Gospel passion narratives. All of the Gospels, including John, describe the events of Jesus's arrest, trial, and execution in an apocalyptic register, not merely to drive home the catastrophe of the injustice done to Jesus, but to illumine the larger confrontation occurring between YHWH and the powers of sin and death.

The Apocalyptic Context of the Passion

Why then does Jesus die? We must acknowledge that alongside the human actors, the regnant powers and principalities, and above all the powers of sin and death, there is also in the scriptural witness an indication of divine involvement. Though Jesus is the victim of fear-filled and death-dealing human and superhuman powers, he is neither unwitting nor passive in the fateful drama of the cross. We mentioned earlier that Jesus's life and ministry were a kind of provocation of the various enemies arrayed against God and God's anointed. What we mean by this is that through Jesus's life, the enemies of God are fully drawn out into the open to engage in a public struggle with God's reign as embodied in Jesus. It means that God *anticipates* and *appropriates* this rejection to reveal the true depths of the enslavement of creation and the unyielding divine determination to liberate the cosmos. In the collision between God and the powers, the depths of God's compassion expressed in the abject weakness of the cross swallow up death, dealing it a fatal blow. The way of the kingdom is always already the way of the cross. Not because God demands of Jesus a sacrifice to propitiate divine anger. To the contrary, God anticipates the rejection of the reality embodied in Jesus, and in turn uses that rejection to expose the depths of sin and death, to declare God's own solidarity with all who suffer, to

---

35. See Martinus C. de Boer, *The Defeat of Death: Apocalyptic Eschatology in 1 Corinthians 15 and Romans 5* (Sheffield: Sheffield Academic Press, 1988), 114-40.

overthrow the powers of sin and death through Jesus's abandonment and weakness, and to reconcile the world to Godself.

The language of conflict places us in the realm of apocalyptic modes of thought, and as with the life of Jesus (as we have already shown in chap. 4), apocalyptic confrontation is one of the dominant lenses by which the New Testament describes and understands the crucifixion (and resurrection) of Jesus.[36] As we outlined in chapter 3, during the Second Temple period (515 BCE–70 CE), apocalyptic eschatology arose, transforming the prophetic expectations of God's rescue of the people Israel. Apocalyptic texts were often concerned to reveal that God would ultimately vindicate those who were faithful to God's compassionate justice, by rescuing them from the powers that assaulted them, and by overthrowing the powers themselves. The conflict between the rule of the living One and the reign of death embodied in the nations that would conclude with the liberation of Israel was universalized and given a cosmic scope, such that the liberation of Israel was a portent that all of humanity—even the nations![37]—would be set free from the powers of death.

The various apocalyptic traditions and texts that emerged during this period emphasized the total priority of divine action. Only YHWH could save Israel, as the forces arrayed against the faithful were cosmic, even heavenly or supernatural, and easily outmatched any merely human resistance. The impending conflict is described as a confrontation between two ages, or realms, or forms of rule: the old age dominated by evil, suffering, and violence contrasted with the new age of God's reign marked by life with God. God's campaign of liberation, the invasion of the old order by the new, was marked by tribulations of various sorts. These represented the last-ditch effort of resistance by the powers and principalities but were also the means by which YHWH removed the power of sin from among the faithful. Tribulation was tantamount to testing, and testing was meant to remove that which was impure. In other words, tribulation was linked with liberation.

As we noted in regard to the Jubilee legislation in Leviticus 25, an old form of life (one marked by the power of sin and death and a communal life in disarray) must pass away for a new one to emerge; purgation/conversion was constitutive of the new world. Likewise, through a brief survey, it will

---

36. For this argument, see, for example, Dale C. Allison Jr., *The End of the Ages Has Come: An Early Interpretation of the Passion and Resurrection of Jesus* (Philadelphia: Fortress, 1985).

37. See, for example, the so-called Isaiah Apocalypse, Isa. 25:6-10.

become clear that the death (and resurrection) of Jesus Christ should be understood as an apocalyptic event: a revelation of God's conflict with the powers and principalities for the purpose of establishing Jubilee justice and a humanity set at liberty.

The Tribulations of the Son of Man

In the flow of the gospel narratives, the entwining of kingdom and cross is displayed in a variety of ways. Among them is Jesus's anticipation that his life will culminate in his being "lifted up" (cf. John 3:14; 8:28; 12:32), his being handed over to suffer by means of the cross. In the Synoptic Gospels, Jesus's first anticipation of a rejection that leads to death occurs on the heels of the disciples' confession of the messianic status of Jesus:

> Jesus went on with his disciples to the villages of Caesarea Philippi; and on the way he asked his disciples, "Who do people say that I am?" And they answered him, "John the Baptist; and others, Elijah; and still others, one of the prophets." He asked them, "But who do you say that I am?" Peter answered him, "You are the Messiah." And he sternly ordered them not to tell anyone about him. Then he began to teach them that the Son of Man must undergo great suffering, and be rejected by the elders, the chief priests, and the scribes, and be killed, and after three days rise again. (Mark 8:27-31)

This is the first of three predictions in the Gospel of Mark of Jesus's impending passion (cf. 9:31; 10:33-34). As Marcus notes, all the predictions share a similar structure: "(a) a reference to the Son of Man, (b) a reference to those who will be responsible for his death, (c) a prophecy of his death, and (d) a prophecy of his resurrection 'after three days.'"[38] The final prediction, in chapter 10, fills out Jesus's impending ordeal by noting the nature of his sufferings and the fact that he would be executed by the gentiles (cf. 10:33-34).

The appearance of the apocalyptic figure of the "Son of Man" on the lips of Jesus immediately places the events of his suffering in an apocalyptic context. All four Gospels are remarkably consistent on this fact: Jesus's predictions of suffering all feature the self-designation "Son of Man."[39]

---

38. Joel Marcus, *Mark 8-16: A New Translation with Introduction and Commentary* (New York: Doubleday, 2009), 604.

39. Cf. Matt. 16:13-23; 17:22-23; 20:17-19, 28; 26:2, 24; Mark 8:31; 9:12, 31; 10:33-34, 45; Luke 9:21-22, 44; 18:31-33; John 3:14; 8:28; 12:23-34.

Jesus's allusion to this figure gives us an important clue as to the meaning and significance of his death.

As we described in chapter 3, the Son of Man was a figure discussed in the apocalyptic texts 1 Enoch and 4 Ezra, and especially in Daniel 7. As recounted in Daniel's vision, the Son of Man would appear on the Day of YHWH "with the clouds of heaven," a reference to a theophanic appearing of God indicating the arrival of the Great King and Judge. In Daniel's vision, the appearance of YHWH, the Ancient of Days, marks the final liberation of the people of God from demonic powers that have subjected the people to suffering (cf. Dan. 7:25). In typical apocalyptic style, the demonic powers are also identified with political actors and cosmic powers. In Daniel 7:13-14, the Son of Man is given "glory and kingship," becoming a co-regent with YHWH in the unfolding of God's Jubilee reign. His appearing signifies "the great change of the ages, inaugurating the judgement and the new aeon."[40] In other words, the appearing of the Son of Man in the apocalyptic tradition signified the final great conflict between God and the powers and principalities, a conflict whose denouement included the judgment and overthrow of the powers of sin, death, and evil, and the simultaneous liberation of the people of God.

Why must the "Son of Man," who is depicted as a kingly figure who will inherit the kingdom of God, serving as God's co-regent, suffer? Why does Jesus now associate this figure with suffering? What is the meaning of this? The answer of the gospel witness is that Jesus's death and resurrection are key to the unfolding apocalyptic conflict between God and the powers that oppose God.

Reflecting a large body of historical Jesus scholarship, Brant Pitre argues that "Jesus understood his own imminent death in eschatological terms, as part of the long-expected and much-dreaded time of tribulation."[41] Pitre contends, in effect, for an "eschatological doctrine of atonement"[42] in which the sins of Israel and humanity are borne and borne away by YHWH's anointed. In keeping with our focus on the reign of God and the apocalyptic context of Jesus's passion, the argument we are developing here follows a similar trajectory, though we will emphasize the cosmic

---

40. Sigmund Mowinckel, *He That Cometh: The Messiah Concept in the Old Testament and Later Judaism* (Grand Rapids: Eerdmans, 2005), 389.

41. Brant Pitre, *Jesus, the Tribulation, and the End of the Exile: Restoration Eschatology and the Origin of the Atonement* (Grand Rapids: Baker Academic, 2005), 382.

42. Pitre, *Jesus, the Tribulation*, 507.

conflict between God and the powers as the major theme within which a qualified understanding of atonement can be said to occur. In other words, Jesus's death and resurrection is the concrete historical expression of God's overthrow of the powers and principalities. Through his death and resurrection he overcomes "the one who has the power of death, that is, the devil, and free[s] those who all their lives were held in slavery by the fear of death" (Heb. 2:14-15).[43]

Gethsemane

The trials and sufferings of the Son of Man can be said to begin from his birth. As the infancy narratives of the Gospels of Matthew and Luke are eager to show, as one who is from among the powerless and dispossessed, Jesus is placed in a situation of vulnerability from the very beginning.[44] The temptation accounts in the Gospels, as well as the various sayings predicting the impending execution of the Son of Man, build on the themes of vulnerability, rejection, and suffering found already in the beginning of the Gospels.[45] A number of scholars have pointed to the Gethsemane episode as especially illustrative of the apocalyptic context of Jesus's suffering.

In the flow of the synoptic narratives, the episode functions as a kind of "opening scene" of the "definitive apocalyptic confrontation."[46] In the Gospel of John, though there is no parallel Gethsemane scene, descriptions of Jesus afflicted by a troubled spirit function in a similar fashion,[47] and the striking description in the book of Hebrews that "in the days of his flesh, Jesus offered up prayers and supplications, with loud cries and tears, to the

43. Though we will return to this later, it is here that the cultic language of atonement finds an appropriate outlet. As an act aimed against the powers of sin and death, Jesus's death (and resurrection) can be understood as an event of expiation wherein sin and death are purged and humanity is released from the power of sin and death and translated into a new reality.

44. Cf. Matt 2:1-23; Luke 2:1-7.

45. Cf. Matt. 4:1-11; 16:13-23; 17:22-23; 20:17-19, 28; 26:2, 24; Mark 1:12-13; 8:31; 9:12, 31; 10:33-34, 45; Luke 4:1-13; 9:21-22, 44; 18:31-33; John 3:14; 8:28; 12:23-34.

46. Rutledge, *The Crucifixion*, 373. In similar language, Barth notes that "In this story there is already compressed the whole happening of Good Friday to the extent that it already speaks of a passion of Jesus, but of a passion which has to do strictly with the establishment of His definitive willingness for the real passion which comes upon Him immediately after. In this respect the story forms the turning-point between the two parts of the whole Gospel record." Karl Barth, *Church Dogmatics* IV/1 (Edinburgh: T&T Clark, 1956), 264.

47. Cf. John 11:33-35, 38; 12:27-28a; 18:11.

one who was able to save him from death" (5:7) also echoes the Gethsemane episode. The most unflinching description of the Gethsemane scene can be found in Mark's Gospel:

> They went to a place called Gethsemane; and he said to his disciples, "Sit here while I pray." He took with him Peter and James and John, and began to be distressed and agitated. And he said to them, "I am deeply grieved, even to death; remain here, and keep awake." And going a little farther, he threw himself on the ground and prayed that, if it were possible, the hour might pass from him. He said, "Abba, Father, for you all things are possible; remove this cup from me; yet, not what I want, but what you want." He came and found them sleeping; and he said to Peter, "Simon, are you asleep? Could you not keep awake one hour? Keep awake and pray that you may not come into the time of trial; the spirit indeed is willing, but the flesh is weak." And again he went away and prayed, saying the same words. And once more he came and found them sleeping, for their eyes were very heavy; and they did not know what to say to him. He came a third time and said to them, "Are you still sleeping and taking your rest? Enough! The hour has come; the Son of Man is betrayed into the hands of sinners. Get up, let us be going. See, my betrayer is at hand." (Mark 14:32-42)

In this remarkable account, Jesus the servant of YHWH is shown to struggle with the terrible fate which he has already predicted for himself on a number of occasions. Several commentators have noted that one of the key differences between Mark's account and those found in Matthew and Luke is that the latter writers seem to soften the theme of struggle depicted so graphically in Mark.[48]

Literary development aside, the scene is saturated with apocalyptic motifs. First, we should call attention to the preceding pericope, which points to Peter's impending denial of Jesus, where several allusions to the prophet Zechariah appear. Jesus and the disciples are said to make their way to the Mount of Olives, which Zechariah depicted as the point of departure for God's eschatological overthrow of the powers (Zech. 14:4).[49] Entwined

48. The most comprehensive discussion of this difference can be found in Raymond E. Brown, *The Death of the Messiah: From Gethsemane to the Grave*, 2 vols. (New York: Doubleday, 1994), 1:110-236.

49. I am following the argument of Brant Pitre here. See his *Jesus, the Tribulation*, 480-81. See also Joel Marcus, *The Way of the Lord: Christological Exegesis of the Old Testament in the Gospel of Mark* (London: T&T Clark International, 1992), 154-59.

with this is a direct reference to Zechariah 13:7, which speaks of the affliction of God's anointed that will be instrumental in God's reclamation of the faithful.

This apocalyptic and eschatological context is not abandoned when Jesus and his disciples enter Gethsemane. Rather, apocalyptic motifs also deeply shape the Gethsemane scene, the most significant of which are the repeated use of the Greek terms *peirasmos* (translated as "testing," "trial," or "tribulation") and *hōra* (translated as "hour"), and the image of the "cup." In the context of Mark's Gospel, the term "trial" or "tribulation" carries apocalyptic connotations, referring to the final eschatological trial. Marcus notes that "*peirasmos*, especially in conjunction with *hora* ('hour'14:35, 41), is a technical term,"[50] referring to the final eschatological testing that is meant to come upon humanity. In fact, all the struggles recounted in this scene—his terror at the prospect of what faces him (Mark 14:34);[51] his falling to the ground (14:35);[52] his prayer that the "cup," also an allusion to eschatological judgment, be taken from him (14:36);[53] the growing sense that he will face the impending sufferings alone (14:37–41); and the "increasing frenzy"[54] at the end of the scene (14:41–42)—echo apocalyptic and eschatological themes, pointing in one inexorable direction: the Son of Man is entering into and is *now* engaged in the final conflict with the powers of sin and death.

When one brings together the description of Jesus as "deeply grieved, even to death," with his request to "remove this cup from me," and his concluding statement, "the hour has come; the Son of Man is handed over into the hands of sinners," one is brought face-to-face with the mystery of the kingdom of God. Jesus is indeed asking if the divine will that God's Jubilee justice triumph over the forces of evil can occur without suffering. But God's answer is silence. Indeed, the Son of Man will be handed over to those who wish to do him harm.

The mystery at the heart of the gospel is clearly seen here: God's war for the liberation of humanity will not be waged with weapons or instruments that are normally associated with power. No. It is in the form of weakness and the compassionate self-offering of the Son of Man that God's righ-

---

50. Marcus, *Mark 8–16*, 988.
51. See Brown, *Death of the Messiah*, 1:153–57. See also Marcus, *Mark 8–16*, 975, 983–84.
52. See Marcus, *Mark 8–16*, 977.
53. See Brown, *The Death of the Messiah*, 1:168–72. See also Marcus, *Mark 8–16*, 985.
54. Marcus, *Mark 8–16*, 988. See also Brown, *Death of the Messiah*, 1:157–62, 167–68.

teousness and justice will ultimately triumph. But this will not be a path that leaves God unaffected. Rather, the passion of Jesus is the outworking of the cost of God's struggle with the powers of sin and death. Scripture refers to Jesus's passion as a mutual surrender of the Son, one in which both Father (cf. Rom. 8:32) and Son (cf. Gal. 2:20) actively participate. In this mutual surrender of the Son of God, God reveals that God is willing to hazard death to become and remain the God of the godforsaken, the condemned, and the cursed.[55] "In giving up the Son he gives 'everything' and 'nothing' can separate us from him."[56] Furthermore, the passion reveals that God's weakness is more powerful than the energies and strategies of the powers and principalities; the former issues in life, while the latter can only issue in death.

The book of Hebrews describes Jesus's experience here and his prayer on Golgotha as a single history of faithfulness. Through his trials he "learned obedience" (5:8); he was made "perfect through sufferings" (2:10). Though these and other texts have been used to justify various forms of masochism and oppression—especially gendered forms[57]—both within the church and beyond, they need not be.[58] Rather, they refer to the fullness of Jesus's active faithful commitment to God's will, to a whole life lived in total faithfulness to God's Jubilee vision, a willingness, and even more, a determination to tread the path of faithfulness even in the face of death. In face of the death-dealing powers, Jesus's faithfulness is declared to be "life giving" because it is representative. It is representative because it is done on behalf

---

55. "The Father who sends his Son through all the abysses and hells of God-forsakenness, of the divine curse and final judgment is, in his Son, everywhere with those who are his own; he has become universally present." Jürgen Moltmann, *The Trinity and the Kingdom: The Doctrine of God* (Minneapolis: Fortress, 1993), 82.

56. Moltmann, *Trinity and the Kingdom*, 82.

57. For a brief discussion of some of the broad Enlightenment and modern critiques of the cross, see Vítor Westhelle, *The Scandalous God: The Use and Abuse of the Cross* (Minneapolis: Fortress, 2006), 60-75. Some of the most significant and searching criticisms along this line have come from feminist theologians. For a discussion of this theme, see Arnfríður Guðmundsdóttir, *Meeting God on the Cross: Christ, the Cross, and the Feminist Critique* (Oxford: Oxford University Press, 2010), 27-55, and Lisa Isherwood, *Introducing Feminist Christologies* (Sheffield: Sheffield Academic Press, 2001), 87-102.

58. For a discussion of recent feminist retrievals of "active suffering" as an expression of divine solidarity meant to affirm human beings caught in suffering, while also energizing the same for resistance in the face of meaningless or unjust suffering, see Elizabeth A. Webb, "Power in Weakness: Feminist Reclamations of the Suffering of Christ," in *Religious Studies Review* 38, no. 4 (December 2012): 199-205.

of others in such a way as to include them rather than to exclude them. A substitute takes the place of another, excluding them from a given action, while a representative acts on behalf of another so as to include them in the action.[59] The faithfulness of Jesus, which ultimately leads to his death, is an act of profound friendship because it is done on behalf of others and brings life to others.[60] Jesus takes his path neither for God nor for himself alone, but so that "he might destroy the one who has the power of death, that is, the devil, and free those who all their lives were held in slavery by the fear of death" (Heb. 2:14-15).

The Trial

In the characteristic apocalyptic imagery already discussed, the Gethsemane scene ends with Jesus's dual declarations, "The hour has come" and "the Son of Man is turned over to the hands of sinners" (Mark 14:41).[61] This is not merely an observation by Jesus regarding those who have come to arrest him. To the contrary, it is a broader statement about Jesus's impending trial and eventual execution. As such, it marks "a striking reversal of Dan. 7:13-14, in which the 'one like a son of man' is 'given dominion and glory and kingship, that all peoples, nations, and languages should serve him,' including the evil nations that have oppressed Israel."[62] Rather than the nations being handed over to the Son of Man for judgment, the reverse has happened. The trial scenes across all four Gospels are consistent in this regard, evoking the image of the Son of Man from Daniel 7 in this grotesque and inverted form. It must be said, though, that at the same time, there is a rather clear sense in the gospel accounts that there are in fact two trials occurring.

On the one hand, Jesus is on trial. Here the paradox could not be more striking: God's anointed co-regent, the Son of Man, whom Daniel 7 depicts as bringing the divine rectification of all injustice, has been placed into the hands of the unjust. He will be rejected, condemned to death, mocked,

---

59. For a detailed discussion of the differences between "substitution" and "representative," see Darrin W. Snyder Belousek, *Atonement, Justice, and Peace: The Message of the Cross and the Mission of the Church* (Grand Rapids: Eerdmans, 2012), 265-91.

60. See Deanna A. Thompson, *Crossing the Divide: Luther, Feminism, and the Cross* (Minneapolis: Fortress, 2004), 155-61.

61. In the second clause, I am following Marcus's translation. See Marcus, *Mark 8-16*, 981, 989-90.

62. Marcus, *Mark 8-16*, 989.

spat upon, tortured, and executed by the Romans (cf. Mark 10:32-34). He will, in other words, take the visage of the suffering servant of Isaiah,[63] the righteous one upon whom falls an undeserved death. Put bluntly, the death of the so-called Son of Man will be "like so many people before and after him."[64] Of course, the deeper meaning of this event is yet to be revealed in the light of the resurrection of this crucified one, where the entwining of the apocalyptic (and royal) Son of Man with the royal suffering servant in the fate and identity of Jesus tells us that the reign of God that he has proclaimed is to be understood as an act of profound self-giving (cf. Mark 10:45), and as God's unabashed identification with the tortured, the excluded, and the damned.

Nowhere is this made clearer than in one of the most dramatic scenes found in the Gospel of John. In the fifth act of Jesus's trial as recounted by John, after the innocent Jesus has been scourged and mocked, and donning a purple robe and crown of thorns, he is brought out by Pilate and presented to the crowd with the acclamation: "Here is the man!" (John 19:5), an oblique reference to Jesus's identity as the Son of Man.[65] In the sharpest possible contrast with Daniel 7, where the Son of Man is presented before the royal throne of God and given "dominion and glory and kingship" (Dan. 7:14), we see here a broken, tortured human being. The man of sorrows. Any and all pretense to royalty, as we usually understand it, is stripped away and the visage of an innocent, poor, dark-skinned man—one subjected to the violence of the state and the powers that be—is set before us as the apocalypse of God's reign. Our conceptions of God, power, rule, and authority are all overturned. God is not found among the politically or religiously powerful, but among the victims of the powerful. God exercises God's reign in weakness.

On the other hand, however, Pilate, the religious authorities, and the powers that they represent are also on trial. In the synoptic accounts of Jesus's trial, this fact is signified by Jesus's answer to the question of the chief

---

63. And not only the visage of the suffering servant. As Joel Marcus has pointed out, the figures of the righteous sufferer in the psalms and the humble king in Zech. 9–14 are also important intertextual allusions at work in Mark. See Marcus, *Way of the Lord*, 153-98.

64. Sobrino, *Jesus the Liberator*, 209.

65. "He [Pilate] hits the truth accidentally (as Caiaphas did, 11.50-2). Jesus, in his complete humiliation, is set forth as the heavenly Man (and this is the essence of John's teaching about the Son of Man)." C. K. Barrett, *The Gospel according to St. John* (London: SPCK, 1975), 450.

priest: "Are you the Messiah, the Son of the Blessed One?" (Mark 14:61). The answer given in Mark's account is as follows:

> "I am; and
> 'you will see the Son of Man
> seated at the right hand of the Power,'
> and 'coming with the clouds of heaven.'" (Mark 14:62)

This saying—one that combines portions of Psalm 110, a royal psalm, with Daniel 7—indicates that, contrary to appearances, God's justice will be done to the powers arrayed against him; that "Jesus' condemnation is not the last word in the story."[66] The image of the Son of Man descending with the clouds of heaven is a direct reference to the ushering in of God's reign, an event that, counter to all appearances, the gospel witness understands to be unfolding right in the midst of the unjust condemnation of Jesus. In other words, "in, with, and under" (to borrow the Lutheran sacramental phrasing) the tragic and paradoxical inversion of the image of the royal Son of Man that Jesus's trial performs, there is another paradox: the powers themselves are being judged.

This same double paradox is also seen in John's account of Jesus before Pilate. In the second scene, Pilate questions Jesus regarding his status as a king, a status that the religious authorities had used as a basis for denouncing Jesus to the Roman authorities. The scene unfolds as follows:

> Then Pilate entered the headquarters again, summoned Jesus, and asked him, "Are you the King of the Jews?" Jesus answered, "Do you ask this on your own, or did others tell you about me?" Pilate replied, "I am not a Jew, am I? Your own nation and the chief priests have handed you over to me. What have you done?" Jesus answered, "My kingdom is not from this world. If my kingdom were from this world, my followers would be fighting to keep me from being handed over to the Jews. But as it is, my kingdom is not from here." Pilate asked him, "So you are a king?" Jesus answered, "You say that I am a king. For this I was born, and for this I came into the world, to testify to the truth. Everyone who belongs to the truth listens to my voice." Pilate asked him, "What is truth?" (John 18:33–38)

Jesus's first response to Pilate has often been understood to mean that Jesus's kingdom is spiritual, and thus otherworldly. But this is an unfortunate

66. Marcus, *Way of the Lord*, 167.

misreading. What is at issue here is not whether or not the kingdom that Jesus has preached and embodied *is present in this world*, but whether or not *it functions like the kingdoms of this world*.[67] As we noted in our discussion of YHWH's kingship as seen in the psalms, the prophets, and the apocalyptic traditions, at issue was the difference between the *way* in which God rules and the *way* that the kings and emperors of the world (and the cosmic powers behind them) exercise their power. God's way is fundamentally a just and compassionate way, a movement that sides with, and is found (almost exclusively) among, the lowly. In contrast, the powers and principalities traffic in violence and death.

In a similar fashion, Jesus's declaration that his kingdom is "not of this world" is not meant to displace God's reign from this world. To the contrary, it is a revelation that the reign of God proclaimed and embodied in Jesus *takes a path and exercises a power that is fundamentally different from this world*. The first fruit of this declaration is to create a distinction, or contrast. The contrast is between the reign of God embodied in Jesus—the servant of the poor and the dispossessed who proclaims and performs God's Jubilee justice—and the injustice and violence visited upon Jesus and embodied in the Roman prefect. This is itself an event of revelation, an initial unmasking of the violent and illegitimate rule of the powers of death represented by Jesus's accusers. His death brings into "clear public view the violence and injustice of the reigning powers."[68] As Moltmann puts it, "*Jesus, the Son of Man*, means . . . *Ecce Homo*; behold the true man in an inhuman world. *Jesus the Son of Man* also means at one and the same time: *Ecce Deus*: behold the true God in a world of evil spirits and false gods."[69] The world of violence, a world ordered by the powers of sin and death—represented by the political and religious powers and elite—has rejected the compassionate justice of God's Jubilee reign. In so doing, it has shown the true depths of its love affair with death. It is an inhuman world, one that is destined to collapse in on itself as the final outcome of

---

67. "It is not a question of *whether* Jesus' kingship exists in this world but of *how* it exists; not a certification that the interests of Jesus' kingdom are 'otherworldly' but a declaration that his kingship has its source outside this world and so is established by methods other than those of this world." Rensberger, *Johannine Faith*, 97.

68. Darby Kathleen Ray, "A Praxis of Atonement: Confounding Evil through Cunning and Compassion," *Religious Studies and Theology* 18, no. 1 (June 1999): 43.

69. Jürgen Moltmann, "The Passion of the Son of Man and His Call to Follow Him," in *Meditations on the Passion: Two Meditations on Mark 8:31–38*, by Johann-Baptist Metz and Jürgen Moltmann, trans. Edmund Colledge (Eugene, OR: Wipf & Stock, 2012), 10.

the trial of Jesus makes clear, where the instruments of death and violence ultimately lead to the undoing of the power of death (cf. Col. 2:14b–15).

Passion Portents

As a final, brief observation, the death of Jesus on the cross is also associated with more conventional signs of apocalyptic tribulation. These other apocalyptic motifs come in the form of cataclysmic events or signs that are associated with Jesus's suffering and death. The book of Matthew gives the most expansive description of these occurrences:

> From noon on, darkness came over the whole land until three in the afternoon. . . . Then Jesus cried again with a loud voice and breathed his last. At that moment the curtain of the temple was torn in two, from top to bottom. The earth shook, and the rocks were split. The tombs also were opened, and many bodies of the saints who had fallen asleep were raised. After his resurrection they came out of the tombs and entered the holy city and appeared to many. Now when the centurion and those with him, who were keeping watch over Jesus, saw the earthquake and what took place, they were terrified and said, "Truly this man was God's Son!" (Matt. 27:45, 50–54)

The passage "makes plain the eschatological meaning of the crucifixion,"[70] through the various apocalyptic signs reported. The darkness that covers "the whole land" is especially evocative of Amos 8:9–10, a text that describes the onslaught of the Day of the Lord. As one commentator has noted: "The parallel between Amos 8:9–10 and Matt. 27:45 is substantial: darkness falls in both; in both that darkness is at noon; and whereas there is mourning as for 'an only son' or 'a beloved one' in Amos, Jesus is, in Matthew, God's beloved Son (cf. 3:17; 12:18; 17:5), and he is confessed to be God's Son precisely at the crucifixion itself (27:54)."[71] Additionally, the rending of the temple veil, the earthquake, resurrection occurrences, and the acclamation by a gentile of God's anointed are all elements that can

70. W. D. Davies and Dale C. Allison Jr., *The Gospel according to Saint Matthew*, vol. 3 (Edinburgh: T&T Clark, 1997), 628.

71. Dale C. Allison Jr., *Studies in Matthew: Interpretation Past and Present* (Grand Rapids: Baker Academic, 2005), 80–81.

be found in expectations for the coming Day of the Lord, a day filled with both judgment and new life.[72]

The point, in keeping with our overall theme, is that the apocalyptic conflict between the reign of God and the powers of sin and death that resist God that we have seen in the life and ministry of Jesus is also characteristic of Jesus's final fate. The death of Jesus on the cross belongs alongside the events of exorcism and healing as an event of apocalyptic significance.

GOD OF THE OPPRESSED

The passion of Jesus was the climax of the confrontation of God's Jubilee reign against the reign of the powers of sin and death. In this light, Jesus's death is but an extension of his life. Both represent a scandalous divine incursion into the territory of violence and death to set free the captives. In this incursion, God reveals the depth and extent of God's identification with those who are hounded by the powers that organize our world. In the words of James Cone: "By electing Israelite slaves as the people of God and by becoming the Oppressed One in Jesus Christ, the human race is made to understand that God is known where human beings experience humiliation and suffering."[73] Humanity is made to know that "The Jesus story is the poor person's story, because God in Christ becomes poor and weak in order that the oppressed might become liberated from poverty and powerlessness."[74] In keeping with the witness of the Torah, the prophets, and the apocalyptic writings, in Jesus, God is the God of the oppressed.

An Innocent Man Was Lynched

The death of Jesus was accompanied by signs and portents that highlight its apocalyptic significance and cosmic uniqueness. And yet, this poor man, whose life was driven by a commitment to God's compassionate justice, was also killed, "like so many people before him and after him. . . . In this sense there is nothing mysterious in Jesus' death, because it is a frequent

---

72. See Brown, *Death of the Messiah*, 2:1097–1152, and Allison, *End of the Ages*, 40–50.
73. Cone, *Black Theology of Liberation*, 67.
74. James H. Cone, *God of the Oppressed*, rev. ed. (Maryknoll, NY: Orbis, 1997), 74.

occurrence."[75] His sufferings are consonant with the sufferings of the poor, the oppressed, and the disinherited; those who cannot afford to defend themselves, those who find both legal and extralegal violence aimed at their body, their person, and their community. Throughout his life Jesus had identified himself with the poor, with those considered traitors to their people, with women of any station in life, with the diseased and afflicted, with children and the differently abled. In his final tribulations, he is identified with criminals (whether guilty or not) and especially with all those who are unjustly persecuted. On this account, it is important to note that though multiple trials were convened in an attempt to find a legal basis for executing him, Jesus was in effect, lynched.

Speaking about the racial regime in the United States, and specifically about the racial persecution of African Americans, James Cone observes that "Lynching was an extra-legal punishment sanctioned by the community."[76] In the modern West, the symbolic order—or the regnant powers and principalities of the cultural, social, political order—configures the able-bodied, white, heterosexual, male citizen, usually of some means (and almost always Christian) in positions of privilege; while the differently abled, persons of color, women, the poor (and especially the undocumented or underdocumented poor), LGBTQIA2S+ persons, and non-Christians are placed on the margins of the social order. From the perspective of this symbolic order, which continues to shape much of contemporary society, Jesus's passion experience is radically similar to the kind of death-dealing control, exploitation, torture, and dehumanization that those on the bottom of the social order of our age continue to experience. The passion of Jesus "is the revelation of the freedom of God, taking upon himself the totality of human oppression."[77] As such, it is an affirmation of the humanity of those society and the social order push to the margins.

Thus, it can be said that from a historical point of view, Jesus was poor, he was an immigrant from a questionable region (Galilee), and he had questionable paternity. However, from within the perspective of the symbolic order of our contemporary world (i.e., white supremacy and racial capitalism), we must add to this description that Jesus is also like the undocumented migrant hounded by legal regimes who question his very humanity. He is like the person of color whose body has been the object

---

75. Sobrino, *Jesus the Liberator*, 209.
76. James H. Cone, *The Cross and the Lynching Tree* (Maryknoll, NY: Orbis, 2011), 3.
77. Cone, *Black Theology of Liberation*, 124–25.

of unjust labor extraction and sexual predation, whose culture has either been eradicated or appropriated for economic gain, and whose person has been associated with animality and criminality. He is like the many women who continue to labor under patriarchal regimes, where their exploitation is virtually guaranteed, their full humanity denied, and access to a flourishing life blocked. He is like the LGBTQIA2S+ person who is styled and attacked as diseased, disordered, and a contagion to be feared, shunned, mocked, and persecuted. He is, in other words, like every person who is daily assailed in their very humanity, and not just because he voluntarily aligns himself with outsiders and those who suffer. Rather, it is because he allows himself to be driven into the same godforsaken spaces where the oppressed are *forced* to live on a daily basis; he allows himself to be made subject to the same kind of injustice and dehumanization—whether legal or extralegal—with which much of humanity is involuntarily made to deal moment by moment.[78]

The Dehumanization of the Cross

Nowhere is God's identification with the lowly seen more clearly than in a consideration of the mechanism used to put Jesus to death. From both a historical and theological perspective, the cross "means human beings rejecting human beings. It is human beings abandoning human beings. It shows how human beings, in the grip of demonic powers, are inflicting

---

78. Jon Sobrino develops this insight under the broad heading of "the poor": "On the one side are those who groan under some type of basic need in the tradition of Isaiah 61:1ff. So the poor are those who hunger and thirst, who go naked, strangers, the sick, those in prison, those who mourn, those weighed down by a real burden (Luke 6:20-21; Matt. 25:25ff.). In this sense, the poor are those who live bent (*anawin*) under the weight of a burden—which Jesus often interpreted as oppression—those for whom life and survival is a hard task. In modern parlance, we could call these the *economic* poor, in the sense that the *oikos* (the hearth, the home, the symbol of what is basic and primary in life) is in grave danger, and that they are thereby denied the minimum of life.

"On the other side, the poor are those despised by the ruling society, those considered sinners, the publicans, the prostitutes (Mark 2:16; Matt. 11:19; 21:23; Luke 15:1ff.), the simple-minded, the little ones, the least (Matt. 11:25; Mark 9:36ff., Matt. 10:42; 18:10-14; 25:40-45), those who carry out despised tasks (Matt. 12:31; Luke 18:11). In this sense, the poor are the marginalized, those 'whose religious ignorance and moral behavior closed, in the conviction of the time, the gate leading to salvation for them.' These could be called the *sociological* poor, in the sense that being a *socium* (the symbol of basic interhuman relationships) is denied them, and with this, the minimum of dignity." Sobrino, *Jesus the Liberator*, 80.

injustice on each other, tearing each other apart, destroying each other."[79] The cross was by far one of the most diabolical instruments of torture and execution ever devised. An obscenity against any human being, crucifixion was once described by Origen as "*mors turpissima crucis* ('the utterly vile death of the cross).'"[80] Generally thought to have arisen among the Persians,[81] it came to be widely used in the Roman Empire and represented the most severe penalty that could be bestowed by the state, one usually reserved for slaves, dangerous criminals, and political revolutionaries.[82]

Crucifixion functioned in the Greco-Roman world as a legal means to exclude and execute those the Roman authorities deemed inhuman or unfit for the social order. "It was a religious-political punishment, with the emphasis falling on the political side."[83] Fleming Rutledge's observation here is worth quoting at length: "Crucifixion as a means of execution in the Roman Empire had *as its express purpose* the elimination of victims from consideration as members of the human race. It cannot be said too strongly: that was its function. It was meant to indicate to all who might be toying with subversive ideas that crucified persons were *not of the same species* as either the executioners or the spectators and were therefore not only expendable but also deserving of ritualized extermination."[84] In the ancient world, because the political and the religious were bound together, the cross did indeed carry religious connotations, but not as an object of devotion. Rather, it was a political symbol of power—meant to illustrate and make plain Roman might (and by extension, Roman claims to divine sanction)[85] and what happens to those who question the same.

Such a horrific form of execution was retained, even by peoples who were themselves shocked at the cruelty of crucifixion, because it was an especially potent deterrent.[86] As noted above, crucifixion was a kind of public "ritualized extermination." The actual hanging of the victim on the

---

79. C. S. Song, *Jesus, the Crucified People* (Minneapolis: Fortress, 1996), 99.

80. Martin Hengel, *Crucifixion in the Ancient World and the Folly of the Message of the Cross* (Philadelphia: Fortress, 1977), xi. See also Rutledge, *The Crucifixion*, 93–96.

81. See Hengel, *Crucifixion*, 22.

82. See Hengel, *Crucifixion*, 39–63.

83. Hengel, *Crucifixion*, 46.

84. Rutledge, *The Crucifixion*, 92.

85. For a historical development of these claims, see Allen Brent, *A Political History of Christianity* (Edinburgh: T&T Clark, 2009), 78–128.

86. "The chief reason for its use was its allegedly supreme efficacy as a deterrent; it was, of course, carried out publicly. As a rule the crucified man was regarded as a criminal who was receiving just and necessary punishment. There was doubtless a fear that to give

wooden beams was the final stage in a longer drama of dehumanization. Flogging, jeering, and other physical and psychological torment were supposed to accompany the event, including having the victim paraded through the streets prior to their execution.[87] Taunting the victim while on the cross was also a standard component of crucifixion. The cumulative effect was to push the victim outside the boundaries of acceptability. The fact that it was an instrument not only of the state, but one that elicited, even required, the cooperation of average people as onlookers and mockers, points to its function as a policing mechanism and further highlights its parallels with the phenomenon of lynching discussed above. The person being executed was pronounced, and was supposed to be interpreted as, *accursed* (cf. Gal. 3:13; Deut. 21:22–23). The process was meant to literally strip the victim of their status as a human being.

This is the situation and posture into which God enters. In the well-known words of Bonhoeffer, "God consents to be pushed out of the world and onto the cross; God is weak and powerless in the world and in precisely this way, and only so, is at our side and helps us."[88] In the crucified Jesus, God enters into the furthest reaches of the dehumanized, the realm of sin and death par excellence. Jesus becomes a criminal, accursed (cf. Gal. 3:13; Deut. 21:22–23), identified with sin itself (2 Cor. 5:21), demonstrating unequivocally that no one and nothing is beyond God's reach.

By reaching into the realm of the godless or the accursed in the form of one who was accursed, in Jesus God overturns the structures that maintain the *cordon sanitaire* between that which is acceptable and that which is not. God, the Creator and source of life, allows Godself to be identified with the dehumanized *not* to underwrite their dehumanization, but rather to call into question every and all forms of dehumanization. The author and sustainer of life would rather hazard death by coming alongside those who suffer to suffer with them than allow the enslavement, disfigurement, and destruction of human beings by nefarious powers to go unchallenged.

In the state-sanctioned murder of Jesus, the critique is clear: the powers that determine what is legitimate, acceptable, and pure (and conversely, what is not) are shown to be fundamentally unjust and capable only of

---

up this form of execution might undermine the authority of the state and existing law and order." Hengel, *Crucifixion*, 87.

87. "It included a flogging beforehand, and the victim often carried the beam to the place of execution, where he was nailed to it with outstretched arms, raised up and seated on a small wooden peg." Hengel, *Crucifixion*, 25.

88. Dietrich Bonhoeffer, *Letters and Papers from Prison* (Minneapolis: Fortress, 2010), 479.

dealing in death. Thus, God takes up the cause of the weak, the poor, the excluded, and the oppressed, to reveal the injustice at the heart of the world, for the purpose of delegitimizing the powers and principalities and overthrowing them.

God Crucified—the God of the Godforsaken

In the midst of this struggle and confrontation, God is not unaffected. In the Gospel of Mark, the nadir of Jesus's crucifixion is saturated with apocalyptic motifs. Ensconced in this climactic moment, Jesus, the Servant of YHWH, the one who has been faithful unto death, is displayed at his most vulnerable.

> When it was noon, darkness came over the whole land until three in the afternoon. At three o'clock Jesus cried out with a loud voice, "Eloi, Eloi, lema sabachthani?" which means, "My God, my God, why have you forsaken me?" When some of the bystanders heard it, they said, "Listen, he is calling for Elijah." And someone ran, filled a sponge with sour wine, put it on a stick, and gave it to him to drink, saying, "Wait, let us see whether Elijah will come to take him down." Then Jesus gave a loud cry and breathed his last. And the curtain of the temple was torn in two, from top to bottom. Now when the centurion, who stood facing him, saw that in this way he breathed his last, he said, "Truly this man was God's Son!" (Mark 15:33-39)

In the midst of a "cosmic darkness,"[89] Jesus cries out in desolation and abandonment. "My God, my God, why have you forsaken me?" (Mark 15:34). It is "perhaps the greatest blues line of all time,"[90] and is indicative of Jesus's identification with the human experience of divine abandonment in a world filled with crosses. Jesus's cry makes evident the truth that Jesus is "the brother and saviour of the condemned and the cursed."[91] Mark's account of the passion narrative, in particular, brings together a variety of traditions, including Daniel's Son of Man, the suffering king of Zechariah 9-14, the suffering servant of Isaiah 53, and the potent image of the righteous sufferer

89. Marcus, *Mark 8-16*, 1054.
90. Stanley Crouch, "Do the Afrocentric Hustle," in *The All-American Skin Game, or the Decoy of Race: The Long and the Short of It, 1990-1994*, by Stanley Crouch (New York: Pantheon Books, 1995), 44.
91. Jürgen Moltmann, *The Trinity and the Kingdom: The Doctrine of God* (Minneapolis: Fortress, 1993), 81.

found especially in Psalm 22, the text from which Jesus's cry of dereliction is drawn.[92] The cumulative effect is that Jesus is understood to be the Son of Man—the eschatological figure whose appearance is meant to mark the end of days, the judgment of the nations, and the coming new life—who takes up the posture of those upon whom judgment was meant to fall. The suffering of Jesus "is not just the prelude to God's eschatological victory but already in a sense *is* that victory."[93] The Day of the Lord has come; "The judgement predicted by the Prophets has fallen on Jesus."[94] Jesus—the Son of God—will bear the sin of the world, and bear it away.

But what is the meaning of the death of Jesus for God? Does the fact that the Son of God has entered into the human experience of divine abandonment in solidarity actually impinge on God? Is this only something that is experienced by the human Jesus? Is God actually affected by the death of Jesus, and not simply as an onlooker? Jürgen Moltmann—a key theologian who has wrestled with these questions since the middle of the twentieth century—offers a carefully nuanced yes to these questions, developing a Trinitarian theology of the cross. He writes,

> When the crucified Jesus is called the "image of the invisible God," the meaning is that *this* is God, and God is like *this*. God is not greater than he is in this humiliation. God is not more glorious than he is in this self-surrender. God is not more powerful than he is in this helplessness. God is not more divine than he is in this humanity. . . . The Christ event on the cross is a God event. And conversely, the God event takes place on the cross of the risen Christ. Here God has not just acted externally, in his unattainable glory and eternity. Here he has acted in himself and has gone on to suffer in himself. Here he himself is love with all his being.[95]

The Father and the Son participate in the event of the cross, each suffering, though in a differentiated fashion.

> In the forsakenness of the Son the Father also forsakes himself. In the surrender of the Son the Father also surrenders himself, though not in the

---

92. For an extensive discussion of these traditions and their role in Mark, see Marcus, *Way of the Lord*, 153–98.

93. Marcus, *Way of the Lord*, 196.

94. Marcus, *Mark 8–16*, 1062.

95. Jürgen Moltmann, *The Crucified God: The Cross of Christ as the Foundation and Criticism of Christian Theology* (Minneapolis: Fortress, 1993), 205.

same way. For Jesus suffers dying in forsakenness, but not death itself; for men can no longer "suffer" death, because suffering presupposes life. But the Father who abandons him and delivers him up suffers the death of the Son in the infinite grief of love. . . . The suffering and dying of the Son, forsaken by the Father, is a different kind of suffering from the suffering of the Father in the death of the Son. . . . The Son suffers dying, the Father suffers the death of the Son.[96]

Moltmann's point is to intensify and underline the fact that it is in the cross that we truly know God, and that the God we come to know is the crucified God and no other. The event of the cross, the abandonment and suffering of Jesus so graphically captured in the cry of dereliction, and the passion and pain of the Father rendered in the form of cosmic darkness establish the fact that God has indeed hazarded death to reclaim the universe for Godself.[97]

THE COSMIC CONFRONTATION

The act of solidarity that God has performed in the life and death of Jesus is nothing less than the apocalypse of the righteousness of God. The divine will that there should be a creation, and that such a creation should live in a flourishing and free relationship to its Creator, draws God into confrontation with that which oppresses and enslaves creation. The confrontation, however, occurs under the form of its opposite, as Jesus, the eschatological and royal Son of Man, is enthroned in and through the cross, by which he disarms "the rulers and authorities and made a public example of them, triumphing over them in it" (Col. 2:15).

The Apocalypse of the Righteousness of God

As we noted in chapter 3, the apocalyptic traditions conceived of the event of God's confrontation with the powers and principalities as a confrontation between different *ways* of being and ruling. The rulers of the earth, in keeping with the fact that they are enthralled to the powers of sin and death, rule through the logic of death dealing and fear. YHWH, however,

---

96. Moltmann, *The Crucified God*, 243.
97. See Moltmann, *Trinity and the Kingdom*, 82.

rules through the establishment of divine righteousness and justice, which, following the psalms, we have conceptualized along the lines of Jubilee. The appearing of God's Jubilee reign means the overthrow of the powers. Likewise, the life, death, and resurrection of Jesus should be seen as a confrontation of cosmic dimensions.

As we have detailed in our survey, the life and ministry of Jesus, and the events surrounding his death, should be understood as the apocalypse of God's Jubilee reign, an event of cosmic dimensions. The cosmic nature of the confrontation between God's reign and the powers of death is clearly portrayed in the teaching of Jesus, and his ministry of healing and exorcism, but it was not absent from the narrative descriptions of Jesus's crucifixion. Throughout the various Gospels, the passion narratives describe the story of Jesus's arrest, trial, and execution on a Roman cross not only as a historical event—pointing to the injustice of the powerful—but also as an apocalyptic event wherein God enters into the human situation at its most vulnerable. The purpose of this expression of solidarity is to liberate humankind from the powers and principalities of sin and death.

In his letter to the Romans, Paul describes this confrontation as the apocalypse of the righteousness of God. In the programmatic statement of the letter, Paul writes: "For I am not ashamed of the gospel; it is the power of God for salvation to everyone who has faith, to the Jew first and also to the Greek. For in it the righteousness of God is revealed through faith for faith, as it is written, 'The one who is righteous will live by faith'" (1:16-17). "The idea that God's 'righteousness' at this place is an expression of God's wrath or justice would be misleading."[98] To the contrary, the event of the cross and resurrection of Jesus—an event Paul describes as a "revelation" or apocalypse—is the apocalyptic divine expression and disclosure of God's faithfulness to creation; it is God's righteousness, or *faithfulness* to the divine decision that creation should live, and should live in flourishing fellowship with its Creator.[99] This is why Paul links the appearance of God's righteousness with salvation.

It is apposite here for us to remember that in the biblical context, "righteousness" is not an abstract quality. As Ernst Käsemann points out, "From the outset it will be noticed that in the field of the Old Testament and of

---

98. Arland J. Hultgren, *Paul's Letter to the Romans: A Commentary* (Grand Rapids: Eerdmans, 2011), 75.

99. See Ernst Käsemann, *Commentary on Romans*, trans. Geoffrey W. Bromiley (Grand Rapids: Eerdmans, 1980), 21-32.

Judaism in general, righteousness does not convey primarily the sense of a personal, ethical quality, but of a relationship; originally signifying trustworthiness in regard to the community, it came to mean the rehabilitated standing of a member of a community who had been acquitted of an offense against it."[100] Thus, God's righteousness does not refer to an abstract quality that God possesses but denotes a relationship. It refers, in other words, to God's faithfulness, first to Godself and God's determination to be Creator, and then to the creature that God has determined should live, and live in a flourishing fashion in fellowship with God and creation as a whole.[101] Thus, the apocalypse of God's righteousness that occurs in the cross (and resurrection) is the demonstrative and effective act whereby God reveals God's own determination that creation should have life in fellowship with God, even in the face of death and the human collusion with death, which is called sin. God willingly hazards death to ensure that this relationship not only remains but can and will be made whole.

The Doxa *of the Kingdom—the Enthronement of the King*

In Jewish apocalyptic texts, anticipation of God's Jubilee reign is a central component. As God's reign moves against the death-dealing powers that oppress God's people, and by extension the whole of humanity, tribulations occur. Apocalyptic modes of thought are animated by an intense longing and hope for God's kingdom to dawn. We have highlighted the apocalyptic contours of Jesus's life and teaching, and we have pointed to the apocalyptic character of his sufferings and death, precisely because these events are the historical embodiment of the divine will that humanity should be set free from the powers that hold it in thrall. In the life history of Jesus, God confronts the powers of sin and death in order that humanity (and creation itself) might be set at liberty. Jesus *is* the reign of God.

Of course, there is a significant twist here—God's overthrow of the powers does not occur through a simple display of power. Rather, in Jesus, and supremely in his sufferings, the reign of God is found in the weakness of the Crucified One. "In and through Jesus, God is understood to struggle against evil, but not with the tools of evil itself—not with coercive power or unjust force—but unconventionally, indirectly, immanently, incarna-

---

100. Ernst Käsemann, "'The Righteousness of God' in Paul," in *New Testament Questions of Today*, by Ernst Käsemann (Philadelphia: Fortress, 1969), 172.

101. See Karl Barth, *Church Dogmatics* II/1 (Edinburgh: T&T Clark, 1957), 376-77.

tionally, using 'weakness' to confront and confound 'dominance.'"[102] In keeping with the humble king of Zechariah,[103] whose death ultimately coincides with the victory of YHWH and the cleansing of the people,[104] or the suffering servant of Isaiah,[105] whose representative suffering on behalf of the people leads to their restoration, so also is Jesus's crucifixion his glorification.

This is not a glorification of death or suffering per se, but rather a revelation of the God who lives in solidarity, the God who lifts up all those who are downtrodden. In faithful solidarity with all those who find and have found themselves harried, enslaved, crushed, and executed in a world organized by violence and death, God walks the path of human despondency, suffering, and the loneliness of a godforsaken death. In so doing, God takes up the cause of creation over against those powers that would seek to undo the cosmos. God undergoes the frontal assault of the powers of sin and death, and in and through utter weakness, undoes them.

One of the most powerful images that brings together the reign of God with the trial of crucifixion in the New Testament is found in the Gospel of John. In a series of passages, John brings together the themes of divine presence, exaltation, and crucifixion, the cumulative effect of which is a vision of the enthronement of Jesus in and through the cross. The result is an identification of the Crucified One with the reign of God, which is contrasted with human conceptions of power and rule (i.e., triumphalism) by emphasizing God's identity with those who suffer, who are oppressed and excluded, thus making plain that the *way* of God's kingdom is in and through the self-giving love of the Crucified. We are speaking here of Jesus's description of his crucifixion as an event of exaltation, in which he would be "lifted up" (cf. John 3:14; 8:28; 12:32-33). It is in the final example where this imagery is used that the themes of kingship and crucifixion become fused:

> Jesus answered them, "The hour has come for the Son of Man to be glorified. Very truly, I tell you, unless a grain of wheat falls into the earth and dies, it remains just a single grain; but if it dies, it bears much fruit. . . .

102. Ray, "A Praxis of Atonement," 41.

103. E.g., Zech. 9:9.

104. E.g., Zech. 12:10-13:1.

105. E.g., Isa. 52:13-53:12. For a discussion of how the images from Zechariah and Isaiah are linked, see Anthony R. Peterson, *Behold Your King: The Hope for the House of David in the Book of Zechariah* (London: T&T Clark, 2009), 213-45.

Now my soul is troubled. And what should I say—'Father, save me from this hour'? No, it is for this reason that I have come to this hour. Father, glorify your name." Then a voice came from heaven, "I have glorified it, and I will glorify it again." The crowd standing there heard it and said that it was thunder. Others said, "An angel has spoken to him." Jesus answered, "This voice has come for your sake, not for mine. Now is the judgment of this world; now the ruler of this world will be driven out. And I, when I am lifted up from the earth, will draw all people to myself." He said this to indicate the kind of death he was to die. (12:23-24, 27-33)

Both the discourse of "glory" and the imagery of being "lifted up" carry royal connotations. *Doxa*, or "glory," is a particularly important word in the New Testament, especially in the Gospel of John. It is the translational equivalent of the Hebrew word *kavod*, a word that frequently refers to the "divine presence," and especially to the royal splendor that accompanies the same.[106] The word, especially in its verbal form, carries royal connotations.[107] Likewise, the imagery of being "lifted up" evokes the installation or enthronement of a king.

Jesus's descriptions of his death as a "glorification" (e.g., John 12:23) and a "lifting up" (12:32), then, are clearly meant to construe the tragedy of the cross as a coronation, overturning our normal understanding of what royal splendor and glory look like.[108] Coupled with these images of kingship, we also have a declaration that the enthronement of the king coincides with the judgment of "the ruler of this world" (e.g., 12:31). As in the synoptic accounts, so also in John, the cross of Jesus is an apocalyptic event of judgment. Even more clearly perhaps, it is an event of the reign of God.[109] Contrary to appearances, the unjust "world" and the diabolical "ruler of this world" both meet their own end in the event. As we discussed in chapter 1, the psalmists picture YHWH's enthronement as a movement or history of events wherein God overthrows the powers and is simultaneously enthroned. John envisions the cross of Jesus in a similar fashion, such

106. See Carey C. Newman, "Glory, Glorify," in *The New Interpreter's Dictionary of the Bible* (Nashville: Abingdon, 2007), 2:576-80.

107. See J. Terence Forestell, *The Word of the Cross: Salvation as Revelation in the Fourth Gospel* (Rome: Biblical Institute Press, 1974), 65.

108. "The verb δοξάζειν appears 22x in the latter part of the fourth gospel, generally in reference to the passion as the hour of Jesus' glorification." Forestell, *Word of the Cross*, 65.

109. "The kingship of Jesus is clearly the principal theme of the passion narrative in the fourth gospel." Forestell, *Word of the Cross*, 83.

that, to use Paul's words, to preach "Christ, and him crucified" (1 Cor. 2:2) is synonymous with preaching the gospel of God's reign.

Very important though is the fact that God's glory here is not revealed in the normal guise of power but in the form of weakness and self-giving love.[110] Here it is worth emphasizing that "glory" carries with it connotations of revelation. That a king is "enthroned in glory" refers to the revelation or making known of the power of the king. In the case of Jesus, though, his exaltation is in the form of the death of a common criminal. Why? Among other reasons, because the suffering of Jesus, the apocalyptic Son of Man, is an expression of divine solidarity and compassion with the "wretched of the earth."[111] As with the incognito suffering servant in Isaiah 52:13–53:12, "The cross is where the Son of Man is exalted because it is where he most fully reveals the Father."[112] Evocative of the suffering servant described in Isaiah,[113] the tribulations, sufferings, and execution of the Son of Man are events in which God has taken the side of the dispossessed over against the powerful and the powers of death that underwrite their regimes. The cross is an event that is in keeping with Jesus's basic life-orientation of service and self-giving, and is therefore the climactic epiphany of the reign of God. In keeping with the themes found in the psalms, the prophets, and the apocalyptic traditions, but now deepened, God's reign is an expression of the most far-reaching compassion, of the most revolutionary love, of the deepest faithfulness, of the most expansive friendship.

CONCLUSION

Jesus's life and ministry is marked by conflict from its very inception. The powers arrayed against him are multilayered and, in the New Testament, are named under the heading "powers and principalities," which signifies

---

110. See Margaret Pamment, "The Meaning of *Doxa* in the Fourth Gospel," *Zeitschrift für die neutestamentliche Wissenschaft und die Kunde der ältern Kirche* 74, no. 1–2 (1983): 12–16.

111. See Fanon, *The Wretched of the Earth*.

112. John W. Romanowsky, "'When the Son of Man Is Lifted Up': The Redemptive Power of the Crucifixion in the Gospel of John," *Horizons* 32, no. 1 (Spring 2005): 110.

113. A number of scholars have called attention to the suffering servant, who is also "exalted and lifted up" (52:13), as a key background figure for understanding the various "lifted up" sayings in John (3:14; 8:28; 12:32–33). See, for instance, Raymond E. Brown, *The Gospel according to John I–XII* (Garden City, NY: Doubleday, 1966), 478.

the historical actors, reigning ideologies, and cosmic powers that seek to thwart God's intention to renew creation. On a historical level, Jesus's adversaries come primarily from the ruling classes and those with power. The religious and political authorities from Jesus's context were bitter rivals and enemies who, nevertheless, worked together to remove the threat that Jesus's commitment to God's Jubilee justice represented. These historical actors were driven by larger forces, which we might call the reigning ideologies, structures, institutions, and cultural assumptions that organize daily life. Behind these, however, stands the real enemy against which Jesus protested, the chthonic powers of sin and death. These are the enslaving powers against which human protest is ultimately powerless, without divine intervention.

The conflict between Jesus and the powers reaches its climax in his crucifixion. Across all four Gospels, Jesus's sufferings are put in an apocalyptic framework of confrontation and tribulation. In the Gethsemane scene, Jesus's inner turmoil, including physical symptoms, demonstrates the apocalyptic nature of the trial that he faces. The scenes with Pilate, especially in the Gospel of John, draw on the imagery of Daniel 7 and the cryptic figure of the Son of Man; though now the Danielic vice-regent of YHWH is merged with the suffering servant of Isaiah, such that the Son of Man is displayed in weakness, undergoing judgment while also, at the same time, judging the powers who render the death penalty against the innocent Son of Man. There are also numerous apocalyptic allusions in the scenes recounting the actual suffering and death of Jesus. The point, in keeping with our overall theme, is that the apocalyptic conflict between the reign of God and the powers of sin and death that resist God that we have seen in the life and ministry of Jesus is also characteristic of Jesus's final fate. The death of Jesus on the cross belongs alongside the events of exorcism and healing as an event of apocalyptic significance.

Of signal importance is the fact that the apocalyptic battle that occurs in the cross is an expression of divine solidarity with the powerless. Drawing on the African American experience in the United States, James Cone develops the insight that Jesus's execution was both legal and extralegal—an act of social policing that has a profound continuity with the vile practice of lynching that has been sanctioned and perpetrated against African Americans by the white social order.

In the ancient world, the cross was an instrument of social torture and death, meant to demarcate the line between the human and the nonhuman. Dehumanization was part of its aim. In the crucified Jesus, God takes up a posture that demonstrates the divine unwillingness to allow anyone to be truly lost. For in Jesus, God enters into the realm of the accursed in solidarity, with the ultimate intention of liberation and rescue. Furthermore, this event of solidarity is not performed at a distance, but in profound nearness and love, as God willingly suffers death and godforsakenness precisely to become the friend of the victims and the innocent, but also of the godless, the rejected and accursed, and those filled with enmity and hatred.

The act of solidarity that God has performed in the life and death of Jesus is nothing less than the apocalypse of the righteousness of God. Righteousness is not an abstract moral quality. Rather, it is a relational category that refers to living in faithful fellowship with oneself and others. The divine will that there should be a creation, and that such a creation should live in a flourishing and free relationship to its Creator, draws God into confrontation with that which oppresses and enslaves creation.[114] This apocalyptic and royal confrontation between YHWH and the powers and principalities, however, occurs under the form of its opposite. Jesus, the eschatological and royal Son of Man, is enthroned in and through the cross, for it is in and through the cross that God "disarmed the rulers and authorities and made a public example of them, triumphing over them in it" (Col. 2:15).

The proclamation of the cross as an act of triumph, however, is tied to the reality of the resurrection of Jesus. The resurrection is God's act of vindication of the faithfulness unto death of Jesus; it is God's protest against the crosses of this world, indicating that evil and death will not finally have the last word. But it is important to remember that the one who is raised is none other than the Crucified. Jesus returns bearing the nail marks of his struggle for faithfulness in the face of the powers of sin and death. As such, he calls all of humanity, and especially those upon whom the Spirit of resurrection and abolition is poured out, to join in the struggle for God's Jubilee justice in the here and now, even as we await the coming cosmic transformation that Jesus's resurrection portends.

---

114. "The message is that in electing to have a world and love it into freedom God rejects all that stands in the way of this destiny." Christopher Morse, *Not Every Spirit: A Dogmatics of Christian Disbelief* (Valley Forge, PA: Trinity Press International, 1994), 248.

Chapter Six

"THY KINGDOM COME!"

The conflict between Jesus and the powers and principalities ends in crucifixion. Instead of a glorious triumph over his enemies, Jesus suffers the fate of the crucified of the world. He is trampled underfoot, so to speak, taking his place among the downtrodden, the losers in a world organized by power and death. The beautiful dream that was encapsulated in his ministry under the idea of Jubilee justice is snuffed out as he cries from his gibbet, "My God, my God, why have you forsaken me?" (Mark 15:34). His beautiful dream has ended in the nightmare of the cross.

Nevertheless, this is not the end. Across the whole of the New Testament, Jesus's solidarity with the "wretched of the earth,"[1] and his fate as one of the crucified, is not understood as the final end of the man from Nazareth. His willing identification with the godforsaken of this world—and who is not or who has not felt that they are godforsaken?—does not simply hallow or affirm godforsakenness as such; rather, it indicates that God has hazarded death that life and love might be brought even to the lowest depths of existence—to the pit of human degradation and the grave.

What leads to this statement? How does the Christian gospel have the temerity to make such claims? There is, quite simply, only one reason: that Jesus lives. That the Crucified One lives as the Resurrected One. That the one who poured himself out in faithfulness even unto death now pours out the Spirit of life. That the vile event of crucifixion can also be seen and understood as an event of royal coronation can only be said in the light of the resurrection of Jesus. Without it, the cross of Jesus remains

---

1. See Frantz Fanon, *The Wretched of the Earth* (New York: Grove, 2004).

yet another event of tragedy in which, at best, a good person has died (cf. 1 Cor. 15:14).

In this final chapter, we consider the resurrection and the outpouring of the Spirit in the context of our consideration of the reign of God embodied in Jesus, paying special attention to the theo-political dimensions of God's ongoing liberative action on behalf of humanity, especially the poor and oppressed. Of course, our task has definite challenges, not the least being that we do not intend to offer a full-scale theology of the resurrection, nor a fully developed pneumatology.

One challenge that we need to name from the outset has to do with a besetting temptation that has often attended Christian reflection on the resurrection of Jesus. What I am referring to is the proclivity within Christian theology to understand the resurrection as only an act of triumph, which Christians, as witnesses to the resurrection, have often used to construct a theology of triumphalism. Of course, there is little doubt that such an event—a genuine resurrection from the dead—is indeed an event of power and even a triumph. But this fact has led many in the history of Christianity to assume a posture of superiority—sometimes even a self-justified dominance—vis-à-vis religious and nonreligious others. This is an attitude and posture that is strikingly different from the one displayed in the life of the humble Jesus.

To avoid such triumphalism, one need only remember that the one who returns does so as the one he was. That is, it is as the Crucified that Jesus returns, bearing in his body the marks of his own history, a history of faithfulness unto death, the history of the kingdom of God enfleshed. There is, therefore, little justification for Christians or the Christian church to become triumphalistic. For the life history of Jesus—a life marked by humility, striving for justice, and extending forgiveness and fellowship to those on the margins of society; a life of vulnerability in companionship with the vulnerable—is the life that returns, and this is the life that has become life-giving (cf. 1 Cor. 15:45).

The resurrection, then, marks the *divine vindication* of the *shape* and *way* of the kingdom that Jesus was. Death, the powers that collude with death, and the all-too-human proclivity to prefer to live without the God of life (i.e., human sin)—these have not, cannot, and will never be able to overcome the humble, loving, life-affirming way of the living God at work in Jesus (cf. Heb. 7:16).

With Paul, we affirm that the *way of life that Jesus is* has become a "life-giving Spirit" (1 Cor. 15:45). Through the outpouring of the Spirit of the resurrection, humanity comes to experience and glimpse Jesus's victory over the powers and principalities. People are invited into a praxis of resurrection that requires a reorientation to the histories of violence that all too often distort human and creaturely life. What is more, they are called into the way of discipleship, the way of freedom, and as such have a share in Jesus's resurrection in the here and now.

Without denying the ongoing reality of death and the continual resistance to God that hangs on in deadly and deathly ways, the Christian community, and all those communities upon whom God pours the Spirit, is enveloped with a holy, righteous, and fervent longing to resist; to imagine and struggle toward a different world; to see to it that death and the death-dealing and sinful ways that continue to enslave find their end in their own abolition. For the Spirit of the resurrection is also the Spirit of abolition, because its outpouring at Pentecost represents the first fruits of the abolition of death and the ways of death.

The Vindication of the Just and Compassionate One

In the resurrection, God has acted to vindicate Jesus and the way of kingdom that he embodies. The resurrection of Jesus is the announcement and demonstration that the ways of death have met their end, and the way of life that Jesus is has triumphed.

God Acted . . . Jesus Rose from the Dead

Of all the many actions, vignettes, events, trials, sayings, etc., that constitute the life history of Jesus given to us in the witness of Scripture, none is more directly apocalyptic and eschatological than the event of his resurrection. For it is here that one of the central expectations of Jewish apocalyptic is displayed and confessed: "God raised Jesus from the dead" (cf. Acts 2:24; Rom. 10:9). As we noted in chapter 3, in the apocalyptic book of Daniel, YHWH offers the promise of resurrection to the wise and those who through wisdom keep themselves from being defiled by the rapacious and idolatrous imperialism personified in Antiochus IV Epiphanes (cf. Dan. 12:2–3). This promise constitutes a declaration of YHWH's sole sovereignty over death, marking off resurrection as a divine prerogative.

Likewise, Jesus's resurrection is understood to take "place as a sovereign act of God."[2] But there is more. For the event of Jesus's resurrection is variously narrated as qualitatively different from other events, such as the raising of Jairus's daughter in the Gospel of Mark (cf. Mark 5:21-34) or the resurrection of Lazarus as described in John (cf. John 11:1-54). Those events are more like resuscitations—Jairus's daughter will eventually die again, as will Lazarus. But Jesus is no longer subject to death (cf. Rom. 6:9). He has been transitioned from the sphere that is enslaved by death into the new creation made free through God's life-giving love.

In a similar fashion, the resurrection of Jesus ought not to be understood as a simple break in the causal nexus, like a miracle. This is because resurrection doesn't just *disrupt the normal processes of life and nature*. Rather, the resurrection of Jesus brings forth in the midst of our history, which is bounded and determined by death, *a life that is no longer subject to death* but *determined only by the irrepressible life of God* (cf. Rom. 6:10; Heb. 7:16). The new creation has appeared in the midst of the old. This is nothing short of a *novum* in history.[3]

Jesus has been transitioned from death to life by an act of God that is definitive. This is a proleptic, cosmic, and eschatological act. The word "proleptic" comes from *prolepsis* and means "to anticipate." Jesus is the "firstborn from the dead" (Col. 1:18), the "first fruits of those who have died" (1 Cor. 15:20). As such, the act of God displayed in Jesus has to do with more than Jesus—it anticipates a new heaven and a new earth. It has to do with the whole of humanity and indeed creation itself. It inaugurates the larger process of resurrection,[4] which will enfold the whole of humanity and creation, and which opens up present history to a new future—one no longer bound by the fear of death and the powers and principalities.[5]

---

2. Karl Barth, *Church Dogmatics* IV/1 (Edinburgh: T&T Clark, 1956), 300.

3. "The 'divine event' character of the resurrection of Jesus Christ is underlined by the fact that it breaks all categories of expectation, of historical methodology, and of language. It was a new and unexpected act of God." Thorwald Lorenzen, *Resurrection and Discipleship: Interpretive Models, Biblical Reflections, Theological Consequences* (Maryknoll, NY: Orbis, 1995), 116; see also Jürgen Moltmann, *The Coming of God: Christian Eschatology* (Minneapolis: Fortress, 1996), 27-29.

4. See Jürgen Moltmann, *The Way of Jesus Christ: Christology in Messianic Dimensions* (Minneapolis: Fortress, 1993), 240-45.

5. "Resurrection doesn't mean a closed fact. It means a way: the transition from death to life." Jürgen Moltmann, *Jesus Christ for Today's World* (Minneapolis: Fortress, 1994), 81.

Here the symbol and reality of resurrection make plain its connection to hope, for "In Christ, as testimony to him bears witness, all God's words and all his works breathe of the *abolition of death*."[6] In the encounters of the disciples with Jesus after his resurrection, "The eternal life of the kingdom of God appeared to them in the flesh. The eternal life of the kingdom, which though still with the Father [in its perfection], had asserted itself in and through Jesus as a [kind of] *harbinger* of the abolition of death."[7] The act of God that raised Jesus from the dead, which vindicated his life and confirmed its divine imprimatur, is a harbinger of the eventual total destruction of death, as well as the divine source and impetus for the search for justice in the here and now. God has acted in Jesus's resurrection and, as such, has displayed the unyielding divine intention to transfigure the cosmos.

Here Jürgen Moltmann's observations regarding the human role played in God's act of resurrection are relevant. As he notes, not only does God raise Jesus from the dead, but Jesus also arises in his own power (cf. John 10:18). "The person who is wakened has to get up. Unless he does, the waking is ineffective."[8] To be sure, there is only one subject who performs the act of resurrection—God, for even on the human side, one can and must say, "God was in Christ" (cf. 2 Cor. 5:19). But Moltmann helpfully points out that though the act of raising Jesus from the dead is a divine act, it encloses within it a space for human response.

This subsequent human response by the man Jesus that is enclosed within the divine act of resurrection *foreshadows* the space and energizing power of the Spirit of the resurrection that has now been poured out into history. It means that even in the here and now, as the Spirit of the resurrection is given and received, human agents are given the opportunity to *participate* in the ongoing work of resurrection that is happening in history through the struggle for God's Jubilee justice—a struggle that can experience real advances but that also finds its true and final end in the universal resurrection of the dead and the transfiguration of creation.

Satisfying the Hunger and Thirst for Justice and Righteousness

Christian theology has often been tempted to move into the realm of the abstract, and in so doing to have nothing to say to those who live with their

---

6. Christoph Blumhardt, *Make Way for the Spirit: My Father's Battle and Mine* (Walden, NY: Plough, 2019), 144.

7. Blumhardt, *Make Way*, 144 (emphasis mine).

8. Moltmann, *Way of Jesus Christ*, 247.

"backs against the wall . . . the poor, the disinherited, the dispossessed."[9] Partly for this reason, Karl Marx once described religion as the "opiate of the masses,"[10] offering only illusions of pie-in-the-sky while the powerful continue to rule the world with impunity. When theology and the life of faith loses its connection to the concrete, it risks becoming a mere ideology, rather than a living witness to the God who acts in radical and surprising ways on behalf of the downtrodden.

The temptation to escape into a posture of otherworldliness is seen nowhere more forcefully than in reference to the resurrection. After all, resurrection or the "return of that which was dead" intersects with larger existential questions about things like "life after death," "the immortality of the soul," and other issues related to ultimate meaning. And to be sure, such longings and questions are indeed engaged in through contemplation of the resurrection—but they must be done so very carefully.

The Uniqueness of Jesus's Resurrection

In chapter 4 we discussed the difference that Jesus makes, arguing that it is Jesus who ultimately defines what the reign of God is in his life, death, and resurrection, notwithstanding the long prehistory of the concept of the kingdom of God in the scriptural memory of Israel that was sketched out in our first three chapters. So also, here, we must remember that what is first and foremost at issue in the Christian gospel is not so much a "resurrection" abstractly conceived, but the "resurrection of *Jesus*."

Our emphasis here is justified not only because of the necessity to avoid abstraction, but also, as we have already noted, because the biblical authors talk about the resurrection of Jesus as qualitatively different from other events. In the New Testament, "the Crucified Christ is transfigured by God into a new mode of existence"[11] through his resurrection, indicating an event that is radically distinct, no mere corporeal resuscitation. This is an event of a different order from the raising of Lazarus or the daughter of Jairus, for instance.[12]

---

9. Howard Thurman, *Jesus and the Disinherited* (Boston: Beacon, 1996), 11, 13.

10. Karl Marx, introduction to "Contribution to the Critique of Hegel's *Philosophy of Right*," in *The Portable Karl Marx*, ed. Eugene Kamenka (New York: Viking Penguin, 1983), 115.

11. Lorenzen, *Resurrection and Discipleship*, 119.

12. "The resurrection is not a revival, as in the case of Jairus's daughter, or Lazarus, whom Jesus brought back to this life but who later died once more." Moltmann, *Way of Jesus Christ*, 222.

The Life History of Jesus Is Vindicated

In the context of our theme of the reign of God, attending to the specific identity of Jesus as the one who was raised, however, helps us to pick up on two key interrelated points. The first is that the resurrection of Jesus is not simply an affirmation of some eternal enduring aspect of Jesus's personality or soul. Rather, the Christian gospel affirms that what is raised up in Jesus is the whole person. "The Risen One is *not* described as quasi-disembodied; he has 'flesh and bones.' He shows the disciples his 'hands and feet.' He urges them to touch him; indeed, he even asks them to give him something to eat, and before their eyes he consumes 'a piece of broiled fish' (Luke 24:36–43)."[13] To speak of the whole person means first to speak of the body. Jesus comes back in an embodied form that has both continuity and discontinuity with his previous form.

The continuity is seen in the fact that the disciples come to recognize Jesus as *Jesus*. "It is I myself" (Luke 24:39), declares Jesus to the disciples. Each of the postresurrection narratives found in the NT is keen to emphasize that after the disciples get over the understandable shock of encountering Jesus alive after his execution, they come to realize that they are now in the living presence of the same Jesus whom they had known, with whom they had lived, and from whom they had learned. At the same time, discontinuity is also evident, as this Jesus suddenly appears and disappears (cf. Matt. 28:9; Luke 24:34, 36; John 20:19). In regard to the body of Jesus, then, continuity and discontinuity come together to create a productive dialectic.

We can see this dialectic at work in the letters of Paul. For instance, in his struggle with the Corinthian community, Paul was especially keen to emphasize the embodied nature of resurrection but also to acknowledge that the body that is raised will be a glorified body (cf. 1 Cor. 15:35–58). The overall point of the dialectic, however, is to emphasize not only that Jesus was raised bodily but that such an action by God in regard to the body of Jesus is indicative of the divine valuing of embodiment in general and creation as a whole.

The bodily resurrection of Jesus means our bodies and creation matter, but perhaps even more importantly, what we do *in* and *with* our bodies also matters. In other words, our affirmation that it was the whole person of

---

13. Gerhard Lohfink, *Is This All There Is? On Resurrection and Eternal Life* (Collegeville, MN: Liturgical Press Academic, 2018), 117.

Jesus who was raised ought not to be taken as a concern only with embodiment or corporeality as such. Rather, the bodily resurrection of Jesus refers especially to the *life history* he lived out in his body, and for which he died. The resurrection of Jesus means "that the whole person of Jesus with all his accomplishments and relationships, i.e., that person which was formed in and through his relationships and ministries, has arrived in the presence of God."[14] As such, the resurrection of Jesus must be understood as the resurrection of his whole life: a life that embodied the reign of God.

The Jesus Who Is Raised Is the Crucified Victim

This leads into our second point: the resurrection of Jesus is an act of God on behalf of a victim of injustice. As we recounted in chapters 4 and 5, Jesus pursued God's Jubilee justice, which meant he dedicated himself to setting free the captives, restoring those in need of wholeness, and extending table fellowship to the downcast, the forsaken, the outcasts, and the godless. He denounced the powerful and was put on trial through false testimony and trumped-up charges, was made a pawn in a larger game played by the powerful, was lynched by the state, and was dehumanized through the process of crucifixion. From any vantage point, Jesus was a victim of radical injustice. As Jon Sobrino notes, "Not just anyone was resurrected, but Jesus of Nazareth, who proclaimed the kingdom of God to the poor and defended them, who denounced and unmasked oppressors, and who was persecuted by them, condemned to death and executed, and who throughout all this kept his trust in God who is Father and his openness to the will of a Father who always showed himself as God, ineffable, beyond manipulation."[15] His resurrection, therefore, is not first and foremost about the broad questions of "life after death," nor is it about God's ability to revive a corpse; rather, the resurrection of the Crucified is above all concerned with the burning question of justice.

The resurrection of Jesus "means first and foremost doing justice to a victim."[16] Jesus was *subjected to a specific history of violence* because of his *very specific commitment to pursue, proclaim, and embody God's Jubilee justice.*

---

14. Lorenzen, *Resurrection and Discipleship*, 246; see also Jürgen Moltmann, *Sun of Righteousness, Arise! God's Future for Humanity and the Earth* (Minneapolis: Fortress, 2010), 54.

15. Jon Sobrino, *No Salvation outside the Poor: Prophetic-Utopian Essays* (Maryknoll, NY: Orbis, 2008), 101.

16. Sobrino, *No Salvation*, 101.

The scars with which Jesus returns signify the history of violence to which he was subject. His was a *marked* body—a body *marked* and *scarred* by very specific events.[17]

At the same time, though, seeing Jesus as the now-living one who is no longer subject to the history of violence signified by his scars underlines the fact that it is his *specific form of life*—a form of life in pursuit of God's Jubilee justice and compassion, a form of life that is itself the kingdom of God come among us—that *no history of death can now master* (cf. Heb. 7:16).[18] As such, the resurrection of Jesus marks the initial satisfaction of the hunger and thirst for justice and righteousness spoken of in the Sermon on the Mount (cf. Matt. 5:6) and longed for in the prophets and apocalyptic texts.

The Lifting Up of the Lowly

Understanding the resurrection as an act of vindication of the life history of Jesus—a life lived in conformity with and pursuit of God's Jubilee justice—also surfaces a nuance in the language of resurrection because it echoes royal or kingdom imagery.[19] As we have already noted, in the context of apocalyptic and prophetic texts, resurrection was an expression of God's sovereignty over the lawlessness of the nations who persecute and kill faithful Israel. Resurrection is an expression of God's faithfulness and justice.[20] In the visions of the apocalyptic seers, the arrival of God's reign is marked by the entrance into the world of God's justice and righteous-

---

17. This statement is a gloss on Shelly Rambo, who writes, "Thinking of Jesus' return in terms of a marked *body*, we see him as one subjected to the socio-material realities of his day. He was crucified under Roman imperial rule. This history is singular, in that he entered history and was subject to it." Shelly Rambo, *Resurrecting Wounds: Living in the Afterlife of Trauma* (Waco, TX: Baylor University Press, 2017), 40.

18. "What is specific about Jesus' resurrection is, therefore, not what God does with a dead body but what God does with a victim. The raising of Jesus is direct proof of the triumph of God's justice, . . . for once, justice has triumphed over injustice." Jon Sobrino, *Christ the Liberator: A View from the Victims* (Maryknoll, NY: Orbis, 2001), 84.

19. For a background discussion, see Colin Brown, "Resurrection," in *The New International Dictionary of New Testament Theology*, ed. Colin Brown (Grand Rapids: Zondervan, 1986), 3:259–309.

20. "The central message of apocalyptic, and its most important one in our own history, has nothing to do with the esoteric but responds to a human longing that in the end there will be justice, that the butcher will not triumph over the victim." Sobrino, *Christ the Liberator*, 39.

ness. These are the instruments by which God overcomes the powers and principalities. Thus, resurrection was conceived as the supreme expression of divine justice, which would mark the entrance of the reign of God into the world.

Jesus's resurrection is described in similar fashion in the New Testament in passages like Acts 2:32–33, Romans 8:34, or Ephesians 1:20, where resurrection and the royal imagery of the installation of a king are combined, drawing on important passages and scenes in Daniel 7 and Psalm 110. Likewise, the imagery of exaltation found in passages like Acts 5:31 and Philippians 2:9 also carries royal connotations, further reinforcing the idea that the resurrection is constitutive of the identity of Jesus and of the reign he embodied.

When we combine the fact that constitutive of Jesus's identity is his being a victim of injustice, with the additional notion that the resurrection is an event of royal exaltation, we come to see that in the resurrection of Jesus God has raised up the lowly. The exaltation of Jesus the victim in resurrection, then, is indicative of God's intention to stand with the outsider and the lowly, to affirm that the last will indeed be first, and the first last.

The Hospitality of the Way of Jesus the Resurrected

In the resurrection of Jesus from the dead, then, we see the first instantiation of the satisfaction of the longings of the prophets and the apocalyptic visionaries that God would step forth into the world and begin to right all wrongs.[21] Jesus's resurrection means that the form of life he lived, one committed to God and neighbor, is now beyond the reach of the power of death. All the ways in which Jesus *was*—ways that we indicated in some detail in chapters 4 and 5—are also all the ways that Jesus now *is* and *will be*. There is no other Jesus to be known than the lowly, humble, loving, welcoming, and fierce friend of the broken and wounded—the king is the servant.

This fact is made especially poignant in the postresurrection narratives in Luke (and John). In Luke 24:13–35, two disciples of Jesus travel along the road to Emmaus, where they will meet the risen Jesus in the context of their own sadness at his crucifixion, their reminiscences, and a meal.

> Now on that same day two of them were going to a village called Emmaus, about seven miles from Jerusalem, and talking with each other about all

---

21. See Moltmann, *Sun of Righteousness, Arise!*, 41.

these things that had happened. While they were talking and discussing, Jesus himself came near and went with them, but their eyes were kept from recognizing him. And he said to them, "What are you discussing with each other while you walk along?" They stood still, looking sad. Then one of them, whose name was Cleopas, answered him, "Are you the only stranger in Jerusalem who does not know the things that have taken place there in these days?" He asked them, "What things?" They replied, "The things about Jesus of Nazareth, who was a prophet mighty in deed and word before God and all the people, and how our chief priests and leaders handed him over to be condemned to death and crucified him. But we had hoped that he was the one to redeem Israel. Yes, and besides all this, it is now the third day since these things took place. Moreover, some women of our group astounded us. They were at the tomb early this morning, and when they did not find his body there, they came back and told us that they had indeed seen a vision of angels who said that he was alive. Some of those who were with us went to the tomb and found it just as the women had said; but they did not see him." Then he said to them, "Oh, how foolish you are, and how slow of heart to believe all that the prophets have declared! Was it not necessary that the Messiah should suffer these things and then enter into his glory?" Then beginning with Moses and all the prophets, he interpreted to them the things about himself in all the scriptures.

As they came near the village to which they were going, he walked ahead as if he were going on. But they urged him strongly, saying, "Stay with us, because it is almost evening and the day is now nearly over." So he went in to stay with them. When he was at the table with them, he took bread, blessed and broke it, and gave it to them. Then their eyes were opened, and they recognized him; and he vanished from their sight. They said to each other, "Were not our hearts burning within us while he was talking to us on the road, while he was opening the scriptures to us?" That same hour they got up and returned to Jerusalem; and they found the eleven and their companions gathered together. They were saying, "The Lord has risen indeed, and he has appeared to Simon!" Then they told what had happened on the road, and how he had been made known to them in the breaking of the bread.

Though this text has been rightly used for reflection on the Christian liturgical practice of sharing the Lord's Supper, its broader theme is hospitality, which was central to Jesus's kingdom ministry, as he had eaten with his disciples, with publicans, with tax collectors, and even with his enemies.[22]

Table fellowship offered the opportunity for welcome, nourishment, and care, and was one of Jesus's central practices for drawing people into God's *shalom*. Now, in his return, this same practice is taken up, and "the Kingdom comes now as it had come earlier in Jesus' ministry with the powerful weapons of meals shared with outcasts, meals which broke down barriers that separated people from one another."[23] The act of taking bread, giving thanks, and breaking it establishes continuity with the life history of Jesus and his words and deeds, as it echoes the feeding of the multitudes (Luke 9:10-17), as well as the last meal Jesus shared with his disciples before his crucifixion (Luke 22:19).

What is especially unique, however, is that here and later in the same chapter, Jesus is now eating with his disciples, something he said he would not do until the kingdom had arrived (Luke 22:15-18). When this scene is brought together with the additional scenes in Luke and in John, where Jesus shares a meal with his disciples, one is left to conclude that the resurrection marks the reappearing of the reign of God on earth, following after its first appearance in the life of Jesus himself (cf. Mark 1:15; Luke 11:20; 17:21).[24]

The implication seems clear—for the community of disciples called to live into the resurrection, hospitality will be central to their way of being. As Letty Russell succinctly states, for the church to be relevant and faithful in any age, including our own, "we must become a community that practices God's Welcome and hospitality in a world of difference and danger."[25] To do so is to find oneself caught up in the great drama of the resurrection and the reign of God at work in our own time and history.

When viewed in the broader argument we have been developing regarding the reign of God enfleshed in Jesus, this scene offers yet another indication that the one who returns is the Crucified who is to be identified both with the violent death that he was subject to and with the life he lived and for

---

22. Justo L. González, *Luke* (Louisville: Westminster John Knox, 2010), 278.

23. Robert J. Karris, "Luke 24:13-35," *Interpretation* 68, no. 2 (January 1987): 59.

24. See Sharon H. Ringe, *Luke* (Louisville: Westminster John Knox, 1995), 289.

25. Letty M. Russell, *Just Hospitality: God's Welcome in a World of Difference* (Louisville: Westminster John Knox, 2009), 115.

which he was rejected and crucified. In the resurrection of Jesus, God has indeed taken sides in the struggle against injustice, dehumanization, and the powers and principalities, and, having overcome death, violence, and destruction, reveals that the God and Father of Jesus is none other than the God of the lowly, the oppressed, the victim. The God who lifts up the lowly, welcomes the stranger, and embraces the dispossessed.

The One Who Lives toward God

Jesus's resurrection marks God's vindication of his life. It makes unmistakable the fact that God identifies with Jesus, one who was himself a victim of injustice, and "thus solidifies God's commitment to the restoration of life for the 'crucified class' of people."[26] It makes plain that Jesus's pursuit of God's Jubilee justice, and the embodiment of God's reign evident in his life history, cannot finally be subdued by violence or the power of death. The resurrection marks the reappearing of the kingdom of God enfleshed in Jesus.

At the same time, the resurrection also breathes of the future. In the resurrection of Jesus, the new creation has appeared in the midst of the old, and in so doing has opened up our history, our age—an age still bounded and enthralled by death and violence—to the life-giving energies of God's own future. For "the death he died, he died to sin, once for all; but the life he lives, he lives to God" (Rom. 6:10). Jesus is the one who now lives toward God. His whole life is now present in and with God,[27] and his reappearing in the midst of history constitutes a promise that moves toward a definite future.

That future is the future of Jesus Christ, wherein God's name is hallowed, God's kingdom has come, and God's will is done definitively for the whole of creation. The future of Jesus Christ is the consummated reign of God (cf. 1 Cor. 15:24–28) in which God dwells with creation (cf. Rev. 21:3–4), in which righteousness and justice are established and God's mercy and *shalom* reign supreme. It is the realm of divine and human cooperation, in which human and creaturely flourishing is realized and the power of death no longer reigns, for God has destroyed

26. Kelly Brown Douglas, *Stand Your Ground: Black Bodies and the Justice of God* (Maryknoll, NY: Orbis, 2015), 188.

27. See Ernst Käsemann, *Commentary on Romans*, trans. Geoffrey W. Bromiley (Grand Rapids: Eerdmans, 1980), 170.

the shroud that is cast over all peoples,
the sheet that is spread over all nations;
he will swallow up death forever. (Isa. 25:7–8)

Humanity finds nourishment (cf. Isa. 25:6), creation finds rest in God's *shalom* (Isa. 11:1–9), violence and dehumanizing destruction come to an end (cf. Isa. 2:4; Rev. 22:2)—in short, all things are made new (cf. Rev. 21:5).

It is this future that presses in on the present with the resurrection of Jesus. Paul's language is replete with the image that the resurrection makes a difference in the here and now, as a new future is opened up, one in which we become partakers of God's life and freedom, taking our place alongside Jesus and his struggle with the powers of sin and death. "The power of Christ's future coming and the vision that it bestows upon the people is the key to why the oppressed can 'keep on keepin' on' even when their fight seems fruitless."[28] For, "If the Spirit of him who raised Jesus from the dead dwells in you, he who raised Christ from the dead will give life to your mortal bodies also through his Spirit that dwells in you" (Rom. 8:11). One can certainly read this text in reference to the future resurrection, but Paul elsewhere makes it clear that his reference is to the *future* resurrection, *but also* to the future that presses in on the *now* (cf. Rom. 6:1–13; 8:12–14).

It is here that the category of justification is important. Paul notes that Jesus was "raised for our justification" (Rom. 4:25), meaning that we have together become sharers in the faithfulness of Jesus unto death. God's righteousness, life, and final reign are bound together in the future of Jesus that presses into history. As we sketched out in chapter 1, God's righteousness refers to God's faithfulness to Israel and to the whole of creation, that there should be a creation and a creature that live a flourishing life in fellowship with God and the whole inhabited earth. Divine righteousness, then, refers to *God's keeping faith* both with God's own intentions *and* with the creation God has called into being. This same righteousness has now been made evident in the faithfulness of Jesus unto death.

In his faithful pursuit of God's Jubilee justice, Jesus shows himself to be the true human covenant partner, so that in his resurrection, his righteousness or faithfulness has reappeared and made possible "the reconciliation of the unreconciled by God"[29] and the beginning of the deliverance of justice to both the just and the unjust. The resurrection is a sign that vic-

---

28. James H. Cone, *God of the Oppressed*, rev. ed. (Maryknoll, NY: Orbis, 1997), 120.
29. Jürgen Moltmann, *Theology of Hope* (Minneapolis: Fortress, 1993), 205.

tims will receive real restitution, and that the unjust will be set on a path of *metanoia*, or transformation.[30] Breath will be given to those deprived of it— people like Eric Garner or George Floyd, whose lives were taken by official representatives of the social order. It is a sign that the terrible end inflicted on these and so many other victims of state and extrajudicial violence is neither just nor the final end. Rather, the true and final end is life with God and the vindication of the unique humanity of all victims of injustice. God's No to violence, death, and injustice—whether legal or illegal—is heard with resounding finality, even as it awaits its final consummation.

The faithfulness of Jesus unto death becomes the pattern of life to which all those who have become witnesses of the resurrection are called to cor- respond. They are "to be conformed to the image of his Son, in order that he might be the firstborn within a large family" (Rom. 8:29), entering into the same process of transition from death to life that constitutes the resur- rection of Jesus the Crucified. Their way of life is meant to be offered within its particular contexts and limitations as a kind of improvisational riff on the way of life that Jesus himself lived, the one who sought out and indeed embodied God's reign (cf. Rom. 12:1–2). Disciples are called into a form of life that is allied with those who suffer. They are called into solidarity with those who are erased from view, like the migrant worker who toils sixty to seventy hours a week collecting food in the fields of industrial agriculture, or the transwoman of color who is discriminated against and rejected at every turn, with no health care, access to affordable housing, or fresh food. The company of disciples can enter into relationships of solidarity—in fact, many disciples are themselves *already* in situations of deprivation and op- pression and *so don't need to "enter into" such situations*—and become par- ables of the reign of God, offering joyful and persistent resistance to the vile and violent powers and principalities that distort, dehumanize, and corrupt human life and the life of the earth.

Moreover, Jesus's resurrection makes plain God's intention to reclaim history and to re-create the cosmos itself. As Jesus returns in the fullness of his person—embodied with clear indications of his life history etched in his glorified body—so also does the whole history of his interactions and the contexts in which he lived his life. As one human being among

---

30. For a discussion of how the divine preferential option for the poor and oppressed can intersect with the possibility of the justification of sinners—both victims and agents— see Jürgen Moltmann, *The Spirit of Life: A Universal Affirmation* (Minneapolis: Fortress, 2001), 123–38.

the many billions of creatures who have lived, Jesus has a place within a vast interconnected web. His history includes not only singular individual actions but also a multitude of interactions in which he was sometimes active, sometimes passive, and sometimes both. He is fully human, fully a creature, and therefore he belongs fully to the history of creation. When he is raised, therefore, it is not only Jesus's history that is reclaimed, it is the history of all creatures, and especially of those who have suffered injustice. Those who have struggled for a meager existence, those who have not always known love or care but who have managed somehow to survive, and those whose existence is threatened with being snuffed out like a smoldering wick. His resurrected appearing means that even in the midst of a history still ruled by violence, injustice, and death, God's power can and does bring life (cf. Rom. 8:11)—that God's promise to abide with the earth and its creatures, to transfigure and set at liberty all who have been held in thrall (cf. Luke 4:18), will in fact be fulfilled.

Of course, the future that presses in on the now is still qualified. For the life-giving power of the resurrection still occurs in the midst of a world where crosses proliferate on a daily basis. And yet, the truth that the resurrection of Jesus has happened kindles hope and strength to struggle for God's Jubilee justice in the here and now and constitutes a promise that the future will actually be crowned by God's justice and righteousness.[31]

The Spirit of the Resurrected One

The Crucified lives. In the event of resurrection God has vindicated Jesus's faithfulness unto death. In his unyielding love for his neighbor, his words and actions were directed to the liberation of creation from the powers and principalities, from the power of sin and death. In being faithful to this path even unto death—in loving God, creation, and his neighbor—Jesus showed that he was solely concerned with doing the will of God (cf. John 6:38). It is this Jesus who has returned, and no other. And yet, his resurrection also means that the daybreak of God's future reign is pressing into the present. Jesus's reappearing is itself a promise that moves toward the fulfillment of God's future, which is a new heaven and a new earth where God dwells with humankind and the creation as a whole (cf. Rev. 21:3-4). God's final

---

31. "We struggle because it is a sign of Jesus' presence with us and of his coming presence to redeem all humanity." Cone, *God of the Oppressed*, 122.

intention is that all things will be made new (cf. Rev. 21:5), and that the process of reclamation and repair is already beginning in the new future opened up in history through Jesus's resurrection.

The past and the future of Jesus Christ converge in the present in and through the Spirit of the resurrection, which has been poured out on communities of faith, and which, in the end, will be poured out on all flesh. In the biblical witness, the identity and work of the Spirit are tightly bound up with Jesus, especially in his ministry and his resurrection. He is the one who bears the Spirit, who is commissioned to proclaim good news to the poor, to lift up the lowly, to set free the captives, and to establish God's Jubilee justice (cf. Luke 4:18–21).[32] It is through the Spirit of God that Jesus performs many of his miracles (cf. Matt. 12:28). But of all the events that constitute the life history of Jesus, it is in the context of the resurrection that discussion of the Spirit is foregrounded most prominently. Even before his death, Jesus links the coming of the Spirit with his departure (cf. John 16:5–15), and with his resurrection (and ascension), both the giving and the promise to give the Spirit are conspicuous.

In the discussion that follows, we do not offer a full-fledged theology of the Spirit. Rather, our focus is on the ways in which the way of Jesus is offered and energized by the Spirit. Jesus gives the Spirit precisely so that communities and people of good will and faith can enter with Jesus into the way of the kingdom.

Reconfiguring Histories of Violence

In the Gospel of John, the giving of the Spirit is directly linked to Jesus's personal breathing on his disciples, imparting to them the promised Comforter:

> When it was evening on that day, the first day of the week, and the doors of the house where the disciples had met were locked for fear of the Jews, Jesus came and stood among them and said, "Peace be with you." After he said this, he showed them his hands and his side. Then the disciples rejoiced when they saw the Lord. Jesus said to them again, "Peace be with you. As the Father has sent me, so I send you." When he had said this, he breathed on them and said to them, "Receive the Holy Spirit. If you forgive

32. See Michael Welker, *God the Spirit* (Minneapolis: Fortress, 1994), 108-24.

the sins of any, they are forgiven them; if you retain the sins of any, they are retained." (John 20:19-23)

The disquieting presence of the wounded Jesus requires a double dose of God's *shalom*. The significance of the passage becomes even clearer when Jesus later appears to Thomas and urges him to touch his hands, and even to thrust his hand into Jesus's side (cf. John 20:24-29). Shelly Rambo has insightfully pointed out that what is at issue in the Johannine accounts is an interlinking of the knowledge or revelation of the Crucified, reconciliation, the Spirit, and the praxis required of those who will follow after him.

The disciples are confronted with the living Christ, who stands in their midst, and yet they cannot see him for who he is. They do not yet understand the significance of the wounded Jesus's appearance—especially of what it will mean for them—and so they must be addressed *twice*. "The repetition of the statement is unusual, if read as a mere greeting. It causes us to think that they may *not* have heard it the first time. They claim to see. But his repetition may be an indication that he is not so certain that they comprehend what is taking place."[33] In the Thomas episode, the situation is even more graphically presented. There the disciple demands to see Jesus on his terms. Rambo notes that Jesus's response doesn't so much have to do with Thomas's doubts as is usually thought, nor is it a mere capitulation on Jesus's part to the demands of Thomas. Rather, it is a confrontation between the history of violence that struck Jesus down and Thomas, who is himself capable of violence—indeed his demand to see Jesus's wounds is in itself an act of control.[34]

But Jesus's invitation to touch the wounds, when paired with the breathing of the Spirit described in the earlier episode, creates an opening—the possibility of seeing Jesus for who he really is and was, one wounded by the humanity who rejects God's reign; *but also* one who now lives *differently in relation to that very history of violence*. "The Jesus who returns cuts through fear and exposes his wounds. And he makes the wounds visible on his body, marking the impossibility of erasure. . . . This return of wounds does not just resurface past trauma but provides a site of encounter in which wounds, surfaced, can be tended."[35] Thus the declaration by Jesus that "if

33. Rambo, *Resurrecting Wounds*, 80.
34. See Rambo, *Resurrecting Wounds*, 82-92.
35. Rambo, *Resurrecting Wounds*, 88-89.

you forgive the sins of any, they are forgiven them; if you retain the sins of any, they are retained" (John 20:23), speaks of a specific praxis. *Knowing* the Crucified means *following* the Crucified—and that means embracing and embodying the praxis of forgiveness, or release.

As we noted in chapter 4, *aphiēmi*, the Greek word for forgiveness, also means "to release," and is used in a variety of contexts, including economic, political, social, and cultic. This range of meaning gives to the word a more complex nuance than one often encounters in its typical translation as "forgiveness." Of course, to speak of the praxis of release in the context of wounds and trauma—as Rambo does in reference to John 20:23—does not mean erasing, forgetting, or pretending that the wounding we have received or doled out is capable of being plunged into a subterranean realm where it no longer has ongoing effects. To forgive in this case, rather, means releasing the debt owed, so that the freedom of the Spirit can enliven one, and one can breathe.[36] Forgiveness allows for the release of the history of violence and sin, not into the realm of the forgotten but into a new relation, in which those who have suffered are no longer bound by the cycle of violence, revenge, and death.

Imagining a different relationship to a history of violence for a culture shaped by the dynamics of racial capitalism and its varied expressions sounds both inviting and dangerous. But, as Rambo points out, the dangerous memory of the Crucified is the place where both seen and unseen wounds are surfaced. Not to be relived (if we are thoughtful and careful enough), but to be accounted for and integrated into our ongoing narratives and lives. "In the experience of trauma, what is not integrated returns."[37] At the same time, this does not mean that repair, restitution, and justice are to be set aside. Not in the least, for victimizers should be held to account so that wounds do not fester, and in the hope that a fully orbed transformation for all might occur.

What a new relationship to histories of violence can mean is that the binding powers of history can no longer harm the victims of injustice. The scars in Jesus's body mark a profound constellation of traumas—that he returns with them means that they are not erased but surfaced offering the possibility of a new relationship to the many histories of violence that have shaped the lives not only of those on the margins but much of the human community.

---

36. "Retaining the sins of others who have harmed you literally drains life from you. It takes away breath." Rambo, *Resurrecting Wounds*, 82.

37. Rambo, *Resurrecting Wounds*, 78.

The Life-Giving Spirit

The interweaving of revelation, reconciliation, praxis, and the Spirit, which is developed in the biblical witness (cf. Rom. 8:1-17; Gal. 4:6; 2 Cor. 4:13-14; etc.), finds a potent expression in Paul's declaration that the risen Christ has become "a life-giving Spirit" (1 Cor. 15:45). In contrast to the "first Adam," whose life is bounded and determined by death and the ways of death, the "second Adam," or Jesus, lives as one who "gives life." In and through the Spirit, witnesses of the resurrection "enter into Christ's saving and life-giving fellowship. In the experience of the life-giving Spirit they recognize Jesus as the Lord of God's rule."[38] They become those who begin to truly see Jesus for who he was, is, and will be—the reign of God enfleshed—and find themselves enfolded in God's reconciling righteousness. What is more, in and through the Spirit, witnesses of the resurrection are conscripted into God's good work of bringing the Jubilee justice of the kingdom to bear on the present.

In chapter 15 of 1 Corinthians, Paul is concerned to correct problematic teaching regarding the embodied nature of the resurrection—or the "resurrection of the flesh."[39] Presumably some in Corinth have moved away from this conception, the result of which from Paul's perspective has been a corresponding devaluing of the body and of what one does in the body, which in turn is leading to a breakdown of communal relations. Thus, here, as elsewhere in the New Testament, the theological and the ethical are intimately bound together. This becomes especially clear in the variant textual reading that brings to a completion the paragraph where Paul's description of the risen Christ as a "life-giving Spirit" occurs: "Just as we have borne the image of the man of dust, *let us* also bear the image of the man of heaven" (1 Cor. 15:49). The variant reading, "let us" instead of "we will," gives the concluding statement a more decidedly ethical reading. As Hays and others have pointed out, "such an ethical twist would not be incongruous with other conclusions of paragraphs within 1 Corinthians 15 (see, e.g., vv. 33-34, 58),"[40] nor would it be strange within the wider context of the letter as a whole (cf. 1 Cor. 6:12-20; 11:23-34).

Paul's exhortation, then, speaks of a *praxis of resurrection*—if the way of Jesus Christ has been vindicated and made present now in the midst

---

38. Moltmann, *The Spirit of Life*, 68.
39. The Greek can literally be translated: "resurrection of the corpses."
40. Richard B. Hays, *First Corinthians* (Louisville: Westminster John Knox, 2011), 273.

of history, then a corresponding action by those who have become witnesses is urged, "without compulsion, without being anxiously tied to the 'letter,' without overemphasizing their own works and achievements or those of other persons (cf. Gal. 5:18). . . . In the community of these persons, peace is created in the power of the Spirit by the diverse spread of love."[41] Those who have been encountered by the living Christ, and enfolded into God's reconciling righteousness, are impelled forward to *practice resurrection*.

Of course, this does not mean that the actions of the community of witnesses are on the same order as that of God's act of raising the dead Christ, but it does mean finding ways to *analogously* or *parabolically* witness through both word and deed so as to proclaim the truth that justice has been done to a victim of injustice. It means to become God's partners in struggle who seek in practical ways to take "the crucified people [in our ongoing history] down from the cross."[42] To become willing partners who in the power of the Spirit of the resurrection follow after Jesus means realizing that our actions are at "service of the resurrection of the *dead*, so of the resurrection of the *many*."[43] To become those who practice resurrection means to embark on a course of action that is social and political so as to raise up those who have been trampled underfoot.[44]

Such action will obviously mean the critique and judgment of unjust structures and those who support them, but within the divine economy into which humanity is invited, such judgment is not the last word, for "God is just because he creates justice for people who are deprived of it, *and puts the unjust on a just path*. He creates justice for the people who suffer violence, and he saves through his righteousness. Through this justice and righteousness God brings about the shared peace which also means true life: *shalom*."[45] Setting free the captives also means setting free the captors; though the former are at the center of God's intention, the latter are not left out. The final aim of God's freedom is a creation set at liberty to participate in God's own irrepressible life.

---

41. Welker, *God the Spirit*, 258.
42. Sobrino, *Christ the Liberator*, 48.
43. Sobrino, *Christ the Liberator*, 48.
44. See Sobrino, *Christ the Liberator*, 48.
45. Moltmann, *The Spirit of Life*, 141 (emphasis mine).

THE SPIRIT OF FREEDOM—TOWARD A PNEUMATOLOGICAL POLITICS OF THE CROSS AND RESURRECTION

The Holy Spirit of which the New Testament witness speaks, and which Christians have come to experience in a variety of ways, is variously identified as the Spirit of light, life, love, and freedom. In the context of a theo-political reading of God's reign, the identification of the Spirit with the imbricated actions of light, love, life, and freedom is significant. When seen through the lens of the enlivening power of the Spirit, the cross and resurrection of Jesus together point toward a politics of solidarity and the struggle for justice.

The Outpouring of Freedom

In the outpouring of the Spirit, witnesses to the resurrection become those who, to some extent, know and see not only who Jesus was, is, and will be, but even more importantly, they come to discern the shape and character of the God who raises the dead, and find themselves invited into the process of becoming disciples.

Discerning the Light

As we noted above, recognition of Jesus is central to the various resurrection narratives. To recognize that in Jesus God has vindicated one who was trampled underfoot by the powerful—by overcoming the power of death and the various machinations of injustice that wield that power—is central to understanding the meaning of the resurrection. Justice is actually done. Evil will not finally triumph. The oppressed have a champion in God; a champion who has hazarded death that humanity might live. It is the Spirit who opens the eyes to see this truth.

In the Gospel of John, the Spirit is described as one who will lead into "all truth" (cf. 16:13)—the truth here being who Jesus is and what it means to follow in his footsteps.[46] Jennifer McBride comments on the scene in John 16: "What Jesus communicates is that the coming of the Spirit is not the end to their discipleship journey but is the beginning of a movement—one rooted just as firmly in incarnational existence and bodily engagement

46. See Francis J. Moloney, SDB, *The Gospel of John* (Collegeville, MN: Liturgical Press, 1988), 440–42.

as before. . . . The disciples must live out the weight of Jesus' prior claims—those demands of the gospel to make peace, have mercy, do justice, and love enemies."[47] To recognize that in Jesus God has acted on behalf of the poor and the oppressed is to recognize the basic shape of God's reign, and thereby to recognize the form of life that God is calling for humanity to inhabit. Thus, the Spirit's role in offering light is not merely about making communities and individuals aware of the identity of Jesus per se; rather, it is about helping communities of faith and individuals see the *way* that God is God in Jesus. In Jesus, God is the God of the oppressed, the liberator of the enslaved, the healer of the broken, the One who exercises power in the form of self-giving and loving-kindness.

Neighbor Love

That form of life into which witnesses of the resurrection are invited by the Spirit is one marked by the same love and self-giving that marked the life of Jesus—a life that is now no longer bound by the power of death. In the Pauline and Deutero-Pauline literature, a central function of the gift of the Spirit is to energize and enable Christian communities to live like Jesus, to follow after him (cf. Phil. 2:1–11; Eph. 5:1–2). In the fifth chapter of his letter to the Galatians, Paul identifies the first fruit of the Spirit as love. What is often missed in popular interpretation of the passage is the profoundly communal nature of the love being described. Love is not simply a fellow feeling of regard; rather, it is an action lived out in community. This becomes especially clear when the passage in which the fruits of the Spirit are enumerated is placed in its proper context.

In verses 22–23 we read: "By contrast, the fruit of the Spirit is love, joy, peace, patience, kindness, generosity, faithfulness, gentleness, and self-control. There is no law against such things." As the NRSV helpfully draws out, this is a contrast list, meant to mark off a stark difference to what is described just prior in verses 19–21. There we read: "Now the works of the flesh are obvious: fornication, impurity, licentiousness, idolatry, sorcery, enmities, strife, jealousy, anger, quarrels, dissensions, factions, envy, drunkenness, carousing, and things like these." The two lists describe different visions of community—one marked by violence, impunity, and the devouring of one's neighbor; the other by the love of God, which regards

---

47. Jennifer M. McBride, *Radical Discipleship: A Liturgical Politics of the Gospel* (Minneapolis: Fortress, 2017), 230.

and respects the humanity of the other, a love that knits the community together in a bond of fellowship and mutuality made concrete by action. What is more, Paul makes it clear that the basis for living in this fashion is the Spirit whom God gives.

But the love that is meant to be central in the life of the community also spills out, transgressing boundaries as the "love of neighbor." This is made clear in the parable of the Good Samaritan. As recounted in Luke (see Luke 10:25-37), Jesus is queried by a legal scholar regarding how to find salvation. The conversation immediately circles around the greatest commandments: Love the Lord your God with all your heart, soul, strength, and mind; and love your neighbor as yourself. As the text tells us: "But wanting to justify himself, he asked Jesus, 'And who is my neighbor?'" (v. 29). Jesus responds to this clever question with the parable of the Good Samaritan, which recounts the act of compassion given by a Samaritan (i.e., one who would have been considered an outsider) to a stranger who had been robbed and beaten. The actions of the Samaritan include not only stopping to care for the man but also subsequently taking him to find shelter, food, and medicine, for which the Samaritan agrees to pay. These actions are all placed in striking contrast to a priest and a Levite, both of whom are said to have passed by the man in order to preserve their ritual purity. As Sharon Ringe notes, "The parable changes in a fundamental way how the question about neighbors is usually framed."[48] By the end of the parable, Jesus makes it clear that the question is not "who is my neighbor?," and therefore, what are the limitations of my love?, but rather, "am I being a neighbor to everyone I meet?"

The impelling force of the Spirit of love, then, aims at a "borderless love," a love that is not bound or enclosed but rather free and filled with energy. A love that is in stark contrast to the policies pursued at the southern border of the United States, or in areas like Israel/Palestine. In these places, borders mean separation and deprivation. At the southern border in the United States, children, even infants, are separated from parents, travelers from fellow travelers, and the human beings who guard borders from those who seek to pass over them. It is precisely such violent policing and surveillance that Jesus's border-transgressing love calls into question.

Furthermore, as the love of Jesus, the Crucified, it is a love that is always pushing the community of faith to turn toward those who have been neglected or made invisible. Much like the man who was robbed in the

---

48. Ringe, *Luke*, 160.

parable of the Good Samaritan and left for dead because of the religious codes of the day, there are many people our social order renders invisible and disposable. One need only think of the migrant, the sex worker, women of color, and any number of persons whom state policies and local practices render useless and disposable. It is to these that the Spirit of Jesus seeks to lead the church. It is these that the Spirit of Jesus calls members of the church-community to see as already loved by God and full members in God's people of faith. As Leonardo Boff observes: "The world is full of such people: nameless economic losers who carry no weight in the present system, because they produce very little and consume almost nothing. They are the ones who matter to Jesus. They are the ones we must love as our nearest neighbors, the ones we must love as we love ourselves."[49] The love of the Spirit lays a claim on those who receive it, such that any prior allegiances that may have guided who or how we love are qualified and set to the side. The love of God given in the Spirit finds its true end in genuine mutuality, a shared sense of common humanity, and the recognition that every human being—indeed, the creation as a whole—belongs to the living God whose love for creation will never end.

Freedom *for* Life

The Spirit, then, enlightens and empowers communities of faith in the way and praxis of Jesus. But the Spirit also brings freedom and life. If we take seriously that in the resurrection of Jesus God has indeed vindicated and set free a victim of the powers and principalities that seek to enslave and enclose humankind—and if we keep in mind that this same God is the one who led the people Israel out of bondage in Egypt—then we can understand why the biblical authors continually link the experience of God with the interlocking experiences of freedom and life.[50]

The Spirit of the resurrection who is poured out, energizing witnesses of the resurrection to live and seek a new life, is the Spirit of freedom, for "where the Spirit of the Lord is, there is freedom" (2 Cor. 3:17). But the living of this new life is not to be confused with the problematic assertions that have often characterized Christian conceptions of the Spirit's work in

---

49. Leonardo Boff, *Come, Holy Spirit: Inner Fire, Giver of Life, and Comforter of the Poor* (Maryknoll, NY: Orbis, 2015), 172.

50. See Moltmann, *The Spirit of Life*, 99-100.

the lives of people. In those conceptions, the Spirit is often only the energizing power that makes piety possible. This is, unfortunately, "a hopelessly impoverished view. The working of God's Spirit in the life of the believer means an involvement in the world where men are suffering."[51] Speaking from the context of the Black church tradition, J. Deotis Roberts describes the holistic and socially engaged work of the Spirit: "The spirit that comforts and heals in Black worship, renews and empowers us as we oppose the evils in the society which would humiliate and destroy us."[52] Rather than an empowerment for piety individualistically construed, the Spirit works to set communities and individuals free to forge relationships of solidarity and friendship that affirm the common humanity of all; they are set free to struggle for and imagine a world marked not by repression and dispossession but rather by mutuality, where access to a flourishing life is made available to all.

In contrast to the many forms of freedom discussed in the wider world, freedom as understood within a biblical framework is not so much a "freedom from" as a "freedom for." "God's freedom is essentially not freedom *from*, but freedom *to* and *for*."[53] To be more precise, the content of the Spirit of freedom and life who is poured out is none other than Jesus of Nazareth, who was free for God *and* the pursuit of God's Jubilee justice, and was therefore free to love and serve his neighbor. This is the form of freedom that is given in the power of the Spirit.

As we have endeavored to show in chapters 4 and 5, and in the preceding discussion in this chapter, the life, death, and resurrection of Jesus are bound up with the struggle for the liberation of humankind from the abstract and concrete manifestations of bondage, injustice, death dealing, and dehumanization. God's justice and righteousness refer to God's faithfulness that there should be a creation and that all creatures should have access to a flourishing life. This is the basic vision of the Jubilee. The return of land, the setting free of captives, the remission of debts—all of which are enumerated in the Levitical legislation—were concrete actions meant to ensure that all the people of Israel had access to the basic necessities for a

---

51. James H. Cone, *Black Theology and Black Power*, rev. ed. (Maryknoll, NY: Orbis, 1997), 58.

52. J. Deotis Roberts, "The Holy Spirit and Liberation: A Black Perspective," *Mid-Stream* 24, no. 4 (October 1985): 409.

53. Karl Barth, "The Gift of Freedom: Foundation of Evangelical Ethics," in *The Humanity of God*, by Karl Barth (Louisville: Westminster John Knox, 1960), 72.

flourishing life. In his inaugural sermon (see Luke 4:14–30), Jesus took this vision and further expanded it beyond the boundaries of Israel to include gentiles and then set about liberating people caught in a variety of forms of bondage.

For communities and individuals of faith to be set free for this vision means turning and learning to become a neighbor to all and to the whole of creation. But in a world where most human beings do not have access to a flourishing life, "living by the Spirit is impossible unless the believer lives in freedom *and* desires the same for everyone."[54] Just as Jesus went about proclaiming and enacting liberation, so also are disciples of Jesus called to follow after. "The creative power that enables people to struggle against the forces that diminish, oppress and dehumanize people, and to build freer and more just communities, is the power of the Holy Spirit."[55] To live in the Spirit of Jesus is to be caught up in the concrete struggles of those who daily find their lives and very humanity commodified, enclosed, expropriated, and subject to the brutalities of global economic and political dynamics that reach well beyond localized manifestations.

The life, love, and light that the Spirit gives, then, are energized in the power of the Spirit of freedom to take their course in a history marked by death. The disciple and the discipling community find the courage and indeed the freedom not only to recognize that God is among the victims of oppression bearing a cross but is also struggling for justice in the here and now. In the power of the Spirit of freedom, witnesses to the resurrection are empowered to forge relationships of solidarity and follow God into the hells that human beings have created in the midst of God's good earth. That same Spirit empowers them to refuse the borders erected in this world that seek to divide and deplete human sociality; to work for their dismantling and abolition, in order that mutuality may replace protectionism and avarice. That same Spirit empowers them to seek not only their own freedom but the freedom of the whole of creation.

The Struggle for the Commons—the Spirit of Abolition

The second chapter of the book of Acts recounts the event of Pentecost, often regarded as the birth of the church. The account details the outpour-

54. Boff, *Come, Holy Spirit*, 168 (emphasis mine).
55. John P. Brown, "The Holy Spirit in the Struggles of People for Liberation and Fullness of Life," *International Review of Mission* 79, no. 3 (July 15, 1990): 274.

ing of the promised Spirit and subsequent events. Several commentators have drawn attention to the theo-political dynamics at play in the book of Acts, especially the brief summaries of communal life found in chapters 2 and 4.[56] The summary in chapter 2 reads as follows: "All who believed were together and had all things in common; they would sell their possessions and goods and distribute the proceeds to all, as any had need. Day by day, as they spent much time together in the temple, they broke bread at home and ate their food with glad and generous hearts, praising God and having the goodwill of all the people. And day by day the Lord added to their number those who were being saved" (Acts 2:44-47). The significance of this summary cannot be overstated regarding questions about the concrete form of life that the outpouring of the Spirit effected and that the early Christians sought to enact.[57] Though it is beyond the scope of our task here to do justice to this passage in total, let alone to engage the Pentecost narrative, it is important to highlight the key descriptor that begins the passage: "All who believed were together and had all things in common; they would sell their possessions and goods and distribute the proceeds to all, as any had need." The text tells us that the earliest disciples held everything in *common*.

A similar summary appears again in chapter 4:

Now the whole group of those who believed were of one heart and soul, and no one claimed private ownership of any possessions, but everything they owned was held in common. With great power the apostles gave their testimony to the resurrection of the Lord Jesus, and great grace was upon them all. There was not a needy person among them, for as many as owned lands or houses sold them and brought the proceeds of what was sold. They laid it at the apostles' feet, and it was distributed to each as any had need. There was a Levite, a native of Cyprus, Joseph, to whom the apostles gave the name Barnabas (which means "son of encouragement"). He sold a field that belonged to him, then brought the money, and laid it at the apostles' feet. (Acts 4:32-37)

56. See, for example, Justo L. González, *Acts: The Gospel of the Spirit* (Maryknoll, NY: Orbis, 2001); C. Kavin Rowe, *World Upside Down: Reading Acts in the Graeco-Roman Age* (New York: Oxford University Press, 2009); Matthew L. Skinner, *Intrusive God, Disruptive Gospel: Encountering the Divine in the Book of Acts* (Grand Rapids: Brazos, 2015); and Willie James Jennings, *Acts* (Louisville: Westminster John Knox, 2017).

57. Notwithstanding some objections that this is an idealized portrait. See n. 59 below.

The vision put forward here can be described loosely as "commoning"—that is, a communal endeavor not so much to renounce possessions as to hold them differently by holding them cooperatively. When taken together, both passages depict a community in which "those who did possess property did not *claim* it as such but thought of it as property to be shared with those in need."[58] Rather than this being about a theory of political economy, it is about a Spirit-empowered form of voluntary economic redistribution that doesn't mean the eradication of the notion of individual possessions or property, but rather a reorientation of the relationship that communities and individuals have in regard to the same.

Not surprisingly—and especially in the modern era—some commentators have often bent over backward to argue against the vision of "commoning" found in these passages.[59] But such arguments often ignore other early Christian sources as well as the longer history-of-effects, or tradition, that has flowed out from these texts as evidence that many in the early Christian movement did indeed seek to take this communal vision seriously.[60] In addition to the other sources within the New Testament itself (cf. 2 Cor. 8–9; James 2:1–7),[61] one can find numerous theological critiques of injustice and greed that are consistently framed as an abrogation of the common possession of the earth by humanity and the many creatures that inhabit it, well into the early modern period and beyond. Take, for instance, the following passages from the late antique period:

> Mark the wise dispensation of God! That he might put humanity to shame, he has made certain things common, as the sun, air, earth, and water . . . whose benefits are dispensed equally to all as brethren . . . observe, that concerning things that are common there is no contention, but all is peaceable. But when one attempts to possess himself of anything, to make it his

58. Beverly Roberts Gaventa, *The Acts of the Apostles* (Nashville: Abingdon, 2003), 100.

59. See González, *Acts*, 70–74, for a discussion of some of the most typical arguments, as well as a critical response.

60. "Putting the economic teachings of Jesus, based on the principles of the Jubilee and Sabbatical laws, into practice was not optional for the early Christians; it was not something that a Christian might do if he or she feels like being an especially nice person. This was something that a Christian must do, was obligated to do; it was just as central to the early Christians as was refraining from idolatry and fornication." Roman A. Montero, *All Things in Common: The Economic Practices of the Early Christians* (Eugene, OR: Resource Publications, 2017), 122.

61. See Gaventa, *Acts of the Apostles*, 100.

own, then contention is introduced, as if nature herself were indignant, that when God brings us together in every way, we are eager to divide and separate ourselves by appropriating things, and by using those cold words "mine and thine." Then there is contention and uneasiness. But where this is not, no strife or contention is bred. This state therefore is rather our inheritance, and more agreeable to nature.[62]

Or,

Nature has poured forth all things for all people for common use. God has ordered all things to be produced, so that there should be food in common to all, and that the earth should be a common possession for all. Nature, therefore, has produced a common right for all, but greed has made it a right for a few.[63]

Both texts, from John Chrysostom and Ambrose of Milan, respectively, indicate a typical view held by numerous key figures from the history of Christianity. Nevertheless, the persistent appearance of this core assumption in the form of a critical invective and imperative command for Christians to follow indicates that there was indeed significant resistance to it, even within the Christian community itself.[64] Indeed, much like the ministry of Jesus, the form of "commoning" envisioned in Acts met resistance, rejection, and even violent suppression, often from other Christians.

In the modern age, one of the central dynamics of resistance to forms of "commoning" both within the confines of the church and well beyond is often described as "enclosure." Historically speaking, "enclosure" refers to the legal and extralegal process of cordoning off common lands that were open to day laborers, peasants, farmers, fishermen, and all those—both men and women—who "hewed wood and drew water"[65] in Europe begin-

---

62. John Chrysostom, "Homily 12 on 1 Timothy," in *Nicene and Post-Nicene Fathers: First Series*, ed. Philip Schaff (New York: Cosimo Classics, 2007), 13:448.

63. Ambrose of Milan, "Duties of the Clergy," in *Nicene and Post-Nicene Fathers: Second Series*, ed. Philip Schaff and Rev. Henry Wallace (New York: Cosimo Classics, 2007), 10:23.

64. See Martin Hengel, *Property and Riches in the Early Church* (Philadelphia: Fortress, 1974); Susan R. Holman, ed., *Wealth and Poverty in Early Church and Society* (Grand Rapids: Baker Academic, 2008); Peter Brown, *Through the Eye of a Needle: Wealth, the Fall of Rome, and the Making of Christianity in the West, 350–550 AD* (Princeton: Princeton University Press, 2012); and Montero, *All Things in Common*.

65. See Peter Linebaugh and Marcus Rediker, *The Many-Headed Hydra: Sailors, Slaves,*

ning in the thirteenth and fourteenth century.[66] The wealthy and powerful began to seize such lands and to expel the inhabitants who had lived there for generations. Those who were expelled were then rendered much more vulnerable to poverty, exploitation, and enslavement by the same people who had driven them from the land.

One of the earliest attempts to curtail the rapaciousness of the powerful came in the form of the Magna Carta, or "Great Charter," of 1215, and its companion, the "Charter of the Forests." Speaking of the Magna Carta, historian Peter Linebaugh notes, "Its provisions revealed the oppression of women, the aspirations of the bourgeoisie, the mixture of greed and power in the tyranny, an independent ecology of the commons, and the famous chapter 39 from which habeas corpus, prohibition of torture, trial by jury, and the rule of law are derived."[67] Both the Magna Carta and the "Charter of the Forests" sought to assure the rights of individuals vis-à-vis the state and landed and monied interests, and to curtail the greed of the powerful over against the powerless.

Though the process began in the late medieval era, "enclosure" has come to signify the ongoing attempt to control and exploit populations in order to expropriate labor and wealth.[68] The transatlantic slave trade, which began during roughly the same period; the evolution of the prison or workhouse; the factory; the merchant ship; the plantation—all these (and others) have functioned as institutional expressions of "enclosure" either consistently throughout their history, or at one time or another in their development. Racism and racial capitalism; gender and sexual exploitation; colonization and the seizure and expropriation of indigenous lands; the building of impenetrable border walls that facilitate the flow of capital

---

Commoners, and the Hidden History of the Revolutionary Atlantic (Boston: Beacon, 2000), 36–70.

66. See Silvia Federici, *Re-enchanting the World: Feminism and the Politics of the Commons* (Oakland, CA: PM Press, 2019).

67. Peter Linebaugh, *The Magna Carta Manifesto: Liberties and Commons for All* (Berkeley: University of California Press, 2008), 28.

68. I am borrowing this observation from Linebaugh: "The 'English enclosure movement' has belonged to that series of concrete universals—like the slave trade, the witch burnings, the Irish famine, or the genocide of Native Americans—that has defined the crime of modernism, limited in time and place but also immanent with the possibility of recurrence." "Enclosures from Bottom Up," in *Stop, Thief! The Commons, Enclosures, and Resistance*, by Peter Linebaugh (Oakland, CA: PM Press, 2014), 142. See also Federici, *Re-enchanting the World*, 26–33.

and commodity while impeding the migration of vulnerable human be-ings—these can all be seen in some measure as expressions of enclosure: *the attempt to control bodies and material resources, to dispossess others of their rights and freedoms, and to bar access to the resources needed for a flourishing life*. In short, the attempt to steal the bread, water, breath, and freedom needed to truly live.

Though it is beyond the scope of this book to offer a full-scale descrip-tion of the historical development and material dynamics of enclosure, nevertheless, we can say in light of what we have learned about God's reign thus far in our argument, and especially in view of the work of liberation that is central to the work of the Spirit, that against such processes the only possible stance and action is one of revolt and abolition.[69]

In the fateful summer of 2020, events unfolded in Minneapolis that subsequently came to be called "the uprising." On May 20, George Floyd, a forty-six-year-old African American man, was murdered by Minneapolis police. Unlike many other victims of police violence, Floyd's death was different both in its form and in the fact that his execution was filmed by multiple bystanders. Floyd was not shot to death by the police, as has happened to so many black and brown people of color. Rather, he was handcuffed, wrestled to the ground, and pinned down by three police officers, while one of the officers placed his knee into the neck of Floyd for over nine minutes, preventing air from entering his lungs, eventually killing him.

The raw reality of the killing of Floyd sparked understandable outrage, his death being one in a series of police-related deaths in the Twin Cities. Peaceful protests began, which at night sometimes turned violent, as peo-ple and groups with no direct relation to the neighborhood sought to in-flame the situation by starting fires, looting, and inciting violence. After the protests and riots had subsided, it became clear that the protests had been about more than the killing of George Floyd. The neighborhood where Mr. Floyd died has long suffered under a variety of macro- and microdynamics that can be explained through the lens of "enclosure." Redlining, racial housing covenants, disinvestment, and overpolicing have been major dy-namics in shaping the history and geography of Minneapolis. The eruption

69. What Karl Barth once referred to as the revolt against "the lordless powers." See his *The Christian Life: Church Dogmatics* IV/4; *Lecture Fragments* (Grand Rapids: Eerdmans, 1981), 205–33.

of anger and the cry for change were decades long in the making.[70] As one native Minnesotan put it: "This was all inevitable."[71]

Not long after the protests and riots had ended, members of the neighborhood where Floyd was killed by the Minneapolis police began calling for a reimaging of policing and the social, political, and economic dynamics that had contributed to Floyd's death and the social conditions in south Minneapolis. "Defund the police" was a call to reimagine public safety and was rooted in long-standing conversations about abolition democracy.[72] Though the call has yet to lead to meaningful changes, nevertheless, local organizers decided to create a commons of their own.

George Floyd Square, located at East Thirty-Eighth Street and Chicago Avenue, was declared an autonomous zone by residents in the area. Over against the various policies and practices that have done significant harm to community members, the endeavors occurring in George Floyd Square can be understood as an expression of the commons. Medical care, mental health care, food and clothing distribution, and community safety patrols are all organized by local residents, who typically meet twice a day. Art, poetry, dance, song, and even comedy have been employed as tools meant to express pain, pleasure, hope, and despair and to build and reaffirm communal bonds and commitments.

70. For a history of redlining and racial covenants, see the ongoing project Mapping Prejudice: https://mappingprejudice.umn.edu/index.html. For a broader history of the role of the federal government in creating segregated neighborhoods in places like Minneapolis, see Richard Rothstein, *The Color of Law: A Forgotten History of How Our Government Segregated America* (New York: Liveright, 2017). For a discussion of the role that financial institutions and real estate agencies played in keeping communities of color from access to home ownership, see Keeanga-Yamahtta Taylor, *Race for Profit: How Banks and the Real Estate Industry Undermined Black Homeownership* (Chapel Hill: University of North Carolina Press, 2019). For a history of the long and acrimonious history between the Minneapolis Police Department and communities of color, see https://www.mpd150.com/. For a history of the construction of Interstate 35W and its effects on communities of color in south Minneapolis, see *MPD 150: A People's Project Evaluating Policing*, accessed January 27, 2022, https://www.mpd150.com/.

71. Justin Ellis, "Minneapolis Had This Coming," *Atlantic*, June 9, 2020, https://www.theatlantic.com/ideas/archive/2020/06/minneapolis-long-overdue-crisis/612826/.

72. See Christina B. Heatherton, "#BlackLivesMatter and Global Visions of Abolition: An Interview with Patrise Cullors," in *Policing the Planet: Why the Policing Crisis Led to Black Lives Matter*, ed. Jordan T. Camp and Christina Heatherton (London: Verso, 2016), 35–40; Angela Y. Davis, *Abolition Democracy: Beyond Empire, Prisons, and Torture* (New York: Seven Stories, 2005).

Though many of the endeavors can be understood as experimental and therefore open to change or augmentation, when taken as a whole, the autonomous zone can be read as a provisional expression of the Spirit of freedom and abolition. For the Spirit is interested in calling people into the life that God gives indiscriminately. "The Spirit forever calls us out of our captivities, our prisons, our graves—calls us to stand up."[73] The Spirit "calls us to stand up." Choosing to rethink and reject the status quo of city politics and racial capitalism, members of the neighborhood are seeking to make equity and mutuality possible. When they do so, one can discern the Spirit of the resurrection, for "Wherever fear is overcome and human dignity is regained, wherever people reject the death imposed on them by others and struggle in their brokenness and with hope, seeking to build among themselves a new community where there is fullness of life—there we see signs of the breaking in of God's rule and of the Spirit of God, and there we may speak of resurrection."[74] Expressions like George Floyd Square fit within the long history of resistance to enclosure and dehumanization, and resonate with the practices of the early Christians who held all things in common, affirming the basic dignity and value of every human being, and their right to access the flourishing life that God intends.

CONCLUSION

The Crucified lives. Justice has been done, and because justice is done for Jesus the victim, we can know that God intends to do justice on behalf of all victims. Jesus's resurrection makes clear that the God of mercy, justice, and righteousness is faithful not only to the divine intention for creation but also to creation itself, and especially to those creatures who have been denied the flourishing life that God intended. It marks a vindication of Jesus's life and represents a re-presentation of the indestructability of God's reign. Jesus's life was the embodiment of God's reign, and though struck down by faithlessness, nevertheless he lives. And because he lives, because his life history has been released from death's grip, the true power of Jesus's humble, loving, and justice-seeking way is shown to be the way of God. The

---

73. John P. Brown, "The Holy Spirit," 277.
74. John P. Brown, "The Holy Spirit," 277.

resurrection of Jesus offers hope for a different future, a different world, but also a new and different way of living in the world here and now.

The outpouring of the Spirit of freedom is what empowers communities and people to enter into the way of Jesus. By the power of the Spirit, followers of the way of Jesus—and even those who might claim no direct relation to Jesus—gain courage and energy to live out in an improvisational and provisional fashion the very same commitment to God's Jubilee justice that Jesus himself embodied.

Conclusion

In June of 2020, not long after George Floyd's death and the subsequent uprising in Minneapolis and across the country, I joined about two thousand clergy from various denominations in a silent walk to honor Mr. Floyd and to express solidarity with our Black and brown brothers and sisters in their struggle for life and justice. The march began about one-fourth of a mile from Thirty-Eighth and Chicago, the holy ground where Mr. Floyd was murdered. Our walk took a little over nine minutes, the same amount of time that an officer from the Minneapolis Police Department had placed his knee on Mr. Floyd's neck, denying him the breath of life and eventually suffocating him to death.

The mood was somber, but also determined. There was lament, but also deep commitment. As we approached Thirty-Eighth and Chicago, I began to hear the voice of a woman crying out: "Black lives matter! All lives matter! Black lives matter! All lives matter!" As the meeting at the crossroads commenced, different leaders from the community and from the historic Black Protestant churches led us in prayer, as did Mr. Floyd's family. While this was happening, the woman who was crying out shifted into a deeper register. She began to wail: "Black lives matter! Black lives matter! Black lives matter!" There were some in the crowd who seemed intent on trying to get her to tone down her cry, but to no avail. I will never forget the sound of that woman's voice because it came from deep within her, buried in pain, but also longing. It was a searching cry for God to act; to make right a world that is so profoundly wrong; to indeed see to it that Black lives do matter, because when Black lives matter, then all lives will matter.

That woman's cry "Black lives matter! Black lives matter! Black lives matter!" was prayer. It was the only prayer at that moment that could be uttered. It was a riff on the second petition of the Lord's Prayer: "Thy kingdom come!" It was a kingdom prayer. For to dissolve the bondage of white supremacy and to abolish the structures of racial capitalism that have so deeply disfigured all of humanity, indeed the earth, and especially those who have lived on the underside of the modern world, is in such profound continuity with the reign of God that Jesus embodied, the kingdom that he calls his disciples to enter into, that it would be hard to imagine a more urgent task for followers of Jesus to pursue.

There are many places in the world where one can discern God's reign at work, but it can especially be discerned in the struggles of ordinary people for life, dignity, care, fellowship, justice, and peace. And as we have shown, this struggle is a struggle not only for life for some, but for a flourishing life for all.

For God's reign is one where flourishing life is given and affirmed for all. Where fellowship and fellow feeling are the norm. It is a power that confronts this world and its death-dealing arrangements in judgment, but for the purpose of igniting new life—life in fellowship with God, with one another, and with the earth. This is the kingdom about which Jesus spoke, which he lived out, and for which he died, and continues to live. This is the reign of God that people of good will, and those who want to follow Jesus, are invited to seek in the power of the Spirit and to bring to bear on a world that is in deep need of healing, wholeness, justice, peace, and joy.

Let us turn then to the God of life, to the way of Jesus, the way of the kingdom, the way of love! Let us put our hands on the plow to sow God's *shalom*, to seek God's justice, to know and spread God's mercy, so that all people may live freely in genuine fellowship with the earth, with one another, and with the God of life! Amen.

BIBLIOGRAPHY

Ackroyd, Peter R. *Exile and Restoration: A Study of Hebrew Thought of the Sixth Century B.C.* Philadelphia: Westminster, 1968.

Alexander, Michelle. *The New Jim Crow: Mass Incarceration in the Age of Color-blindness.* New York: New Press, 2012.

Allen, Leslie C. "Some Prophetic Antecedents of Apocalyptic Eschatology and Their Hermeneutical Value." *Ex Auditu* 6 (1990): 15–28.

Allison, Dale C., Jr. *The End of the Ages Has Come: An Early Interpretation of the Passion and Resurrection of Jesus.* Philadelphia: Fortress, 1985.

———. *Studies in Matthew: Interpretation Past and Present.* Grand Rapids: Baker Academic, 2005.

Ambrose of Milan. "Duties of the Clergy." In *Nicene and Post-Nicene Fathers: Second Series*, edited by Philip Schaff and Rev. Henry Wallace, 10:1–90. New York: Cosimo Classics, 2007.

Ateek, Naim Stifan. *A Palestinian Christian Cry for Reconciliation.* Maryknoll, NY: Orbis, 2008.

Balthasar, Hans Urs von, ed. *Origen, Spirit and Fire: A Thematic Anthology of His Writings.* Washington, DC: Catholic University of America Press, 1984.

Barrett, C. K. *The Gospel according to St. John.* London: SPCK, 1975.

Barth, Karl. *The Christian Life: Church Dogmatics IV/4; Lecture Fragments.* Grand Rapids: Eerdmans, 1981.

———. *Church Dogmatics* II/1. Edinburgh: T&T Clark, 1957.

———. *Church Dogmatics* III/3. Edinburgh: T&T Clark, 2000.

———. *Church Dogmatics* IV/1. Edinburgh: T&T Clark, 1956.

———. *Church Dogmatics* IV/2. Edinburgh: T&T Clark, 1958.

———. *Church Dogmatics* IV/4. Edinburgh: T&T Clark, 1969.

———. "The Gift of Freedom: Foundation of Evangelical Ethics." In *The Humanity of God*, by Karl Barth, 69–96. Louisville: Westminster John Knox, 1960.

———. "Poverty." In *Against the Stream: Shorter Post-War Writings, 1946–52*, by Karl Barth, 241–46. London: SCM, 1954.

———. *Prayer*. Fiftieth anniversary ed. Louisville: Westminster John Knox, 2002.

Bauckham, Richard. *Jesus and the God of Israel:* God Crucified *and Other Studies on the New Testament's Christology of Divine Identity*. Grand Rapids: Eerdmans, 2008.

———. *Gospel of Glory: Major Themes in Johannine Theology*. Grand Rapids: Baker Academic, 2015.

Beasley-Murray, G. R. *Jesus and the Kingdom of God*. Grand Rapids: Eerdmans, 1986.

Belousek, Darrin W. Snyder. *Atonement, Justice, and Peace: The Message of the Cross and the Mission of the Church*. Grand Rapids: Eerdmans, 2012.

Berkhof, Hendrik. *Christ and the Powers*. Translated by John Howard Yoder. Scottdale, PA: Herald, 1977.

Blenkinsopp, Joseph. "The Theological Politics of Deutero-Isaiah." In *Divination, Politics, and Ancient Near Eastern Empires*, edited by Alan Lenzi and Jonathan Stökl, 129–43. Atlanta: Society for Biblical Literature, 2014.

Block, Daniel I. "My Servant David: Ancient Israel's Vision of the Messiah." In *Israel's Messiah in the Bible and the Dead Sea Scrolls*, edited by Richard S. Hess and M. Daniel Carroll R., 17–56. Grand Rapids: Baker Academic, 2003.

Blomberg, Craig L. "Jesus, Sinners, and Table Fellowship." *Bulletin for Biblical Research* 19, no. 1 (2009): 35–62.

Blumhardt, Christoph. *Ansprachen, Predigten, Reden, Briefe, 1865–1917*. Vol. 2, *1890–1906*. Edited by Johannes Harder. Neukirchen-Vluyn: Neukirchener Verlag, 1978.

———. *Christoph Blumhardt and His Message*. Edited by R. Lejeune. Woodcrest, NY: Plough, 1963.

———. *Make Way for the Spirit: My Father's Battle and Mine*. Walden, NY: Plough, 2019.

Boer, Dick. *Deliverance from Slavery: Attempting a Biblical Theology in the Service of Liberation*. Chicago: Haymarket Books, 2015.

Boer, Martinus C. de. *The Defeat of Death: Apocalyptic Eschatology in 1 Corinthians 15 and Romans 5*. Sheffield: Sheffield Academic Press, 1988.

Boff, Leonardo. *Come, Holy Spirit: Inner Fire, Giver of Life, and Comforter of the Poor*. Maryknoll, NY: Orbis, 2015.

———. *The Lord's Prayer: The Prayer of Integral Liberation*. Maryknoll, NY: Orbis, 1983.

Bonhoeffer, Dietrich. *Letters and Papers from Prison*. Minneapolis: Fortress, 2010.

Bibliography

Boyarin, Daniel. *The Jewish Gospels: The Story of the Jewish Christ.* New York: New Press, 2012.

Braumann, G. "Parousia." In *The New International Dictionary of New Testament Theology*, edited by Colin Brown, 2:898-901. Grand Rapids: Zondervan, 1986.

Brent, Allen. *A Political History of Early Christianity.* Edinburgh: T&T Clark, 2009.

Breslauer, S. Daniel. "Power, Compassion and the Servant of the Lord in Second Isaiah." *Encounter* 48, no. 2 (Spring 1987): 163-78.

Brown, Colin. "Resurrection." In *The New International Dictionary of New Testament Theology*, edited by Colin Brown, 3:259-309. Grand Rapids: Zondervan, 1986.

Brown, John P. "The Holy Spirit in the Struggles of People for Liberation and Fullness of Life." *International Review of Mission* 79, no. 3 (July 15, 1990): 273-81.

Brown, Peter. *Through the Eye of a Needle: Wealth, the Fall of Rome, and the Making of Christianity in the West, 350-550 AD.* Princeton: Princeton University Press, 2012.

Brown, Raymond E. *The Birth of the Messiah: A Commentary on the Infancy Narratives in the Gospels of Matthew and Luke.* Rev. ed. New York: Doubleday, 1993.

———. *The Death of the Messiah: From Gethsemane to the Grave.* 2 vols. New York: Doubleday, 1994.

———. *The Gospel according to John I-XII.* Garden City, NY: Doubleday, 1966.

Brueggemann, Walter. *A Commentary on Jeremiah: Exile and Homecoming.* Grand Rapids: Eerdmans, 1998.

———. *An Introduction to the Old Testament: The Canon and Christian Imagination.* Louisville: Westminster John Knox, 2003.

———. *Israel's Praise: Doxology against Idolatry and Ideology.* Philadelphia: Fortress, 1988.

———. *Like Fire in the Bones: Listening for the Prophetic Word in Jeremiah.* Minneapolis: Fortress, 2006.

———. "Praise to God Is the End of Wisdom—What Is the Beginning?" *Journal for Preachers* 12, no. 3 (Easter 1989): 30-40.

———. *The Prophetic Imagination.* 2nd ed. Minneapolis: Fortress, 2001.

———. "Psalms 9-10: A Counter to Conventional Social Reality." In *The Bible and the Politics of Exegesis*, edited by David Jobling et al., 3-15. Cleveland: Pilgrim, 1991.

———. *An Unsettling God: The Heart of the Hebrew Bible.* Minneapolis: Fortress, 2009.

Buber, Martin. *Kingship of God.* 3rd ed. Amherst, NY: Humanity Books, 1967.

Carmichael, Calum. *Illuminating Leviticus: A Study of Its Laws and Institutions in the Light of Biblical Narratives.* Baltimore: Johns Hopkins University Press, 2006.

Carter, Warren. "Matthew's Gospel: An Anti-Imperial/Imperial Reading." *Currents in Theology and Mission* 34, no. 6 (December 2007): 424–33.

Chrysostom, John. "Homily 12 on 1 Timothy." In *Nicene and Post-Nicene Fathers: First Series*, edited by Philip Schaff, 13:444–49. New York: Cosimo Classics, 2007.

Collins, John J., ed. *Apocalypse: The Morphology of a Genre.* Semeia 14. Missoula, MT: Society of Biblical Literature, 1979.

———. "Apocalyptic Eschatology as the Transcendence of Death." *Catholic Biblical Quarterly* 36, no. 1 (1974): 21–43.

———. *The Apocalyptic Imagination.* 2nd ed. Grand Rapids: Eerdmans, 1997.

———. *The Apocalyptic Vision of the Book of Daniel.* Ann Arbor, MI: Scholars Press, 1977.

———. *Daniel: A Commentary on the Book of Daniel.* Minneapolis: Fortress, 1993.

———, ed. *The Oxford Handbook of Apocalyptic Literature.* Oxford: Oxford University Press, 2014.

Cone, James H. *Black Theology and Black Power.* Rev. ed. Maryknoll, NY: Orbis, 1997.

———. *A Black Theology of Liberation.* Fortieth anniversary ed. Maryknoll, NY: Orbis, 2016.

———. *The Cross and the Lynching Tree.* Maryknoll, NY: Orbis, 2011.

———. *God of the Oppressed.* Rev. ed. Maryknoll, NY: Orbis, 1997.

———. *The Spirituals and the Blues: An Interpretation.* Maryknoll, NY: Orbis, 1992.

Cousar, Charles B. *A Theology of the Cross: The Death of Jesus in the Pauline Letters.* Minneapolis: Fortress, 1990.

Croatto, José Severino. "From the Leviticus Jubilee Year to the Prophetic Liberation Time: Exegetical Reflections on Isaiah 61 and 58 in Relation to the Jubilee." In *God's Economy: Biblical Studies from Latin America*, edited by Ross Kinsler and Gloria Kinsler, 89–111. Maryknoll, NY: Orbis, 2005.

Cross, Frank Moore. *Canaanite Myth and Hebrew Epic: Essays in the History of the Religion of Israel.* Cambridge, MA: Harvard University Press, 1996.

Crouch, Stanley. *The All-American Skin Game, or the Decoy of Race: The Long and the Short of It, 1990–1994.* New York: Pantheon Books, 1995.

Cummings, George C. L. "The Slave Narratives as a Source of Black Theological Discourse: The Spirit and Eschatology." In *Cut Loose Your Stammering Tongue: Black Theology in the Slave Narratives*, edited by Dwight N. Hopkins and George Cummings, 46–66. Maryknoll, NY: Orbis, 1991.

Davidson, Steed Vernyl. *Empire and Exile: Postcolonial Readings of the Book of Jeremiah.* Edinburgh: T&T Clark, 2011.

Davies, W. D., and Dale C. Allison. *A Critical and Exegetical Commentary on the Gospel according to Saint Matthew.* Vol. 1. Edinburgh: T&T Clark, 1988.

———. *Matthew: A Shorter Commentary.* London: T&T Clark International, 2004.

Davis, Angela Y. *Abolition Democracy: Beyond Empire, Prisons, and Torture.* New York: Seven Stories, 2005.

Dekker, Jaap. "The Servant and the Servants in the Book of Isaiah." *Sárospataki Füzetek* 3, no. 4 (2012): 33–46.

DiTommaso, Lorenzo. "Deliverance and Justice: Soteriology in the Book of Daniel." In *This World and the World to Come: Soteriology in Early Judaism,* edited by Daniel M. Gurtner, 71–86. London: T&T Clark, 2011.

Dodd, C. H. *The Parables of the Kingdom.* New York: Charles Scribner's Sons, 1961.

Dorman, Anke. "'Commit Injustice and Shed Innocent Blood': Motives behind the Institution of the Day of Atonement in the Book of Jubilees." In *The Day of Atonement: Its Interpretation in Early Jewish and Christian Traditions,* edited by Thomas Hieke and Tobias Nicklas, 49–61. Leiden: Brill, 2012.

Douglas, Kelly Brown. *Stand Your Ground: Black Bodies and the Justice of God.* Maryknoll, NY: Orbis, 2015.

Du Bois, W. E. B. *Black Reconstruction in America: 1860–1880.* New York: Free Press, 1992.

Dussel, Enrique. *The Underside of Modernity: Apel, Ricoeur, Rorty, Taylor, and the Philosophy of Liberation.* Atlantic Highlands, NJ: Humanities, 1996.

Ellis, E. Earle. "Segregation and the Kingdom of God." *Christianity Today* 1, no. 12 (March 1957): 6–9.

Ellis, Justin. "Minneapolis Had This Coming." *Atlantic,* June 9, 2020. https://www.theatlantic.com/ideas/archive/2020/06/minneapolis-long-overdue-crisis/612826/.

Eskenazi, Tamara C. "Exile and the Dreams of Return." *Currents in Mission and Theology* 17, no. 3 (June 1990): 192–200.

Fanon, Frantz. *The Wretched of the Earth.* New York: Grove, 2004.

Farris, Stephen. *The Hymns of Luke's Infancy Narratives: Their Origin, Meaning, and Significance.* Sheffield: JSNT, 1985.

Federici, Silvia. *Re-enchanting the World: Feminism and the Politics of the Commons.* Oakland, CA: PM Press, 2019.

Fitzgerald, John Thomas. "The Temptation of Jesus: The Testing of the Messiah in Matthew." *Restoration Quarterly* 15, no. 3–4 (1972): 152–60.

Fitzmyer, Joseph A. *The Gospel according to Luke X–XXIV.* Garden City, NY: Doubleday, 1985.

Forestell, J. Terence. *The Word of the Cross: Salvation as Revelation in the Fourth Gospel.* Rome: Biblical Institute Press, 1974.

Frey, Jörg. "Apocalyptic Dualism." In *The Oxford Handbook of Apocalyptic Literature*, edited by John J. Collins, 271–94. New York: Oxford University Press, 2014.

Garroway, Joshua. "The Invasion of a Mustard Seed: A Reading of Mark 5.1–20." *Journal for the Study of the New Testament* 32, no. 1 (2009): 57–75.

Gaventa, Beverly Roberts. *The Acts of the Apostles.* Nashville: Abingdon, 2003.

———. *Our Mother Saint Paul.* Louisville: Westminster John Knox, 2007.

———. *When in Romans: An Invitation to Linger with the Gospel according to Paul.* Grand Rapids: Baker Academic, 2016.

Gilmore, Ruth Wilson. "Fatal Couplings of Power and Difference: Notes on Racism and Geography." *Professional Geographer* 54, no. 1 (2002): 15–24.

Goff, Matthew. "Wisdom and Apocalypticism." In *The Oxford Handbook of Apocalyptic Literature*, edited by John J. Collins, 52–68. New York: Oxford University Press, 2014.

González, Justo L. *Acts: The Gospel of the Spirit.* Maryknoll, NY: Orbis, 2001.

———. *Luke.* Louisville: Westminster John Knox, 2010.

Gowan, David E. *Theology of the Prophetic Books: The Death and Resurrection of Israel.* Louisville: Westminster John Knox, 1998.

Grabbe, Lester L. "'Son of Man': Its Origin and Meaning in Second Temple Judaism." In *Enoch and the Synoptic Gospels: Reminiscences, Allusions, Intertextuality*, edited by Loren T. Stuckenbruck and Gabriele Boccaccini, 169–97. Atlanta: SBL Press, 2016.

Grabbe, Lester L., and Robert D. Haak, eds. *Knowing the End from the Beginning: The Prophetic, the Apocalyptic, and Their Relationships.* London: T&T Clark, 2003.

Granzano, Frank. *The Millennial New World.* Oxford: Oxford University Press, 1999.

Green, Joel B. *The Gospel of Luke.* Grand Rapids: Eerdmans, 1997.

Guðmundsdóttir, Arnfríður. *Meeting God on the Cross: Christ, the Cross, and the Feminist Critique.* Oxford: Oxford University Press, 2010.

Guelich, Robert. *An Introduction for Understanding the Sermon on the Mount.* Dallas: Word, 1982.

Gunkel, Hermann. *Introduction to Psalms: The Genres of the Religious Lyric of Israel.* Macon, GA: Mercer University Press, 1998.

Haber, Susan. "A Woman's Touch: Feminist Encounters with the Hemorrhaging Woman in Mark 5.24–34." *Journal for the Study of the New Testament* 26, no. 2 (2003): 171–92.

Hanson, Paul D. *The Dawn of Apocalyptic: The Historical and Sociological Roots of Jewish Apocalyptic Eschatology.* Rev. ed. Philadelphia: Fortress, 1979.

———. "Prophetic and Apocalyptic Politics." In *The Last Things: Biblical and Theo-*

logical Perspectives on Eschatology, edited by Carl E. Braaten and Robert W. Jenson, 43–66. Grand Rapids: Eerdmans, 2002.

Harink, Douglas. *Paul among the Postliberals: Pauline Theology beyond Christendom and Modernity.* Grand Rapids: Brazos, 2003.

Harper, Matthew. *The End of Days: African American Religion and Politics in the Age of Emancipation.* Chapel Hill: University of North Carolina Press, 2016.

Harrisville, Roy A. *Fracture: The Cross as Irreconcilable in the Language and Thought of the Biblical Writers.* Grand Rapids: Eerdmans, 2006.

Harvey, Jennifer. *Dear White Christians: For Those Still Longing for Racial Reconciliation.* Grand Rapids: Eerdmans, 2014.

Harvey, Jennifer, Karin A. Case, and Robin Hawley Gorsline. Introduction to *Disrupting White Supremacy from Within: White People on What We Need to Do*, edited by Jennifer Harvey et al., 3–32. Cleveland: Pilgrim, 2008.

Hauerwas, Stanley. *Matthew.* Grand Rapids: Brazos, 2006.

Hays, Richard B. *First Corinthians.* Louisville: Westminster John Knox, 2011.

Heatherton, Christina B. "#BlackLivesMatter and Global Visions of Abolition: An Interview with Patrise Cullors." In *Policing the Planet: Why the Policing Crisis Led to Black Lives Matter*, edited by Jordan T. Camp and Christina Heatherton, 35–40. London: Verso, 2016.

Hengel, Martin. *Christ and Power.* Dublin: Christian Journals, 1977.

———. *Crucifixion in the Ancient World and the Folly of the Message of the Cross.* Philadelphia: Fortress, 1977.

———. *Property and Riches in the Early Church.* Philadelphia: Fortress, 1974.

Hertig, Paul. "The Jubilee Mission of Jesus in the Gospel of Luke: Reversals of Fortune." *Missiology* 26, no. 2 (April 1998): 167–79.

Heschel, Abraham J. *The Prophets.* New York: HarperOne, 2001.

Hollenbach, Paul W. "Jesus, Demoniacs, and Public Authorities: A Socio-Historical Study." *Journal of the American Academy of Religion* 49, no. 4 (December 1981): 567–88.

Holman, Susan R., ed. *Wealth and Poverty in Early Church and Society.* Grand Rapids: Baker Academic, 2008.

Horne, Gerald. *The Apocalypse of Settler Colonialism: The Roots of Slavery, White Supremacy, and Capitalism in Seventeenth-Century North America and the Caribbean.* New York: Monthly Review Press, 2018.

Horsley, Richard H. *The Liberation of Christmas.* New York: Continuum, 1993.

———. *Scribes, Visionaries, and the Politics of Second Temple Judea.* Louisville: Westminster John Knox, 2007.

Hultgren, Arland J. *Paul's Letter to the Romans: A Commentary.* Grand Rapids: Eerdmans, 2011.

Hunsinger, George. *The Beatitudes*. Mahwah, NJ: Paulist, 2015.

Isasi-Díaz, Ada María. "Kin-dom of God: A *Mujerista* Proposal." In *In Our Own Voices: Latino/a Renditions of Theology*, edited by Benjamin Valentin, 171–89. Maryknoll, NY: Orbis, 2010.

———. *Mujerista Theology: A Theology for the Twenty-First Century*. Maryknoll, NY: Orbis, 1996.

Isherwood, Lisa. *Introducing Feminist Christologies*. Sheffield: Sheffield Academic Press, 2001.

Janowski, Bernd, and Peter Stuhlmacher, eds. *The Suffering Servant: Isaiah 53 in Jewish and Christian Sources*. Grand Rapids: Eerdmans, 2004.

Jennings, Willie James. *Acts*. Louisville: Westminster John Knox, 2017.

Jenson, Robert W. *Ezekiel*. Grand Rapids: Brazos, 2009.

———. *Systematic Theology*. Vol. 1, *The Triune God*. Oxford: Oxford University Press, 1997.

Jeremias, Joachim. *New Testament Theology*. New York: Macmillan, 1971.

Johnson, Elizabeth. *She Who Is: The Mystery of God in Feminist Theological Discourse*. New York: Crossroad, 1997.

———. *Truly Our Sister: A Theology of Mary in the Communion of Saints*. New York: Continuum, 2003.

Johnson, Luke Timothy. *The Gospel of Luke*. Collegeville, MN: Liturgical Press, 1991.

———. *Hebrews: A Commentary*. Louisville: Westminster John Knox, 2006.

Joyce, Paul. "The Kingdom of God and the Psalms." In *The Kingdom of God and Human Society*, edited by R. S. Barbour, 42–59. Edinburgh: T&T Clark, 1993.

Karris, Robert J. "Luke 24:13–35." *Interpretation* 68, no. 2 (January 1987): 57–61.

Käsemann, Ernst. *Commentary on Romans*. Translated by Geoffrey W. Bromiley. Grand Rapids: Eerdmans, 1980.

———. *On Being a Disciple of the Crucified Nazarene: Unpublished Lectures and Sermons*. Grand Rapids: Eerdmans, 2010.

———. "'The Righteousness of God' in Paul." In *New Testament Questions of Today*, by Ernst Käsemann, 168–82. Philadelphia: Fortress, 1969.

Kazen, Thomas. "Son of Man as Kingdom Imagery: Jesus between Corporate Symbol and Individual Redeemer Figure." In *Jesus from Judaism to Christianity: Continuum Approaches to the Historical Jesus*, edited by Tom Holmén, 87–108. Edinburgh: T&T Clark, 2007.

King, Martin Luther, Jr. "Facing the Challenge of a New Age." In *A Testament of Hope: The Essential Writings and Speeches of Martin Luther King, Jr.*, edited by James M. Washington, 135–44. San Francisco: HarperCollins, 1986.

Kinsler, Ross, and Gloria Kinsler. *The Biblical Jubilee and the Struggle for Life: An Invitation to Personal, Ecclesial, and Social Transformation.* Maryknoll, NY: Orbis, 1999.

Kinukawa, Hisako. "The Story of the Hemorrhaging Woman (Mark 5:25–34) Read from a Japanese Feminist Context." *Biblical Interpretation* 2, no. 3 (1994): 283–93.

Kirk-Duggan, Cheryl A. *Exorcizing Evil: A Womanist Perspective on the Spirituals.* Maryknoll, NY: Orbis, 1997.

Kline, Meredith G. *Kingdom Prologue: Genesis Foundations for a Covenantal Worldview.* Eugene, OR: Wipf & Stock, 2006.

Kloppenborg, John S., with John W. Marshall, eds. *Apocalypticism, Anti-Semitism, and the Historical Jesus: Subtexts in Criticism.* London: T&T Clark International, 2005.

König, Adrio. *The Eclipse of Christ in Eschatology: Toward a Christ-Centered Approach.* Grand Rapids: Eerdmans, 1989.

Kuhn, Karl Allen. *The Kingdom according to Luke and Acts: A Social, Literary, and Theological Introduction.* Grand Rapids: Baker Academic, 2015.

Kümmel, Werner G. *Promise and Fulfillment: The Eschatological Message of Jesus.* Naperville, IL: Allenson, 1957.

Ladd, George Eldon. *The Presence of the Future: The Eschatology of Biblical Realism.* Rev. ed. Grand Rapids: Eerdmans, 1974.

Levenson, Jon D. *Resurrection and the Restoration of Israel: The Ultimate Victory of the God of Life.* New Haven: Yale University Press, 2008.

Lewis, Alan E. *Between Cross and Resurrection: A Theology of Holy Saturday.* Grand Rapids: Eerdmans, 2001.

Lincoln, Bruce. *Gods and Demons, Priests and Scholars: Critical Explorations in the History of Religions.* Chicago: University of Chicago Press, 2012.

Linebaugh, Peter. "Jubilating; or, How the Atlantic Working Class Used the Biblical Jubilee against Capitalism, with Some Success." *Radical History Review* 50 (1991): 143–80.

———. *The Magna Carta Manifesto: Liberties and Commons for All.* Berkeley: University of California Press, 2008.

———. *Stop, Thief! The Commons, Enclosures, and Resistance.* Oakland, CA: PM Press, 2014.

Linebaugh, Peter, and Marcus Rediker. *The Many-Headed Hydra: Sailors, Slaves, Commoners, and the Hidden History of the Revolutionary Atlantic.* Boston: Beacon, 2000.

Lippy, Charles H. "Waiting for the End: The Social Context of American Apocalyptic Religion." In *The Apocalyptic Vision in America: Interdisciplinary Es-*

says in Myth and Culture, edited by Lois Parkinson Zamora, 37–63. Bowling Green, OH: Bowling Green University Popular Press, 1982.

Lochman, Jan Milič. *The Lord's Prayer.* Grand Rapids: Eerdmans, 1990.

Loewen, Susanne Guenther. "'We Are All Meant to Be Mothers of God': Mothering as Embodied Peacemaking." *Vision: A Journal for Church and Theology* 1, no. 1 (Fall 2000): 32–43.

Lohfink, Gerhard. *Is This All There Is? On Resurrection and Eternal Life.* Collegeville, MN: Liturgical Press Academic, 2018.

Lorenzen, Thorwald. *Resurrection and Discipleship: Interpretive Models, Biblical Reflections, Theological Consequences.* Maryknoll, NY: Orbis, 1995.

Lucass, Shirley. *The Concept of the Messiah in the Scriptures of Judaism and Christianity.* London: T&T Clark International, 2011.

Lundström, Gösta. *The Kingdom of God in the Teaching of Jesus: A History of Interpretation from the Last Decades of the Nineteenth Century to the Present Day.* Richmond, VA: John Knox, 1963.

Macaskill, Grant. *Revealed Wisdom and Inaugurated Eschatology in Ancient Judaism and Early Christianity.* Leiden: Brill, 2007.

Marcus, Joel. *Mark 1–8: A New Translation with Introduction and Commentary.* New York: Doubleday, 2000.

———. *Mark 8–16: A New Translation with Introduction and Commentary.* New York: Doubleday, 2009.

———. *The Way of the Lord: Christological Exegesis of the Old Testament in the Gospel of Mark.* London: T&T Clark International, 1992.

Marshall, I. Howard. *Commentary on Luke.* Grand Rapids: Eerdmans, 1978.

Martyn, J. Louis. *Theological Issues in the Letters of Paul.* Nashville: Abingdon, 1997.

Marx, Karl. Introduction to "Contribution to the Critique of Hegel's *Philosophy of Right.*" In *The Portable Karl Marx*, edited by Eugene Kamenka, 115–24. New York: Viking Penguin, 1983.

Mays, James L. *Amos: A Commentary.* Philadelphia: Westminster, 1969.

———. *The Lord Reigns: A Theological Handbook to the Psalms.* Louisville: Westminster John Knox, 1994.

McAllister, Colin, ed. *The Cambridge Companion to Apocalyptic Literature.* Cambridge: Cambridge University Press, 2020.

McBride, Jennifer M. *Radical Discipleship: A Liturgical Politics of the Gospel.* Minneapolis: Fortress, 2017.

McGinn, Bernard, John J. Collins, and Stephen J. Stein, eds. *The Continuum History of Apocalypticism.* New York: Continuum, 2003.

Mettinger, Tryggve. *A Farewell to the Servant Songs: A Critical Examination of an Exegetical Axiom.* Lund: Gleerup, 1983.

Metts, H. Leroy. "The Kingdom of God: Background and Development of a Complex Discourse Concept." *Criswell Theological Review* 2, no. 1 (Fall 2004): 51–82.

Middleton, Richard J. *A New Heaven and a New Earth.* Grand Rapids: Baker Academic, 2014.

Milgrom, Jacob. "Israel's Sanctuary: The Priestly 'Picture of Dorian Gray.'" *Revue biblique* 83, no. 3 (July 1976): 390–99.

———. *Leviticus 1–16.* New York: Doubleday, 1991.

Miller, Patrick D. *The Ten Commandments.* Louisville: Westminster John Knox, 2009.

Miller, Robert J., ed. *The Apocalyptic Jesus: A Debate.* Santa Rosa, CA: Polebridge, 2001.

Moloney, Francis J., SDB. *The Gospel of John.* Collegeville, MN: Liturgical Press, 1988.

Moltmann, Jürgen. *The Coming of God: Christian Eschatology.* Minneapolis: Fortress, 1996.

———. *The Crucified God: The Cross of Christ as the Foundation and Criticism of Christian Theology.* Minneapolis: Fortress, 1993.

———. *Jesus Christ for Today's World.* Minneapolis: Fortress, 1994.

———. "The Passion of the Son of Man and His Call to Follow Him." In *Meditations on the Passion: Two Meditations on Mark 8:31–38,* by Johann-Baptist Metz and Jürgen Moltmann, 3–20. Translated by Edmund Colledge. Eugene, OR: Wipf & Stock, 2012.

———. *The Spirit of Life: A Universal Affirmation.* Minneapolis: Fortress, 2001.

———. *Sun of Righteousness, Arise! God's Future for Humanity and the Earth.* Minneapolis: Fortress, 2010.

———. *Theology of Hope.* Minneapolis: Fortress, 1993.

———. *The Trinity and the Kingdom: The Doctrine of God.* Minneapolis: Fortress, 1993.

———. *The Way of Jesus Christ: Christology in Messianic Dimensions.* Minneapolis: Fortress, 1993.

Montero, Roman A. *All Things in Common: The Economic Practices of the Early Christians.* Eugene, OR: Resource Publications, 2017.

Moore, Anne. *Moving beyond Symbol and Myth: Understanding the Kingship of God of the Hebrew Bible through Metaphor.* New York: Lang, 2009.

Morse, Christopher. *The Difference Heaven Makes: Rehearing the Gospel as News.* London: T&T Clark, 2010.

———. *Not Every Spirit: A Dogmatics of Christian Disbelief.* Valley Forge, PA: Trinity Press International, 1994.

Moss, Candida R. "The Man with the Flow of Power: Porous Bodies in Mark 5:25–34." *Journal of Biblical Literature* 129, no. 3 (2010): 507–19.

Mowinckel, Sigmund. *He That Cometh: The Messiah Concept in the Old Testament and Later Judaism.* Grand Rapids: Eerdmans, 2005.

———. *The Psalms in Israel's Worship.* Grand Rapids: Eerdmans, 2004.

MPD 150. *MPD 150: A People's Project Evaluating Policing.* Accessed January 27, 2022. https://www.mpd150.com/.

Mundle, Wilhelm. "Revelation." In *The New International Dictionary of the New Testament*, edited by Colin Brown, 3:309–16. Grand Rapids: Zondervan, 1986.

Myers, Ched. *Binding the Strong Man: A Political Reading of Mark's Story of Jesus.* Maryknoll, NY: Orbis, 1997.

Najman, Hindy. "The Inheritance of Prophecy in Apocalypse." In *The Oxford Handbook of Apocalyptic Literature*, edited by John J. Collins 36–51. New York: Oxford University Press, 2014.

Nardoni, Enrique. *Rise Up, O Judge: A Study of Justice in the Biblical World.* Peabody, MA: Hendrickson, 2004.

Naveh, Eyal. "Dialectical Redemption: Reinhold Niebuhr, Martin Luther King, Jr., and the Kingdom of God in America." *Journal of Religious Thought* 42, no. 2 (1989–1990): 57–76.

Neusner, Jacob. *Theological Dictionary of Rabbinic Judaism.* Part 3, *Models of Analysis, Explanation, and Anticipation.* Lanham, MD: University Press of America, 2006.

Newman, Carey C. "Glory, Glorify." In *The New Interpreter's Dictionary of the Bible*, 2:576–80. Nashville: Abingdon, 2007.

North, Christopher R. *The Suffering Servant in Deutero-Isaiah: An Historical and Critical Study.* 2nd ed. Oxford: Oxford University Press, 1956.

O'Day, Gail. "Singing Woman's Song: A Hermeneutic of Liberation." *Currents in Theology and Mission* 12, no. 4 (August 1985): 203–10.

Pamment, Margaret. "The Meaning of *Doxa* in the Fourth Gospel." *Zeitschrift für die neutestamentliche Wissenschaft und die Kunde der ältern Kirche* 74, no. 1–2 (1983): 12–16.

Peppard, Michael. *The Son of God in the Roman World: Divine Sonship in Its Social and Political Context.* Oxford: Oxford University Press, 2011.

Perdue, Leo G., and Warren Carter. *Israel and Empire: A Postcolonial History of Israel and Early Judaism.* London: Bloomsbury, 2015.

Pero, Cheryl S. *Liberation from Empire: Demonic Possession and Exorcism in the Gospel of Mark.* New York: Lang, 2013.

Perrin, Norman. *Jesus and the Language of the Kingdom.* Philadelphia: Fortress, 1976.

Peterson, Anthony R. *Behold Your King: The Hope for the House of David in the Book of Zechariah.* London: T&T Clark, 2009.

Pitre, Brant. *Jesus, the Tribulation, and the End of the Exile: Restoration Eschatology and the Origin of the Atonement.* Grand Rapids: Baker Academic, 2005.

Pleins, J. David. *The Psalms: Songs of Tragedy, Hope, and Justice.* Maryknoll, NY: Orbis, 1993.

Portier-Young, Anathea E. *Apocalypse against Empire: Theologies of Resistance in Early Judaism.* Grand Rapids: Eerdmans, 2011.

———. "Jewish Apocalyptic Literature as Resistance Literature." In *The Oxford Handbook of Apocalyptic Literature*, edited by John J. Collins, 145–62. New York: Oxford University Press, 2014.

Powery, Emerson B., and Rodney S. Sadler Jr. *The Genesis of Liberation: Biblical Interpretation in the Antebellum Narratives of the Enslaved.* Louisville: Westminster John Knox, 2016.

Public History of 35W: A Community-Collaborative Oral History and Research Projects on 35W in South Minneapolis. Accessed January 5, 2021. https://35w.heritage.dash.umn.edu/.

Raboteau, Albert J. *Slave Religion: The "Invisible Institution" in the Antebellum South.* Oxford: Oxford University Press, 2004.

Rad, Gerhard von. *Old Testament Theology.* Vol. 1, *The Theology of Israel's Historical Traditions.* New York: Harper & Row, 1962.

———. *Old Testament Theology.* Vol. 2, *The Theology of Israel's Prophetic Traditions.* New York: Harper & Row, 1965.

Radner, Ephraim. *Leviticus.* Grand Rapids: Brazos, 2008.

Rambo, Shelly. *Resurrecting Wounds: Living in the Afterlife of Trauma.* Waco, TX: Baylor University Press, 2017.

———. "Trauma and Faith: Reading the Narrative of the Hemorrhaging Woman." *International Journal of Practical Theology* 13 (2009): 233–57.

Ray, Darby Kathleen. "A Praxis of Atonement: Confounding Evil through Cunning and Compassion." *Religious Studies and Theology* 18, no. 1 (June 1999): 34–46.

Reddish, Mitchell G., ed. *Apocalyptic Literature: A Reader.* Peabody, MA: Hendrickson, 1995.

Reimer, David J. "Political Prophets? Political Exegesis and Prophetic Theology." In *Intertextuality in Ugarit and Israel*, edited by Johannes C. de Moor, 126–42. Leiden: Brill, 1998.

Reiser, Marius. *Jesus and Judgment: The Eschatological Proclamation in Its Jewish Context.* Minneapolis: Fortress, 1997.

Rensberger, David. *Johannine Faith and Liberating Community.* Philadelphia: Westminster, 1988.

Ringe, Sharon H. *Jesus, Liberation, and the Biblical Jubilee: Images for Ethics and Christology.* Philadelphia: Fortress, 1985.

———. *Luke.* Louisville: Westminster John Knox, 1995.

———. "Luke 4:16–44: A Portrait of Jesus as Herald of God's Jubilee." *Proceedings* 1 (1981): 73–84.

Roberts, J. Deotis. "The Holy Spirit and Liberation: A Black Perspective." *Mid-Stream* 24, no. 4 (October 1985): 398–410.

Roberts, J. J. M. "The Enthronement of Yhwh and David: The Abiding Theological Significance of the Kingship Language of the Psalms." *Catholic Biblical Quarterly* 64 (2002): 675–86.

———. "Mowinckel's Enthronement Festival: A Review." In *The Book of Psalms: Composition and Reception,* edited by Peter W. Flint and Patrick D. Miller Jr., 97–115. Leiden: Brill, 2005.

Robinson, Cedric J. *Black Marxism: The Making of the Black Radical Tradition.* Chapel Hill: University of North Carolina Press, 2000.

Roediger, David. *Seizing Freedom: Slave Emancipation and Liberty for All.* London: Verso, 2015.

Romanowsky, John W. "'When the Son of Man Is Lifted Up': The Redemptive Power of the Crucifixion in the Gospel of John." *Horizons* 32, no. 1 (Spring 2005): 100–116.

Rosemont, Franklin. Preface to *Blues and the Poetic Spirit,* by Paul Garon, 7–15. New York: Da Capo, 1975.

Rosenblatt, Marie-Eloise. "Gender, Ethnicity, and Legal Considerations in the Haemorrhaging Woman's Story Mark 5:25–34." In *Transformative Encounters: Jesus and Women Re-viewed,* edited by Ingrid Rosa Kitzberger, 137–61. Leiden: Brill, 2000.

Rossing, Barbara R. "Prophecy, End-Times, and American Apocalypse: Reclaiming Hope for Our World." In *Compassionate Eschatology: The Future as Friend,* edited by Ted Grimsrud and Michael Hardin, 253–66. Eugene, OR: Cascade, 2011.

Rothstein, Richard. *The Color of Law: A Forgotten History of How Our Government Segregated America.* New York: Liveright, 2017.

Rowe, C. Kavin. *World Upside Down: Reading Acts in the Graeco-Roman Age.* New York: Oxford University Press, 2009.

Rowe, Robert D. *God's Kingdom and God's Son: The Background to Mark's Christology from Concepts of Kingship in the Psalms.* Leiden: Brill, 2002.

Rowland, Christopher. *The Open Heaven: A Study of Apocalyptic in Judaism and Early Christianity.* New York: Crossroad, 1982.

Ruether, Rosemary Radford. *Sexism and God-Talk.* London: SCM, 1983.

Russell, D. S. *Divine Disclosure: An Introduction to Jewish Apocalyptic.* Minneapolis: Fortress, 1992.

———. *The Method and Message of Jewish Apocalyptic.* Philadelphia: Westminster, 1964.

Russell, Letty M. *Just Hospitality: God's Welcome in a World of Difference.* Louisville: Westminster John Knox, 2009.

Rutledge, Fleming. *The Crucifixion: Understanding the Death of Jesus Christ.* Grand Rapids: Eerdmans, 2015.

Said, Edward. *Representations of the Intellectual.* London: Vintage, 1994.

Santala, Risto. "The Suffering Messiah and Isaiah 53 in the Light of Rabbinic Literature." *Springfielder* 39, no. 4 (March 1976): 177–82.

Saucy, Mark. *The Kingdom of God in the Teaching of Jesus: In the 20th Century.* Dallas: Word, 1997.

Schulz, Richard. "The King in the Book of Isaiah." In *The Lord's Anointed: Interpretation of Old Testament Messianic Texts,* edited by Philip E. Satterthwaite, Richard S. Hess, and Gordon J. Wenham, 141–65. Carlisle, UK: Paternoster, 1995.

Schwarz, Hans. *Eschatology.* Grand Rapids: Eerdmans, 2000.

Schweitzer, Albert. *The Kingdom of God and Primitive Christianity.* New York: Seabury, 1968.

———. *The Mystery of the Kingdom of God.* Buffalo, NY: Prometheus, 1985.

———. *The Quest of the Historical Jesus.* New York: Macmillan, 1968.

Selman, Martin J. "The Kingdom of God in the Old Testament." *Tyndale Bulletin* 40, no. 2 (November 1989): 161–83.

Sinha, Manisha. *The Slave's Cause: A History of Abolition.* New Haven: Yale University Press, 2016.

Skinner, Matthew L. *Intrusive God, Disruptive Gospel: Encountering the Divine in the Book of Acts.* Grand Rapids: Brazos, 2015.

Smith, Anthony D. *Chosen Peoples: Sacred Stories of National Identity.* Oxford: Oxford University Press, 2003.

Smith, Daniel L. *The Religion of the Landless: The Social Context of the Babylonian Exile.* Bloomington, IN: Meyer-Stone Books, 1989.

Smith-Christopher, Daniel L. *A Biblical Theology of Exile.* Minneapolis: Fortress, 2002.

———. "Reassessing the Historical and Sociological Impact of the Babylonian Exile (597/587–539 BCE)." In *Exile: Old Testament, Jewish, and Christian Conceptions,* edited by James M. Scott, 7–36. Leiden: Brill, 1997.

Sobrino, Jon. *Christ the Liberator: A View from the Victims.* Maryknoll, NY: Orbis, 2001.

———. *Jesus the Liberator: A Historical-Theological View*. Maryknoll, NY: Orbis, 1993.

———. *No Salvation outside the Poor: Prophetic-Utopian Essays*. Maryknoll, NY: Orbis, 2008.

Song, C. S. *Jesus, the Crucified People*. Minneapolis: Fortress, 1996.

Songs of Zion. United Methodist Church Supplemental Worship Resources, 12. Nashville: Abingdon, 1981, 1982.

Stassen, Glen. "The Ten Commandments: Deliverance for the Vulnerable." *Perspectives in Religious Studies* 35, no. 4 (Winter 2008): 357–71.

Still, Todd D. "*CHRISTOS* as *PISTOS*: The Faith(fullness) of Jesus in the Epistle to the Hebrews." In *A Cloud of Witnesses: The Theology of Hebrews in Its Ancient Contexts*, edited by Richard Bauckham, Daniel Driver, Trevor Hart, and Nathan MacDonald, 40–50. London: T&T Clark, 2008.

Stuckenbruck, Loren. "Overlapping Ages at Qumran and 'Apocalyptic' in Pauline Theology." In *The Dead Sea Scrolls and Pauline Literature*, edited by Jean-Sébastien Rey, 309–26. Leiden: Brill, 2014.

Taylor, Joan. *The Immerser: John the Baptist within Second Temple Judaism*. Grand Rapids: Eerdmans, 1997.

Taylor, Keeanga-Yamahtta. *Race for Profit: How Banks and the Real Estate Industry Undermined Black Homeownership*. Chapel Hill: University of North Carolina Press, 2019.

Thompson, Deanna A. *Crossing the Divide: Luther, Feminism, and the Cross*. Minneapolis: Fortress, 2004.

Thurman, Howard. *Jesus and the Disinherited*. Boston: Beacon, 1996.

———. "The Negro Spiritual Speaks of Life and Death." In *Deep River and the Negro Spiritual Speaks of Life and Death*, by Howard Thurman. Richmond, IN: Friends United Press, 1975.

Treat, Jeremy R. *The Crucified King: Atonement and Kingdom in Biblical and Systematic Theology*. Grand Rapids: Zondervan, 2004.

Trocmé, André. *Jesus and the Nonviolent Revolution*. Maryknoll, NY: Orbis, 2003.

Uffenheimer, Benjamin. "From Prophetic to Apocalyptic Eschatology." In *Eschatology in the Bible and in Jewish and Christian Tradition*, edited by Henning Graf Reventlow, 200–217. Sheffield: Sheffield Academic Press, 1997.

University of Minnesota. "Mapping Prejudice: Visualizing the Hidden Histories of Race and Privilege in the Build Environment." Accessed January 27, 2022. https://mappingprejudice.umn.edu/index.html.

Vanhoozer, Kevin J. *Remythologizing Theology: Divine Action, Passion, and Authorship*. Cambridge: Cambridge University Press, 2010.

Voorwinde, Stephen. "The Kingdom of God in the Proclamation of Jesus." In *The*

Content and Setting of the Gospel Traditions, edited by Mark Harding and Alanna Nobbs, 329–53. Grand Rapids: Eerdmans, 2010.

Walker, David. "Walker's Appeal, in Four Articles; Together with a Preamble, to the Coloured Citizens of the World, but in Particular, and Very Expressly, to Those of the United States of America, Written in Boston, State of Massachusetts, September 28, 1829." Accessed January 27, 2022. https://docsouth.unc.edu/nc/walker/walker.html.

Weaver, Alain Epp. *Mapping Exile and Return: Palestinian Dispossession and a Political Theology for a Shared Future*. Minneapolis: Fortress, 2014.

Webb, Elizabeth A. "Power in Weakness: Feminist Reclamations of the Suffering of Christ." *Religious Studies Review* 38, no. 4 (December 2012): 199–205.

Weinfeld, Moshe. "'Justice and Righteousness'—משפט וצדקה—the Expression and Its Meaning." In *Justice and Righteousness: Biblical Themes and Their Influence*, edited by Henning Graf Reventlow and Yair Hoffman, 228–46. Sheffield: JSOT Press, 1992.

Weiss, Johannes. *Jesus' Proclamation of the Kingdom of God*. Philadelphia: Fortress, 1971.

Welker, Michael. *God the Spirit*. Minneapolis: Fortress, 1994.

Westermann, Claus. *Isaiah 40–66: A Commentary*. Philadelphia: Westminster, 1969.

Westhelle, Vítor. *The Scandalous God: The Use and Abuse of the Cross*. Minneapolis: Fortress, 2006.

Wiesel, Elie. "God's Suffering: A Commentary." In *Wrestling with God: Jewish Theological Responses during and after the Holocaust*, edited by Steven T. Katz, Shlomo Biderman, and Gershon Greenberg, 682–84. Oxford: Oxford University Press, 2007.

Williams, Eric. *Capitalism and Slavery*. Chapel Hill: University of North Carolina Press, 1944.

Wink, Walter. *Engaging the Powers: Discernment and Resistance in a World of Domination*. Minneapolis: Fortress, 1992.

———. *John the Baptist in the Gospel Tradition*. Eugene, OR: Wipf & Stock, 2000.

———. *Naming the Powers: The Language of Power in the New Testament*. Philadelphia: Fortress, 1984.

———. *Unmasking the Powers: The Invisible Powers That Determine Human Existence*. Philadelphia: Fortress, 1986.

Witmer, Amanda. *Jesus, the Galilean Exorcist: His Exorcisms in Social and Political Context*. London: T&T Clark, 2012.

Woods, Clyde. *Development Arrested: The Blues and Plantation Power in the Mississippi Delta*. London: Verso, 2017.

Woods, Edward J. *The "Finger of God" and Pneumatology in Luke-Acts.* Sheffield: Sheffield Academic, 2001.

Wright, Christopher J. H. "Year of Jubilee." In *The Anchor Bible Dictionary*, edited by David Noel Freedman and Gary Alan Herion, 3:1027–28. New York: Doubleday, 1992.

Yoder, John Howard. "Exodus and Exile: The Two Faces of Liberation." *Cross Currents* 23, no. 3 (Fall 1973): 297–309.

York, John O. *The Last Shall Be First: The Rhetoric of Reversal in Luke.* London: JSOT Press, 1991.

Ziegler, Philip G. *Militant Grace: The Apocalyptic Turn and the Future of Christian Theology.* Grand Rapids: Baker Academic, 2018.

INDEX OF AUTHORS

Index of Subjects

adventus, 40

adversaries of YHWH, 134-44, 169-70; Jesus's religious and political adversaries, 135-37, 170; "powers and principalities" (reigning ideologies), 137-41, 164-65, 169-70; the powers of sin and death, 142-44, 170

Ambrose of Milan, 201

Americas, European invasion of, 2-3

Amos, 42-45

Antiochus IV Epiphanes, 72n24, 73-74, 79, 174

aphiēmi ("release" or "forgiveness"), 108-9, 190

apocalyptic literature tradition, xv, 9, 68-90, 145, 166; and the Black freedom struggle of the nineteenth century, xv, 84-87, 90; the cosmic confrontation between YHWH and the earthly nations, 9, 71, 72-80, 132, 145, 164-71, 174; cosmological soteriology and apocalyptic epistemology, 74-77; defining "apocalyptic," 9, 69-70; divine agency and God's reign, 89-90; as form

of resistance literature, xv, 82-83; God's re-creation of the heavens and the earth, 78; and imperial regimes of the ancient Near East, 71-72, 72n24, 79-80; and the Jubilee tradition, 9, 74, 166; and modern political movements, xv, 82-87, 90; the priority of divine action, 74-77, 145; Second Temple period literature, 69-70, 145; seeing the world as divine gift, 74-76; the Son of Man figure, xv, 73, 80-82, 90, 136, 147, 152-54, 162-63, 170; and the tribulation of purgation, 78-80, 145; two ages (the present and the "age to come"), 77-80, 89, 145; wisdom and "wise teachers," 83-84. *See also* Daniel, book of

atonement, 148n43; Day of Atonement and Jubilee Year, 27, 29-31, 53; eschatological doctrine of, 147; representative suffering, 49-52, 66, 89, 151-52, 167; substitutionary, 49n38, 134n1

Auschwitz, 48n35

Index of Scripture